THE POPULAR ARTS
A Critical Reader

THE
POPULAR ARTS

A Critical Reader

EDITED BY

IRVING DEER
University of South Florida

HARRIET A. DEER
University of South Florida

Charles Scribner's Sons · New York

B. 8.67 (Col)

Printed in the United States of America
Library of Congress Catalog Card Number 66-24493

ACKNOWLEDGMENTS

"Stone, Steel, and Jazz," *Made in America* by John A. Kouwenhoven (Garden City, 1948), pp. 238-269. Copyright 1948 by John A. Kouwenhoven. Reprinted by permission of Doubleday & Company, Inc.

"[Literature in an Organization Society]," *The Organization Man* by William H. Whyte, Jr. (New York, 1956), pp. 243-263. Copyright, © 1956, by William Whyte, Jr. Reprinted by permission of Simon and Schuster, Inc.

"[Primitivism in *The Family of Man*]," *The House of Intellect* by Jacques Barzun (New York, 1959), pp. 27-30. Copyright © 1959 by Jacques Barzun. Reprinted with the permission of Harper & Row, Publishers.

"The 'Western': Definition of the Myth" by John Williams, *The Nation,* CXCIII (November 18, 1961), 401-405. Copyright © 1961 by John Williams. Reprinted by permission of John Williams.

"Reactors of the Imagination," reprinted from *The Astonished Muse* by Reuel Denney (Chicago, 1957), pp. 186-203, by permission of the University of Chicago Press. Copyright © 1957.

"The Detective Story as a Historical Source" by William O. Aydelotte, *The Yale Review,* XXXIX (Autumn, 1949), 76-95. Copyright, Yale University Press. Reprinted by permission of *The Yale Review* and the author.

(*The following page is an extension of the copyright page.*)

"The Gangster as Tragic Hero," *The Immediate Experience* by Robert Warshow (New York, 1962), pp. 127-133. Copyright, Joseph Goldberg. Reprinted by permission of Joseph Goldberg.

"Pornography Is Not Enough," *The Self-Conscious Society* by Eric Larrabee (Garden City, 1960), pp. 99-118. Copyright © 1960 by Eric Larrabee. Reprinted by permission of the author.

"Kitsch," *A Clerk of Oxenford* by Gilbert Highet (New York, 1954), pp. 210-219. Reprinted by permission of Oxford University Press, Inc.

"The Rebirth of the Musical," from the book *The American Imagination.* Copyright © Times Publishing Company Limited, 1959. First published in *The Times Literary Supplement,* 1959. Reprinted by permission of Atheneum Publishers.

From "Children of Thoth," reprinted from *The Astonished Muse* by Reuel Denney (Chicago, 1957), pp. 169-185, by permission of the University of Chicago Press. Copyright © 1957.

"History on the Silver Screen," *Talents and Geniuses* by Gilbert Highet (New York, 1957), pp. 191-198. Copyright © 1957 by Gilbert Highet. Reprinted by permission of Oxford University Press, Inc.

From "The Film" by Albert Hunt, *Discrimination and Popular Culture,* ed. Denys Thompson (Harmondsworth, Eng., 1964), pp. 102-120. Reprinted by permission of Penguin Books Ltd.

"The Witness Point" by Vernon Young, *New World Writing, Fourth Mentor Selection* (New York, 1953), pp. 270-282. Reprinted by permission of the author.

"Comedy's Greatest Era," *Agee on Film* by James Agee (New York, 1958), pp. 2-19. Copyright © 1958 by The James Agee Trust. Reprinted by permission of Grosset & Dunlap, Inc., New York, N.Y., publishers.

"The Twentieth-Century Best-Seller" by P. N. Furbank, *The Modern Age,* VII, ed. Boris Ford (Harmondsworth, Eng., 1963), pp. 429-441. Reprinted by permission of Penguin Books Ltd.

"The Aesthetics of the Popular Arts" by Abraham Kaplan, *Journal of Aesthetics and Art Criticism,* XXXIV (Spring, 1966), 351-364. Reprinted by permission of The American Society for Aesthetics and the author.

TO THE MEMORY OF WILLIAM DEER

Contents

Introduction

This is a book on the popular arts, not on the mass media. It is important to make a clear distinction between the two. The popular arts are extensions of such arts as the drama, opera, painting, the novel, and the musical arts; western films, musical comedy, the magazine illustrations of Norman Rockwell, and detective fiction are all popular extensions of traditional arts. Some of the popular arts—like jazz—may be popular because they are made available through the mass media, and some—like dramatic films—may even utilize the form and conventions of a mass medium to communicate experience artistically and in an entertaining manner. But the mass media are not arts, popular or otherwise; they are merely mechanical means of communicating to masses of people without regard to what is communicated. Through television, radio, newspapers, and such, mass media indiscriminately transmit amateur hours and Greek tragedies, weather forecasts and color photographs of the Parthenon. They may be used as the means of presenting art works of all kinds, but nothing in their nature limits them to that function; they can just as well be used for communicating pure information or instruction.

Perhaps what most confuses us and leads us to equate the popular arts with the mass media is the large amount of time devoted to entertainment in the mass media. The most cursory examination of a television schedule will reveal that most television time is devoted to entertainment of one sort or another— soap operas, quiz or audience-participation shows, entertaining drama, and variety shows. A glance at the most obviously informative mass medium, newspapers, will reveal that a great deal of its space is similarly devoted to entertainment. Most human interest features, the comics, many of the daily columns (on astrology, for example), and a large portion of the women's and sports pages can justly be classified as entertainment. Even where the mass media are used primarily to inform or instruct us, the information or instruction is made as entertaining as possible. This emphasis upon the entertaining sometimes leads to such consequences as the spectacularization of news or the oversimplification of complex issues. Whatever the consequences, however, the mass media are expected to entertain us. To do so, they are used to present a great many popular arts, including western and detective stories, science fiction, comics, popular songs, and family comedies. But there is no reason to confuse what they do with what they are. Westerns, detective stories, and science fiction are types of popular art; television, magazines, and newspapers are types of mass media. Unless we can clearly distinguish between the popular arts and the mass media, we cannot understand what each is or how to evaluate it.

Historically, the mass media and the popular arts developed from different desires and were expected to serve different ends.

The great progenitor of all mass media, printing, arose as a response to the demand of the Renaissance and the Reformation that knowledge be made freely available to all people. Printing was regarded as a means not of creating anything but rather of conveying information. (In point of fact, as H. Marshall McLuhan has pointed out in "Sight, Sound, and Fury" [in *Explorations in Communication*, 1960], printing itself had a wide impact both upon writing style and upon the patterns of meaning perceived among facts.) But the original printers were interested primarily in making information more easily available. The artistic and the philosophical implications of printing itself were generally of little concern to them.

This same desire to spread information is characteristic of the later inventors who originated the other mechanical devices we know today as the mass media—film, radio, television, the phonograph. Marconi envisioned radio ("the wireless telegraph" as he originally called it) as a means of surmounting distance. He did see, to a certain extent, the potential of radio for communicating to more than one person at a time, since he understood that a radio signal could be received simultaneously by more than one receiving set. But he did not envision radio as a medium of art and entertainment. Edison, whose deafness made him acutely aware of the transitoriness of oral communication, invented the phonograph as a means of preserving and disseminating useful oral communication. He believed that the phonograph was a commercial and educational tool. Today, probably only the secretarial dictaphone corresponds in any way to the uses of the phonograph which Edison originally envisioned. Neither Marconi nor Edison foresaw the possibility that their inventions would eventually become almost exclusively used for art and entertainment. Of the modern mass media, only film, and after it television, were originally conceived as media for art or entertainment.

For the man of the Renaissance and the Reformation, divorcing invention from social responsibility was unthinkable.[1] In contrast, late nineteenth- and early twentieth-century inventors of what we now consider the mass media, however, were not concerned with the social implications of their inventions beyond the realization that these inventions facilitated broader communication. For the technologists of the modern world, responsibility was limited only to the practical applications of an invention, not to the social and moral implications of its use. This divorce between technology and human values has had a profound impact on both the mass media and the popular arts, an impact we shall consider in more detail later.

Whereas the mass media generally arose from a desire for broader communication, the popular arts arose from a desire for art and entertainment that was appropriate for a popular audience.[2] The term "popular arts" itself came into use in the late nineteenth century. New art forms had already been developed as substitutes for or extensions of such traditional arts as drama, poetry, fiction, and painting. The traditional arts had become, because of their cost or their complexity, inaccessible to the general public. For example, the legitimate theatre was generally both too complex and too expensive for the general public. To take its place there arose the genre of drama now called "melodrama," and probably the music hall, burlesque, and vaudeville as well.

[1] In one important respect early printers, such as Caxton and Gutenberg, differed from late nineteenth- and early twentieth-century inventors of the mass media. Early printers were aware, in a limited way, of the social impact of their invention. They were aware that they had some responsibility to make only good or moral knowledge available to the general populace. The books that they came to print show this sense of responsibility clearly —the Bible in Germany and Sir Thomas Malory's *Morte Darthur* (conceived by Malory to be a moral guide for gentlemen) in England.

[2] The editors of this book agree with those critics who believe that, though some things happen to be both art and entertainment, art and entertainment are quite distinct (see, e.g., R. G. Collingwood, *The Principles of Art* [1938]). This distinction has been maintained throughout this Introduction.

Since many popular arts were substitute arts, they necessarily developed along different lines, and used different forms and conventions than their more traditional cousins. Although it is true that some of these substitute arts were, as Gilbert Highet points out with regard to kitsch art ("Kitsch," p. 185), simply cheap imitations of traditional forms, other popular arts sprang to life as entirely new forms. Film, for example, never was a traditional art. It arose at first from the popular desire to see pictures move. It developed its own conventions, its own ways of exploring experience, its own kinds of drama which were only partially related to the stage drama.

Sometimes popular art forms developed because more traditional forms were not well adapted to expressing the popular consciousness. The nineteenth-century American humorists Artemis Ward and Josh Billings, for instance, communicated more fully and directly than did the imitators of sophisticated British drawing-room humor. Ward and Billings drew their strength from the folk humor of lower-class Americans—from the canny New England trader, from the Mike Fink riverboat talk, from the general-store, common-sense approach to life of the newly settled western communities. (Neither Ward nor Billings ever quite succeeded in putting his new style of humor into sustained humorous works. They did succeed, nevertheless, in developing the conventions which were later available to Mark Twain, and which he brought to full flower.) The early American humorists did not represent an imitation or debasement of traditional forms. They represented an attempt to create new forms which were capable of expressing new American experiences.

Although the term "popular arts" did not come into use until the nineteenth century, the popular arts were a fact long before a term existed to describe them. Anyone familiar with world literature can readily cite examples of popular art which eventually achieved the status of classical art. Plautus, for example, was the popular dramatist of the Romans. He created a frank and joyous substitute for the pseudo-Greek closet drama officially approved by the intelligentsia. Shakespeare created his dramas in the midst of and with the aid of flourishing popular folk and religious dramatic traditions. Molière based his entire dramaturgy on the popular Italian *commedia* traditions. Although the plays of Plautus were substitutes for the official Greek drama, the popular traditions employed by Shakespeare and Molière were not substitutes for existing forms, nor were they intended for a specific social class. They were, more properly, simply existing artistic forms from which Shakespeare and Molière developed their dramaturgy. By the eighteenth century, however, popular arts, in the sense in which popular arts competed with traditional arts, were clearly in evidence. The existence of a conflict between traditional and popular art can be clearly inferred from John Gay's *The Beggar's Opera* (1728). In that light opera, Gay satirizes Italian opera—the approved operatic form of the elite; he also purports to satirize street ballads of his era. Although Gay's satire renders Italian opera airs ineffectual and effete, his satirical lyrics for the street ballads merely invest them with more gusto and force than they sometimes possessed originally. Rather than producing a satire of the popular ballads of his day, by implication he defends them at the expense of the approved forms of traditional music.

The conflict between traditional and popular arts was more obvious in the nineteenth century. France affords us the most extreme example. Traditional artists in France banded together into what was known as "the Academy"—originally a body whose function was to investigate art and produce orderly principles for its production, but ultimately a body which set about preserving traditional arts from the encroachments of popular forms. Its control of the legitimate theatre was absolute. No play could be produced without the approval of the Academy; and the Academy chose to approve only classical or, in its liberal moments, lofty verse drama. Such drama was obviously very far from the experience of a population which had revolted because of a romantic desire for political equality. It was inevitable, therefore, that means for circumventing the restrictions of the Academy would be devised. Probably the most colorful of these was the device that gave rise to the generic name "melodrama." Although the Academy controlled the legitimate theatres, it did not control musical productions, and so it became commonplace to evade the dictates of the Academy by placing a fiddler in the wings during the performance of an unapproved play. So long as he played continuously throughout the production, the production could be classified as musical and was therefore legitimate; hence the name for a certain genre of popular nineteenth-century drama: *"melos"* (Greek for "song") + "drama," or "melodrama." And hence the attitude and the actual fact that a good bit of this melodrama was frankly crude and directed toward the least educated segment of the population.

The conflict between traditional and popular art in France was, however, unusually severe and prolonged. A number of popular arts which came into being during the nineteenth century were accepted uncritically and widely. Photographic portraiture, for example, was accepted by the middle and the lower classes, and was certainly tolerated by the upper classes, as an economical substitute for the oil portraits they could not afford. In England, although the music hall was patronized chiefly by the middle and the lower classes, who lacked both the money and the taste to patronize opera and drawing room comedy, it attracted its share of patrons who possessed both wealth and sophistication. In America, P. T. Barnum devised his "museum" as a popular substitute for traditional museum displays that were incomprehensible to the general public. Barnum's exhibits were, in reality, primarily collections of freaks. But, capitalizing on the great American instinct for self-improvement, Barnum advertised his exhibits as "educational," and thereby attracted a large number of educated people who would never have admitted to an interest in freaks.

One should not, of course, conclude that outside of France, the traditional and the popular arts existed in unalloyed harmony. Obviously, they did not. They maintained, at best, an uneasy peace. In evaluating the popular arts, most critics and artists retained an ambivalent attitude. On the one hand, the educated Victorian called the cheap novels of his day "penny dreadfuls." On the other hand, Dickens published a number of his best novels as serials in the popular press. Perhaps this ambivalent attitude was best summed up in the concern of Arnold and Tennyson that good material be found for the popular press. They did not assume that popular literature had to be inferior by nature, only that it generally was. Similarly, they did not assume that the popular artist necessarily had to be an inferior artist; but, again, they also could not help observing that he generally suffered from simple-mindedness and lack of integrity. Nevertheless, they were willing to concede the possibility, to articulate the hope, that popular art could occasionally redeem itself.

Yet, by the early part of our own century, this uneasy truce between the traditional and the popular arts had been shattered, and shattered so completely that for many years it was nearly impossible for an artist to work in both areas without serious risk to his artistic reputation. There was a time when the literary artist who agreed to work for Hollywood was nearly ostracized from the community of serious artists. For many years, a well-known legitimate actor could safely work in radio only if he participated in a cultural program, that is, if he presented on radio some legitimate theatrical role. The assumption behind such an attitude was that traditional and popular arts were unalterably opposed, and that the legitimate artist must necessarily corrupt himself if he chose to work in the popular arts.

The sudden disrepute of the popular arts occurred because of the emergence of the mass media as we know them today.

At the end of the last century and the beginning of this one, a number of new mechanical communication media seized the popular imagination. Yet these media were, at least at the beginning, so crude that they frightened men of taste and sensibility. There was film, so crude in its initial stages that it was considered to be beneath contempt. Early films consisted of simple records of movements—a ballet dancer turning around, a baby eating its breakfast, a couple kissing. Enjoyment consisted entirely in the unsophisticated pleasure of seeing pictures move. Added to the simple entertainment were the conditions under which one viewed pictures, which were generally presented in halls called "nickelodeons" because the viewer paid a nickel to see moving pictures. Since the producers were well aware that their bill of entertainment could satisfy only simple tastes, these halls were placed within reach of the available audiences—in other words, in the slum or other low-rent districts of cities. Early films were therefore destined to bring down upon themselves artistic and social disapproval. Nor did early phonograph recordings fare much better artistically. Anyone who has heard early recordings realizes that they were of such poor quality that they often made familiar sounds unrecognizable. As a result, they were used for the kind of music which depended heavily on rhythm alone for its appeal, not on good technical reproductions of fine musicianship. Very few good artists were willing to subject themselves to the indignities of the phonograph record during its earliest days. Nor was early radio any more sophisticated. It had never been conceived as an art medium, popular or otherwise, but only as a means of emergency communication. It became a popular art medium almost in spite of the efforts of radio operators. The crystal set was a sort of parlor game long before commercial broadcasting stations became a reality. Groups of people gathered and passed the earphones around among themselves, listening with rapt fascination to the signals of ham operators. Even after one of the earliest stations, KDKA, was established in Pittsburgh, radio programming continued to be random, disorganized, and monotonously amateur. During its early years, KDKA sought to build an audience in the Ohio River Valley by bringing in local talent from outlying communities to attract local interest. Although it maintained a studio orchestra of sorts, it had no writers, no real programming schedule, and no dramatic or variety shows. Intellectuals took seriously the communication potential of radio, they recognized that it furnished a crude source of popular entertainment, but they had no grasp of its artistic potential.

Not only were these new mechanical media crude, they suffered all the ills of industrialization. From the beginning, the new media were commercial. Film and radio producers required a great deal of special equipment which they could acquire only by tapping industrial capital. We need only consider, for example, the initial investment required for a film studio or a broadcasting station. Moreover, broadcasts could be received only if mechanical receivers were widely available to translate electrical impulses into meaningful sound patterns. Again, making these receivers available required the use of mass production and distribution techniques. Finally, the production of films and radio programs required the organization of numbers of specialists, only a few of whom could properly be classified as artists. Film and radio both require large numbers of engineers, mechanics, and day laborers as well as actors and directors. In other words, the mass media required both the capital and the methods of mass production in order to exist. But the media paid a price to attract the capital they required. In return for funds, they gave essential control of the media to men who were dominated by the profit motive and by a conviction that the mass media could be profitable only in the ways that other mass-production industries were. These businessmen assumed that to make their huge investments pay off, they must produce and sell as much as possible. This drastically affected the quality of what they produced and imposed essentially quantitative standards on their work. Since mass production is most profitable when great quantities of relatively few designs are produced, producers more and more ignored individual preferences and offered consumers fewer and fewer choices among greater and greater quantities of goods and services. In other words, they produced fewer and fewer different kinds of programs in the media and considered the size of their audiences, the number of consumers they had, rather than the actual quality of their programs, to be the gauge of their success or failure as producers.

This industrialization of the mass media would not have affected the general attitude toward popular arts, however, had not something else happened. In their search for a salable mass-media product, industrialists were not slow to discover that since the popular arts tended to appeal to wide audiences, they had a great commercial potential. The industrialists had the money to offer great financial rewards to popular artists; they had the organization to publicize popular arts and to give popular fame to the artists; they had the resources for distributing popular arts to a very wide audience. Thus, they inevitably took over the popular arts to a startling degree. This take-over of the popular arts by the mass media changed the nature of the popular arts. Popular arts had always appealed to fairly broad audiences. But the audiences had been immediate, not at a distance; the popular artist had known the general personality of his particular audience, the fairly specific attitudes to which he was appealing. For example, until the invasion by the mass media, the music-hall or burlesque comedian had had a number of routines developed for particular kinds of audiences. He had performed for Polish immigrants, or for dock-workers, or for Irish immigrants, or for small-town midwesterners. In any case, he had been free to adapt his material to the situation which faced him, and he could respond to and receive the responses of specific audiences. Today, our closest approximation of this situation is found among the night-club entertainers of the "Borscht Belt" circuit, who appeal to Jewish audiences vacationing in the Adirondacks. But the mass media were distributed nationally, even internationally, to all types of audiences at once; and the only response the performer could expect came in the form of a paycheck, or audience ratings, or, occasionally, fan mail. He was forced to standardize his material on the basis of what seemed to appeal to the broadest possible audience, to find material which dealt with those few areas which were common to many different kinds of audiences. No longer could a comedian invent a routine for a particular ethnic audience; no longer could domestic comedy afford to reflect the specific mores of a particular segment of the population. The days of *Abie's Irish Rose* were gone. The popular artist's material became more general, more stereotyped. He was frequently driven to imitate those who attracted large audiences. If he were a dramatist, he had to produce plays which dealt with only a limited number of subjects, acceptable to and understood by almost everyone; he created broad characters who were readily understood by this great, vague, undistinguishable audience. If he were a film maker, he had to discern which story patterns and character types seemed appropriate to all possible kinds of viewers. The popular artist had, inevitably, to appeal to the lowest common denominator, and his work showed it. The popular artist came to be regarded, with some justification, as a man who sold his artistic birthright for a mess of pottage.

Fortunately for the general health of both the traditional and the popular arts, this absolute divorce between traditional and popular gradually began to disappear. A number of conditions helped to heal the breach to some extent.

First, there were the popular arts themselves. Film, in particular, attracted—almost in spite of itself—some men of great artistic power. There was Charlie Chaplin, whose melancholy gaiety surmounted the prejudices of many otherwise disdainful intellectuals. Perhaps more significant because it was more obviously artistic in intention was D. W. Griffith's *Birth of a Nation* (1915). That film made large audiences aware that the film had a capacity for communicating mature artistic experiences.

But the development of the popular arts themselves was sporadic and uneven during the early part of this century. *Birth of a Nation* was not typical of the period, and Griffith's example was not followed in this country until many years later. The German and the Russian film makers followed his lead and succeeded in producing some classic silent films in the next few years: *Dr. Caligari* (1919) and *The Last Laugh* (1924) in Germany; *Potemkin* (1925) in Russia. In the United States, however, Hollywood was producing *The Sheik* (1921). In this country, at least, the popular taste was indiscriminate. To be sure, there were some exceptions. The classic German film *The Blue Angel* (1930) was highly successful here, and Emil Jannings, the star of that film, became a matinee idol. But so did Rudolph Valentino. A few years later, popular audiences were equally enthusiastic about Greta Garbo and Jean Harlow. The artistic successes could most aptly be described as happy accidents. But the possibility of the popular arts producing artistic successes had been recognized.

During the 1930's, other important changes took place which gradually began to affect the attitude of intellectuals toward the popular arts. For one thing, the nature of the popular audience was gradually beginning to change. The general level of literacy and education in this country rose rapidly during the first half of this century. By the time World War II broke out, a high-school diploma had come to be taken for granted. After World War II, the G.I. Bill enabled hundreds of thousands of young men to complete college educations. Government aid and general affluence made it possible for many young men and women to complete college educations who, a generation before, would have been fortunate to complete high school. This rise in the educational level of the popular audience affected the popular culture market in many ways. For the first time, after World War II, there was a large market for quality paperback books. There was also a large market for classical records, and a significant market for specialized forms of classical records (chamber music, for example). The market for reproductions of paintings boomed. Suddenly the population wanted good art in their homes; no longer did the moralistic reproductions of the twenties suffice; no longer was there a large demand for "The Stag at Bay," or "Song of Spring," or "Blind Hope." Instead, there was a demand for good reproductions by Van Gogh, Utrillo, Picasso, and Gauguin.

One might be tempted to conclude from these changes that the popular audience was gradually developing into the kind of elite which Sir Kenneth Clark suggests in "Art and Society" (*Harpers* [August, 1961]) was the traditional audience for the artist. But to view this new generation of Americans as an elite in the sense that they had a broad familiarity with art is to be unjustifiably optimistic. For this new generation was not educated in the same sense as the educated man of 1900. The educated man of the 1950's and 1960's was most likely to have received a degree that stressed a vocation rather than the arts. His exposure to art was likely to have been limited to a few required courses in art appreciation in college. As a result, although he was likely to know a short list of approved artists, his personal taste was generally of uncertain quality. He frequently acquired a longing for art through his education, but he also carried with him the tastes and attitudes he had developed as a child from devouring comic books and regularly attending the Saturday afternoon movie.

In some ways, this new elite succeeded in alienating both the traditional and the popular artists more deeply than the audience of the 1900's had. Traditional artists frequently sensed that they might reach a larger audience if they could only find ways of communicating with it. So they sometimes attempted to popularize their works in order to reach the popular market.

Popular artists, on the other hand, sensing the increased maturity of their public, frequently attempted to create works capable of gaining the respect attributed to the traditional arts. In both cases, the attempts misfired. Consider, for example, the disastrous policy that Hollywood followed for a number of years after the advent of television, in trying to recapture an audience for the movies. Deciding that television was filling the demand for films conceived primarily as light entertainment, Hollywood felt that its place, therefore, must be to produce serious, adult art. But its producers, directors, and writers had for many years worked in the tradition of light popular entertainment; they were ill-equipped to conceive and execute adult films. They thought of adult art in terms of subject matter, not treatment; as a result, "adult" came for them to mean subjects which were not presented on television because they were unsuitable for family audiences. These subjects, such as prostitution, were still given the sensational glamor treatment popular films had always given their subjects. What emerged was actually the equivalent of the sensational dime novel—*Blackboard Jungle* (1954), *The Wild One* (1954), *War and Peace* (1956), for example. Hollywood directors had good intentions, but they lacked the artistic maturity to realize them. The mature public was repelled by the films; the immature public either wallowed in the sensationalism or shuddered in moral horror. In no case did the audiences stream back to the movie houses. Had it not been for Walt Disney, whose work was blithely popular and moral, Hollywood would have gone bankrupt.

Nor did the new elite create consistent changes in taste. The popular taste was as quixotic and confused in the 1950's and 1960's as it had been in the 1920's. And the popular arts reflected the confusion. Labels meant nothing. A western film might turn out to be possessed of the kind of artistry, integrity, and toughness of *High Noon* (1952). An intentionally adult film might turn out to be possessed of the kind of inadequacy and luridness of

Butterfield 8 (1960). The same confusion prevailed in the other popular arts. A popular recording group might be the Beatles; but it also might be a fine jazz group. A best seller might be *Peyton Place* (1956); but it also might be *Lord of the Flies* (1954). Even within the format of one television series, the quality might vary tremendously. One could, by and large, assume that *Gunsmoke* (1955) would present routinely oversimplified psychological westerns. But the offering might be an exceptionally sensitive and moving western adaptation of Melville's *Billy Budd*.

Given these changes both in the popular audience and in the popular arts themselves, given the confusion and profusion of popular art products, the shifting lines of differentiation between the popular and the traditional arts, and the unreliability of labels, the ability to deal critically with the popular arts became a genuine necessity for most thoughtful Americans. Granted, there had existed two kinds of criticism in the popular arts for several years. There had been the parlor variety, found frequently in newspapers and popular magazines. In this connection, one thinks of the theatre critic George Jean Nathan or many of the reviewers for *Time*; such critics amused their readers with ninety percent wisecrack and ten percent insight and reinforced the traditional attitude of well-educated Americans that popular arts were, as a matter of course, inferior products deserving only of derision. Serious consideration of the popular arts had been left to the social scientists. Many came to believe that the popular arts should be judged almost entirely in terms of quantitative rather then qualitative success. And, for that task, the social scientists were far better equipped than the men of letters. The former were skilled in methods of polling, in compiling statistical data, in audience analysis, in discovering the effect on an audience of a particular idea. The social scientists could answer what were assumed to be the really important questions about the popular arts: what was popular and with whom was it popular? They could also tell a great deal about the ways in which the popular arts influenced the audience. Furthermore, the work of the social scientists was welcomed and frequently sponsored by the communication industry, for it gave the industry concrete information about what subjects and ideas were acceptable to the audience (which TV programs, for example, were commercially successful) and occasionally made the industry feel that it was meeting some vague social responsibility.

But, informative as the social scientists had been, there were some basic questions which they could not answer. They could not explain, for example, why two programs that used essentially the same format and ideas should have such different receptions from the audience. They could not explain why one program seemed to communicate a rich and satisfying experience, while another communicated only emptiness and sterility. They could not explain why a program which included all the "right" ideas should communicate to the audience all the "wrong" impressions. In a word, although they could explain why the popular arts were popular, they could not explain what was or could be artistic about them.

It was this question which concerned men of genuine literary and artistic tastes. They understood well enough the mass-production nature of the popular arts; but they sensed as well the artistic potential of at least some of them. Because there did not exist a body of criticism to help them judge the popular arts, they began to make judgments in the only way they knew how to make them: by asking questions of the popular arts like those they had always asked of the traditional arts. What exactly, they might ask, are the conventions and other elements which distinguish one popular art form from another and from the more traditional arts? In the following articles Vernon Young, James Agee, Albert Hunt, and Gilbert Highet take this approach. Young endeavors to discover and point out the ways in which the movies can successfully express visual experiences; Agee, the ways in which a popular art form (the silent film comedy) sticks within its expressive limits; Hunt and Highet, the ways in which the movies sometimes abuse their own conventions.

The writers of other articles in this collection take other approaches also analogous to those used by literary or art critics of more traditional literary or art works. Reuel Denney, for example, explores the tradition from which two genres of popular art (science fiction and the comics) come, in order to compare some examples of each genre with other examples of the same genre. In his discussion of the comics, he also suggests some of the ways in which a popular art form implies certain social ideas. It is this approach which Norman Podhoretz and Eric Larrabee take also, the former with reference to television drama, the latter with reference to popular pornographic literature. John A. Kouwenhoven does something similar in his discussion of the ways in which American architecture and jazz express specifically American attitudes toward freedom, naturalness, and order. John Williams, in his discussion of the Puritanism expressed by the western story, film, and TV program, and Robert Warshow, in his discussion of the gangster as tragic hero, also take essentially the same approach, except that they deal more fully with the contradictions inherent in our contemporary treatment of the western and gangster heroes.

Among the interesting questions considered by critics included in this collection are those asked by Jacques Barzun, P. N. Furbank, William H. Whyte, Jr., and the critic of the London *Times Literary Supplement*. Barzun and Furbank ask what qualities of the popular arts make them popular and whether these are basically good qualities. Barzun ends by indicting the photographic exhibition *The Family of Man* because it presents what is least human about human beings; Furbank shows the essential cheapness and unimaginativeness of many twentieth-century best-sellers. Whyte asks about the integrity of various works of fiction. In examining organization-man fiction, he con-

cludes that most of the popular fiction of this type, while sham-
ming revolt, is actually urging conformity. The critic of the London *Times* asks questions about the appropriateness of mixed
genres. He deals with the musical comedy both as an independent genre and as a genre that borrows from other popular forms,
concluding that American musical comedy is better than British
because where it borrows, it does so more imaginatively.

These new perspectives on the popular arts are significant,
but not simply because they are new. The social scientists have
been contributing new perspectives to the study of the popular
arts for some time now. The new perspectives presented in this
collection are significant because they embody the kinds of critical principles which have always been applied to the arts. In
other words, this new body of criticism takes into account an
essential fact about the popular arts: whatever limitations are
imposed on them by the necessity to be commercially successful,
they are still art; they ask to be judged as art, and they fulfill, if
even in a limited way, the functions of art in our society. These
critics of the popular arts therefore serve a function that the social scientists have generally been unable to serve. They judge
the popular arts as art. By applying to the popular arts genuine
and appropriate standards, they succeed in showing to a public
for whom the traditional arts have little relevance the values,
insights, and experiences that can be gleaned from the best popular art works. And, finally, by searching for and applying appropriate standards to the popular arts, they are succeeding in
explaining not only the weaknesses of the popular arts but also
their strengths and their unsuspected potential. They are exploring the worth of the values reflected in the popular arts, the
kinds of tastes and attitudes reflected, and the meaning implied
by enjoyment of the popular arts. Such critics, like the best literary and art critics of traditional art, help us to understand the
ambivalences in our own attitudes, to learn what we are and
what we might become. They have brought criticism of the

popular arts to the mainstream of traditional criticism by attempting to explain the relationships between the form and the content of the popular arts, and the relevance of popular art to the best in modern experience.

JOHN A. KOUWENHOVEN

John A. Kouwenhoven (1909-) is a professor of English at Barnard College, Columbia University, and is a well-known critic of American culture. His criticism has earned him the respect not only of scholars in American literature, but of architects and industrial designers internationally. He is author of *Made in America* (1948) and *The Beer Can by the Highway* (1961). The following essay, taken from *Made in America*, defines the vernacular or folk nature of modern architecture, modern industrial design, and jazz. The reader may at first find the inclusion of jazz in a discussion of architectural and industrial forms somewhat puzzling. By comparing music and architecture, however, Kouwenhoven is able to illuminate the nature of both.

Stone, Steel, and Jazz

A civilization shaped by technical and industrial forces like those we have considered in the last chapter, working in collaboration with social and political institutions which—in spite of two world wars and a cataclysmic depression—have retained a degree of democratic equality and personal liberty unparalleled elsewhere, implies cultural values and artistic forms which are not only different from those appropriate to the agricultural and handicraft-commercial civilizations of the past, but have also originated in an altogether different way. For the process by which technological civilization has taken form has reversed that which operated in earlier cultures.

Hitherto, as Santayana pointed out in *Reason in Society*

(1905), civilization has consisted in the diffusion and dilution of habits arising in privileged centers: "It has not sprung from the people; it has arisen in their midst by a variation from them, and it has afterward imposed itself on them from above." But civilization in America, in so far as it can be identified with the vernacular influences this book has sought to define, *has* sprung from the people. What was "imposed on them from above" was the transplanted traditions of an older culture.

From the point of view of those who have been trained in the cultivated tradition, the emergence of a civilization from popular roots has been a phenomenon of dubious merit. The fear of what is often called "popular culture," in all its manifestations, is a notable feature of much historical and critical writing. To Santayana himself it seemed certain that "a state composed exclusively of such workers and peasants as make up the bulk of modern nations would be an utterly barbarous state." Indeed, those who think of culture as "the diffusion of habits arising in privileged centers" are led almost unavoidably to the conclusion reached by an anonymous writer in *Harper's* in 1928, that the future of culture in America is "clearly quite hopeless" because there is no church or aristocracy or other authority to modify or restrain what is assumed to be the human race's "natural taste for bathos."

Back in the 1880s this attitude was already firmly established. Cultivated people everywhere tended to agree with writers like Sir Edmund Gosse that it was from America that the real threat to established values came.

Up to the present time, in all parts of the world [Sir Edmund wrote in 1889], the masses of uneducated or semi-educated persons . . . though they cannot and do not appreciate the classics of their race, have been content to acknowledge their traditional supremacy. Of late there have been certain signs, especially in America, of a revolt of the mob against our literary masters. . . . The revolution against taste, once begun, will land us in irreparable chaos.

Here was one aspect of that "perpetual repudiation of the past" that Henry James had observed. But what Gosse did not see, and could not have accounted for if he had seen, was that this revolt was by no means confined to the mob. Eight years before Gosse wrote, the conservative and staid *North American Review* had published Walt Whitman's famous essay on "The Poetry of the Future" in which he argued that until America produced its own great poetry the "feudalistic, anti-republican poetry" of Shakespeare and the other great writers of the past "will have to be accepted, such as they are, and thankful they are no worse." Even the decorous William Dean Howells was publicly asserting a few years later that at least three fifths of the literature called classic, in all languages, was as dead as the people who wrote it and was preserved only by "a superstitious piety." What was happening, of course, was much more than a mere revolution *against* taste. It was a revolution *in* taste—and it had its roots in the changing bases of civilization itself.

The man who, perhaps more clearly than anyone else in his time, understood what was going on was the engineer, George S. Morison, designer of the first of the great bridges across the Mississippi at Memphis and of many other bridges throughout the country. A powerful man, physically and intellectually, Morison had early abandoned what promised to be a successful career in law to go into engineering. He went to work under Octave Chanute, chief engineer of the Kansas City bridge, in 1867, and by the time the bridge was completed in June 1869, Morison had risen to be associate engineer. By 1875 he was internationally famous as the man who—eighty-six days after fire destroyed the great wooden trestle which carried the Erie Railroad across the Genesee River at Portage—had designed and constructed the steel bridge which replaced it, and at the time of his death in 1903 he was widely recognized as one of the world's great engineers.

Oddly enough, however, few people remember Morison's

book, *The New Epoch as Developed by the Manufacture of Power*, published just after he died but completed—and the preface dated—in Chicago in 1898. It is a strange, forcefully clear book, and an important one, though no historian of our civilization, so far as the present writer has discovered, has taken any note of it. Briefly, it argued that with the discovery of ways to manufacture power mankind entered a new ethnical epoch which would transform civilization. What ultimate form the new epoch would take he did not specify, but he saw clearly that the new mechanical and technical era would in the long run bring about fundamental changes in men's relationship with one another and with their environment. In many ways, he realized, the new epoch would inevitably open as an era of destruction. By its very nature it would destroy "many of the conditions which give most interest to the history of the past, and many of the traditions which people hold most dear." There would be destruction in both the physical and intellectual world—of customs and ideas, systems of thought, and methods of education as well as of old buildings, old boundaries, and old monuments. How this destruction would occur, and how much time it would take, he did not care to guess. The important thing, he argued, was that it would come—"not because the things which are destroyed are themselves bad, but because however good and useful they may have been in the past, they are not adaptable to fulfill the requirements of the new epoch."

Meanwhile there was danger. Some time might elapse after the old had been destroyed before the new was established in its place, and the trouble would lie in the gap between the two. "The next two or three centuries," he warned, "may have periods of war, insurrection, and other trials, which it would be well if the world could avoid." One of the greatest dangers, in this connection, would be the fact that the new epoch would destroy ignorance, spreading education not only to all classes in civilized countries but to savage and barbarous races as well. The most terrible period of all would be that time "when the number of half-educated people is greatest, when the world is full of people who do not know enough to recognize their limitations, but know too much to follow loyally the direction of better qualified leaders."

Whatever the limitations of Morison's 134-page historical essay, it nevertheless succeeded as few if any of its more ponderous successors have done in diagnosing the causes of unrest and chaos in our time. If we bear his thesis in mind we will no longer have any difficulty in understanding the link between Gosse and other cultivated writers of the genteel tradition in the eighties and nineties and their vigorous critics in the 1920s. On the surface, of course, men like J. E. Spingarn, H. L. Mencken, and Ludwig Lewisohn were in open rebellion against almost everything that the exponents of the genteel tradition had stood for. But essentially the writers of the twenties were, in Lewisohn's phrase, trying as their predecessors had done to awaken Americans to "the peril of cutting ourselves off from the historic culture of mankind." Even Irving Babbitt and the new humanists were doing their best to reinforce traditional standards which would correct that "unrestraint and violation of the law of measure" which was at the root of our cultural deficiency. The finest literary talent of a generation was dedicated to the task of setting up some authority which would restrain what inevitably seemed, to anyone who cherished the values inherent in European culture, to be the American's "natural taste for bathos."

Almost nobody among our writers seemed to realize, as Morison did, that destruction of those values was inevitable, however regrettable it might be, and that the great job to be done was to help discover and establish those new values, based upon the actualities of political democracy and industrial technology, which must one day—after who knows what misery and devastation—take their place. Those who sensed that this was so were left to struggle with the problem alone, till many were overcome by the fear of futility. There is no more pitiful record of this fearful loneliness than Sherwood Anderson's *Perhaps Women* (1931). Listen to the note of desperation in these words, for instance:

. . . when mechanical invention followed mechanical invention . . . I at least had not tried to get out of it all by fleeing to Europe.

I had at least not gone to Paris, to sit eternally in cafes, talking of art.

I had stuck and yet . . . all my efforts had been efforts to escape.

Time and again I had told the story of the American man crushed and puzzled by the age of the machine. I had told the story until I was tired of telling it. I had retreated from the city to the town, from the town to the farm.

Watching an intricate machine at work, Anderson thought that the men who designed and built it might "some day be known to be as important in the life swing of mankind as the man who built the Cathedral of Chartres." And yet, he asked, can man, being man, actually stand, naked in his inefficiency before the efficient machine? And his answer was no, it cannot be done— not yet in any event. "They are too complex and beautiful for me. My manhood cannot stand up against them yet."

In his loneliness Anderson questioned whether men any longer had the power to make new values to replace those which the machine was destroying, and the point of his book was the despairing hope that perhaps women could do it for them. But he at least faced up to the challenge, which one woman had thrown at him, to "go and look" at the factories and machines which were shaping the new age, and to "stay looking."

Those who might have been expected to help in the exploration of new values too often spent their time ridiculing or denouncing or lamenting what they called America's bourgeois taste. People like James Truslow Adams, whose study of the downfall of the Puritan theocracy in colonial New England should have taught him better, wrote articles urging "the upper class" to refine and elevate the middle class and not be swamped by its "obscurantist prejudices, its narrow and ignoble prepossessions, its dogmatism, self-righteousness, self-sufficiency." In an article published in a popular monthly in 1932—after Radio City and the George Washington Bridge had both been built— one of the future editors of the *Reader's Digest* declared that anyone who looked at American architecture and manners could see that for a decade or more we had been in the throes of an "uprising of serfs." The middle class, he announced, had delusions of upper-class grandeur to which it was giving expression in structures like the Automat restaurant up near the Bronx with its huge cathedral window and elaborate vestibule, in huge, "insincerely magnificent" movie palaces such as New York's Roxy and Paramount, and in overelaborate business offices designed to cater to what he contemptuously called "the demand for the dignity of industrial pursuits."

That demand was real enough, and the amount of money spent in an effort to satisfy it is a measure of its intensity. It is certainly true that there were plenty of inappropriate guesses as to how that dignity should be expressed. But the failure to find appropriate expressions, in architecture and elsewhere, should not have been taken as evidence that the demand itself was contemptible. The onus for buildings like the Roxy, the Gothic Automat, and the ornate business offices belonged not to those who demanded beautiful surroundings for recreation and work without knowing how to achieve them, but to those who could not, or would not, share Louis Sullivan's faith that it was the architect's job to affirm that which the people really wish to affirm—namely, the best that is in them. For as Sullivan knew, "the people want true buildings, but do not know how to get them so long as architects betray them with architectural phrases."

As one looks back at the twenties and thirties in the light of

the argument which this book has developed, there is something
rather touching about the desperate efforts Americans made to
put utilitarian architecture behind them and to build beautiful
things. We had been effectively taught, by those who we readily
agreed were our betters in aesthetic matters, that what was useful was not beautiful. The architecture of the Chicago school—
the highest manifestation of the vernacular tradition yet achieved
—was discussed by Thomas E. Tallmadge in a chapter of his
1927 history of American architecture entitled "Louis Sullivan
and the Lost Cause." Such architecture was doomed, he said,
because of its demand for originality and for freedom from traditional styles. "What is the culture and genius of America?" he
asked; and promptly answered, "It is European." [1]

It was no wonder, then, that the ordinary citizen who wanted
beauty in his dwelling frequently turned, not to the vernacular
for inspiration, but to the cultivated tradition, convinced that to
be beautiful a design must be both European and useless. It was
in this mood that Americans built during the twenties those
genial horrors that Charles Merz described in *The American
Bandwagon:* the Italian wells that pumped no water, the Spanish
balconies for houses with no rooms upstairs, and all the rest of the
amiable but pointless lies of the Coral Gables era.

There were, of course, fine things being done all through this
period. We were still building grain elevators and industrial plants
which, as the German architect Walter Gropius had written in the
Jahrbuch des Deutschen Werkbundes in 1913, had a natural integrity deriving from their designers' independent and clear vision
of these grand, impressive forms, and which were "not obscured
by sentimental reverence for tradition nor by other intellectual
scruples which prostrate our contemporary European design." But
in the twenties this mechanical architecture, as Lewis Mumford

[1] Nine years later, in a revised edition of his book, Mr. Tallmadge
changed the title of his chapter on Sullivan to "Louis Sullivan, Parent
and Prophet"—a change which concisely expresses the shift in "official"
attitudes toward the vernacular from the twenties to the thirties.

pointed out at the time, had a vocabulary without a literature. When it stepped beyond the elements of its grammar—that is, when it moved from pure engineering construction into the field of architecture proper, it usually could only "translate badly into its own tongue the noble poems and epics which the Romans and Greeks and medieval builders left behind them."

A dispassionate study of the relationships between engineering and architecture in the twentieth century would be of great value to an understanding of our civilization. What apparently happened was that the engineers, feeling the need for something more than the purely utilitarian satisfactions which their designs provided, turned to the architects for help, while at the same time the architects, sensing the vitality of engineering construction in contrast with the sterility of traditional architecture, turned increasingly to the problems of giving architectonic expression to the forms evolved by the engineers.

Any study of these interrelationships would, to be sure, have to reckon with certain questions which are posed by such a structure as the George Washington suspension bridge across the Hudson at New York. As it stands, the bridge is concededly one of the most beautiful structures in America. Other great suspension bridges, like the Golden Gate Bridge, have more spectacular settings; but there is something about the George Washington's lofty yet sturdy towers, curving cables, and slender floor which, as the eminent bridge designer David B. Steinman has said, has made this bridge, to the younger generation of Americans, a symbol of our civilization. . . . Yet, as it stands, the bridge is unfinished; the original design worked out by the engineers and the consulting architect has never been completed.

The bridge as originally designed was the work of O. H. Amman, chief engineer; Allston Dana, engineer of design; and Cass Gilbert, architect. According to the *First Progress Report* on the bridge, issued by the Port of New York Authority January 1, 1928, the guiding motives of the design, from the engineering point of view, were "purity of type, simplicity of structural arrangement, and ease and expediency of construction"—motives which, as we have frequently observed, are characteristic of the vernacular tradition. But, the *Report* continues, in designing this bridge "it was realized that more than the usual attention must be paid to the aesthetic side," because of its monumental size and conspicuous location and because the bridge "should be handed down to posterity as a truly monumental structure, which will cast credit upon the aesthetic sense of the present generation." Here were the reverence for tradition and the intellectual scruples which Gropius had lamented in European design, and which appeared in America wherever the cultivated tradition retained influence. The general outlines and proportions were purely vernacular in origin, dictated, as the *Report* said, "by engineering requirements." But the towers, anchorages, and approaches "called for careful architectural treatment and dignified appearance." It was here, especially in the towers, that the cultivated tradition would be called upon to create the beauty which it was assumed the vernacular alone could not achieve. The steel skeletons of the towers, designed to carry the entire dead and live load of the completed structure, were nevertheless to be imbedded in a concrete casing faced with granite, in the design of which the architect had decorated the main arch with imposts, springers, and voussoirs and had provided other ornamental details which had no reference to the structural forces at work. . . .

However, as the 635-foot steel skeletons of the towers rose from the shores of the river, something unprecedented happened. The "unexpected" functional beauty of the naked steelwork fascinated people, and there was a widespread popular protest against applying the masonry covering which, according to the original plan, was to be the chief element in the aesthetic appeal of the bridge.[2] So far as the present writer knows, the Port of

---

[2] After this chapter was written the author came upon a discussion of this incident in Le Corbusier's recent book, *When the Cathedrals Were*

New York Authority has never taken formal action to abandon the original design, and it is still theoretically possible that the towers will be cased in concrete and stone.[3] The protest which prevented the "aesthetic" treatment of the towers was, after all, almost entirely a popular one, and the time may come when our betters in these matters will decide to go ahead with the design which they believed would best cast credit on our generation's taste. For to many people, apparently, it still seems difficult to believe that pure mathematics and engineering expediency can by themselves produce something beautiful. Even Chief Engineer Amman himself, in his final report on the bridge in 1933, still insisted that the appearance of the towers would be "materially enhanced by an encasement with an architectural treatment" like Cass Gilbert's, though he admitted that the steel towers as they stand lent the structure "a much more satisfactory appearance" than he or anyone else connected with the project had anticipated.

Nor is Mr. Amman the only civil engineer who is unable to accept the statement made fifty years ago by George S. Morison, past president of their society, that "architecture, which as a fine art would consign itself to the museum, . . . will find its highest development in correct construction." For even in suspension

---

White (1947). M. Le Corbusier agrees that the George Washington is "the most beautiful bridge in the world," and that it would have been utterly spoiled if the towers had been faced with stone "molded and sculptured in 'Beaux Arts' style" as the architect had planned. But he seems to have picked up an impression that it was the farseeing wisdom of a single "sensitive" individual which caused the original design to be abandoned. Further, he fails to consider the implications of the fact that the bridge as it stands is a *pure* engineering achievement in the sense that the designer had no aesthetic intentions, but was merely solving functional problems and providing a structure upon which the aesthetic "treatment" could be hung.

[3] The fact that Cass Gilbert's designs for the anchorages and approaches of the bridge were ultimately discarded in favor of much simpler designs by Aymar Embury II suggests, however, that Gilbert's designs for the towers may also have been permanently shelved. The Port Authority will not, however, make public any information on this point.

bridges designed since the George Washington, the engineers have usually felt the need of some sort of architectural treatment for the towers, such as the step-back of Joseph Strauss's Golden Gate Bridge or the steel cupola and spire indicated in Robinson's and Steinman's studies for the proposed Liberty Bridge over the Narrows of New York Harbor. . . . On the other hand, when architects have had a large part in bridge design they have shown increased confidence in the aesthetic force of unadorned engineering forms, as witness the design by Aymar Embury II of the sheet-steel towers of the Bronx-Whitestone Bridge. . . . Mr. Embury, it is perhaps worth noting, was trained as an engineer before he began his work as an architect.

One of the most illuminating architectural careers of this period was that of Raymond M. Hood, who died in 1934. The buildings Hood designed from 1914 to the time of his death offer a startling record of the change from architecture conceived in terms of the cultivated tradition to architecture as the exaltation of vernacular forms.

Born in Pawtucket, Rhode Island, educated at Brown University and the Massachusetts Institute of Technology, Hood worked for a year as a draftsman in the office of Cram, Goodhue and Ferguson, then went to the Beaux Arts in Paris. After his return to this country in 1911, he worked for a while in an architect's office in Pittsburgh, then in 1914 set up as an architect on his own in New York. For years he found little work to do, managing to keep himself going only with sustaining jobs like designing radiator covers. In 1922, however, he suddenly leapt into fame as the co-author of the prize-winning design in the Chicago *Tribune's* $50,000 competition. . . . The contrast between Hood's and Howell's tower, with its drapery of Gothic flying buttresses, and the design submitted in the same competition by the Finnish architect Eliel Saarinen, has often been pointed out. Saarinen's design—"a roaring pile of receding pyramidal masses"—made no compromise with the essential nature of a skyscraper; Hood's tried its best to hide the fact that it was made of concrete and steel and glass.

How much Hood's later work was influenced by the bold design which was defeated by his own in the *Tribune* competition it is impossible now to say. His next big skyscraper was the black and gold American Radiator Tower in New York (1924), which was simpler than the Tribune Tower but essentially in the same vein. Even as late as 1929, in the Scranton Masonic Temple, he was still echoing the Gothic which he had learned in the office of Cram, Goodhue and Ferguson. Then suddenly in 1930 he produced the Daily News Building, with its red stripes accentuating the vertical quality of its step-backed mass, and a year later the McGraw-Hill Building (his favorite) in which the wide strips of windows are separated by horizontal bands of green-blue. . . . Those two great buildings were the last, except for his undetermined share of the Rockefeller Center project, before he died.

What happened to Hood between the Tribune Tower and the McGraw-Hill Building would make a profoundly interesting study. No doubt it was in part the influence of his friend Joseph Urban which encouraged him to use color as an integral part of design. It is probable too that his partnership with the engineer André Fouilhoux taught him a great deal about steel, concrete, and glass construction. But such influences do not by any means answer the questions which his astonishing career raises. What we need to know, and someday may know when Hood's life is properly written, is what he meant when he said, late in life, to Kenneth Murchison, "This beauty stuff is all bunk." On the evidence of his two greatest buildings it seems safe to assume that he meant something very like what the Shaker elder, Frederick Evans, had meant back in the 1870s when he told Charles Nordhoff that Shaker buildings ignored "architectural effect and beauty of design" because what people called "beautiful" was "absurd and abnormal." Like the Shakers, the designer of the

McGraw-Hill Building had an eye to "more light, a more equal distribution of heat, and a more general care for protection and comfort. . . . But no beauty"—if beauty was something apart from such things as these.

In all branches of architecture the influence of the vernacular has been increasingly effective during the past twenty years. First the depression and then the war created pressures which tended to overcome the retarding influence of the cultivated tradition and to encourage a bold acceptance of vernacular forms and techniques. There is increasing awareness that the best work in American architecture grows directly out of the democratic and technological necessities which force us to think in terms of economy, simplification, and fitness for human purposes.

Writing in 1941, Talbot Hamlin listed some of the architectural high spots of the preceding five years: the Farm Security Administration's camps for migratory workers; the Hunter College building; Rockefeller Center; the Bronx-Whitestone Bridge; the new buildings of the Massachusetts General Hospital; the Kaufman house—Falling Water; the planned community of Greenbelt, Maryland; the Norris Dam and its powerhouse; the high school at Idaho Springs, Colorado; the Santa Rita housing project at Austin, Texas; and Frank Lloyd Wright's buildings for the Taliesin Fellowship. Of all these structures, as Mr. Hamlin observed, only Wright's Kaufman house was a private dwelling; all the rest were designed for some socially constructive purpose.

In a technical discussion of the FSA camps in a professional architectural journal Mr. Hamlin observed that the details of actual construction of these buildings were of extraordinary interest "because they show how the need for economy, creatively conceived, can itself become a means to new and beautiful architectural forms," as, for example, in the use of ventilating louvers as an important element of design in the Utilities Building at the Woodville, California, camp. . . .

Apparently [he continued] the San Francisco architectural office of the FSA approached every problem of architectural design, in big as in little ways, with complete freshness and innocence of mind. It had no fixed ideas as to windows or doors or interiors or exteriors. Nothing seems to have inhibited its logical approach to each problem; no fore-ordinated picture of what had been done or what was usual held it back.

Very much the same sort of freedom characterizes the best of our industrial plants, especially those built during the recent war, and here too it is economy which provided the impetus to imaginative construction. The late Albert Kahn, engineer and architect of such magnificent structures as the Chrysler Tank Arsenal in Detroit . . . , the Olds Foundry at Lansing, Michigan, and many others, stated the matter very clearly in an article written for the *Atlantic Monthly* in 1942. Strict economy must, by the nature of the case, prevail in designing factories, especially those which were then called "defense projects." All non-essentials, everything which is not "purely utilitarian," must be eliminated.

The very observance of this requirement, however, often makes for successful design [Mr. Kahn continued]. As a rule, the most direct and straightforward solution produces the best-looking structure. . . . Just as the mere clothing of the skeleton of a modern airplane by designers with an eye for line and a sense of fitness produces an object of beauty, so the frank expression of the functional, the structural, element of the industrial building makes for success. . . .

The triumph during the second quarter of this century of vernacular forms which emerged from a hundred years of first-hand experiments in patterning the elements of a new environment could be traced in many fields besides construction. In writing, for example, it would be easy to show how the tradition of reportorial journalism which first attained literary quality more than a hundred years ago in Dana's *Two Years Before the Mast* had become, since Mark Twain's time, one of the principal shaping forces in our literature and could be traced as clearly in John Dos Passos' *U.S.A.* trilogy as in John Gunther's *Inside U.S.A.* Indeed, journalism in this sense has become a distinctively American phenomenon. As Georges Bataille recently said in the critical journal which he publishes in France, writing like John Hersey's account of the atom bomb's aftermath in Hiroshima illustrates a characteristic American effort "to give reportage a foundation of rigorously factual detail" which is almost unknown elsewhere.

In the movies, again, one could observe the origin and development of an almost purely vernacular art form, the direct product of technology and the commercial organization of popular culture. Those who were sensitive to the changing character of our civilization had anticipated something like the movies long before the technical means had been discovered. As early as 1888 David Goodman Croly, newspaper editor and sociologist, wrote a curious book called *Glimpses of the Future* in which—fifty years before publication of *Finnegans Wake*—he prophesied the disintegration of the novel as an art form and suggested the use of colored pictures (in his day, chromo-lithographs of course) to take the place of descriptions of people and places, and of phonographs to reproduce the conversations between characters. That was as near as he could come, at that stage of technical development, to foreseeing the Technicolor talking picture. But the point worth noting is that long before movie cameras or color film had been invented those who were aware of the vital forces in the new civilization recognized that the traditional art forms would be superseded by forms appropriate to a technological environment.

A study of the development of the movies, furthermore, would provide a striking example of the interaction between the cultivated and vernacular traditions. Earlier in this book that interaction was discussed in terms of architecture, and we saw how the forms which had been inherited from an older civilization were modified by such vernacular influences as balloon-frame construction. In the case of the movies, however, the process was reversed, and a vernacular form was modified by cultivated influences. In the early stages movies were produced without any conscious aesthetic aim; the men and women who made them were in the business of providing mass entertainment in a medium which had been created by machines and science. Then, sometime in the twenties, cultivated critics began discussing the films of D. W. Griffith and Charlie Chaplin as artistic achievements of the first rank. The movie makers themselves began to wonder if they weren't artists and shouldn't behave as such, and artists who had been trained in the techniques of older art forms like the theater began to move over into movie making. With the coming of the talking picture in the late twenties the movies became more and more like photographed plays, and the confusion between what can properly be called cinema values and those of the theater still marks much of Hollywood's output in spite of the success of such movies as *The Informer* and a few of the great documentary films like Pare Lorentz' *The River.*

The role of the vernacular in creating new art forms and altering the basis of old ones could be traced, too, in other fields: in modern dance, in the evolution of the animated cartoon, of the comic strip, and of the radio serial, and in the effect of photographic techniques and movie scenarios upon fiction and poetry. But it is in music, especially in the music loosely known as jazz, that we can most clearly perceive both the extent to which vernacular forms and techniques have succeeded in modifying older traditions and the degree to which the newer forms and techniques are still limited.

Jazz is a subject about which many people have very intemperate opinions, and it will be well, for the purposes of this present discussion, if we can avoid the heated controversies which constantly rage not only between those who dislike it and those who like it, but even between the various cults of its admirers. We may as well avoid, in so far as possible, such bitterly disputed points as the precise relationship between jazz and the music of primitive African tribes and the extent to which jazz has been improved or degraded by its divergence from the instrumental music produced by colored bands in New Orleans sporting houses fifty years ago.

To begin with, then, let us agree that by jazz we mean American popular dance music, exclusive of waltzes, *as it has been performed* for the past quarter century or so. By this definition we mean to include not only the spontaneous instrumental or vocal improvising called hot jazz, epitomized by such a performer as Louis Armstrong, but also the carefully rehearsed performances, featuring improvised solos and "breaks," which professional dance bands like Benny Goodman's or Tommy Dorsey's give to everything they play—whether it be Tin Pan Alley tunes composed in the old operetta or ballad traditions, or melodies lifted from western European concert music, or pieces composed by Tin Pan Alley in imitation of hot-jazz improvisations. In this broad sense jazz is a product of the interaction of the vernacular and cultivated traditions, but its distinctive characteristics as a form of musical expression are purely vernacular.

Jazz is fundamentally a performer's art, and in this it marks itself off decisively from the music of the western European tradition. The composer, who is the dominant figure in Western concert music, is of almost no importance to jazz, for in jazz—in its most distinctive form—invention and performance occur simultaneously as the players have their way with the melodic or rhythmic pattern. It is true, of course, that musical improvisation has flourished in other cultures, and that even Western music of the cultivated tradition had its roots in improvisatory processes. But never before have conditions favored the universal availability of a performer art. The emergence of jazz as what might be called the folk music of the American people is inextricably bound up with such technological advances as phonographic recording and radio broadcasting.

Nor is it only in making jazz available that these technological devices have been important. In the early development of jazz, for example, the player piano not only contributed to the dissemination of ragtime (a rhythmic type which popularized many of the elements of jazz) but also imposed certain characteristics of rhythmic precision and even of tonal quality which became distinctive elements of its techniques. Anyone familiar with the playing of accomplished jazz pianists knows how they can use "pianola" style, though usually only for humorous effect in these latter, more sophisticated days. Similarly, the microphone of the recording and broadcasting studios has had its effect upon the instrumental and vocal performance of jazz. The vocal techniques of singers as diverse as Louis Armstrong and Bing Crosby, Bessie Smith and Dinah Shore, have been devised—often with remarkable inventiveness and sensitivity—to exploit the full range of possibilities in the microphone, and it is largely to the microphone's limitations and possibilities that the typical jazz band owes both its characteristic make-up and its distinctive instrumental techniques. Indeed, these techniques have become such an integral part of jazz that it is seldom performed without the use of a microphone even in small quarters like night clubs and even when the band is not on the air.

It was precisely with the beginning of recorded jazz, in 1918 and the years immediately following, that the instrumentation of jazz bands began to undergo the changes which in the early twenties produced the orchestral combination that is still standard. As long as jazz remained a localized phenomenon in the Storyville district of New Orleans, it retained the instrumentation which had first crystallized with Buddy Bolden's band in the 1890s: a combination of trumpet, valve trombone, clarinet, string bass, drums, and banjo. But as it spread to other parts of the country, and as recordings became increasingly popular after the phenomenal success which Victor made with its records by the Original Dixieland Band in 1918, new instruments were added (notably the piano and saxophone) and the balance of instruments within the ensemble underwent important changes. From about 1921 on the standard jazz orchestra has consisted of three units: the brass (trumpets and trombones), the reeds (saxophones and a clarinet), and the rhythm section (piano, guitar or banjo, string bass or tuba, and drums). All kinds of variants have been tried on this basic arrangement; big "symphonic" bands have been organized, and there have been recurrent experiments with various "small band" combinations built around a piano, and even some highly successful trios, quartets, sextets, and so on. But the three-unit instrumentation remains the standard for both hot and sweet (or commercial) bands.

One of the most interesting aspects of jazz instrumentation is that the rhythm section tends to remain intact, whatever variations may be made in the other units. A fifteen-piece band has four men in the rhythm section, and so has an eight-piece band. What this amounts to, of course, is a recognition of the fundamentally rhythmic nature of jazz. For it is its rhythmic structure that distinguishes it from other types of music.

It is precisely this distinctive rhythmic structure which makes jazz such an extraordinarily effective musical form in our civilization, and we will be better able to understand its significance if we acquaint ourselves with the two rhythmic characteristics which give it its special quality.[5] These characteristics are syncopation and polyrhythm.

Syncopation, in the simplest terms, is the upsetting of rhythmic expectation by accenting a normally unstressed beat and depriving a normally stressed beat of its emphasis. As such it is a device which is fairly common in western European music, and consequently people who do not understand jazz frequently assume that jazz performance has merely borrowed a stock effect

[5] Far and away the most useful analysis of jazz as a musical form is that by Winthrop Sargeant in the revised and enlarged edition of his book, *Jazz: Hot and Hybrid,* published in 1946. I draw heavily on Mr. Sargeant's work in this chapter.

from traditional music and done it to death. But in a Brahms quartet, for example, syncopation is a special effect, consciously used for its striking qualities, whereas in jazz it is—as Winthrop Sargeant says—"a basic structural ingredient which permeates the entire musical idiom."

Even so, syncopation by no means accounts for the special nature of jazz. If it did, musicians trained exclusively in the cultivated tradition would produce jazz merely by continuously employing a device with which they are already familiar— whereas all they would actually produce would be *corn*. For in addition to syncopation jazz is characterized by superimposing of conflicting rhythms which creates a peculiar form of polyrhythm. This polyrhythm, as Don Knowlton was apparently the first to recognize, consists of imposing a *one*—two—three rhythmical element upon the fundamental one—two—three—four rhythm which underlies all jazz.

This formula of three-over-four, with its interplay of two different rhythms, seldom is baldly stated in jazz melody, but it almost invariably affects jazz phraseology and gives it its unique stamp. Here, as in the case of syncopation, we are using a term which is familiar in the cultivated tradition of Western music; but, as with syncopation, the term has a distinctive meaning in relation to jazz. As Sargeant points out, the commonest form of polyrhythm in European concert music—two-over-three—*never* appears in jazz, and the almost universal three-over-four of jazz is very rare indeed in Western music. Furthermore, in European polyrhythm there is no upset of normal rhythmic expectation; strong beats remain stressed and no accent is placed upon unstressed beats. But jazz polyrhythm has the effect of displacing accents in somewhat the same way that syncopation does so.

The domination of jazz by these two characteristics means, as Sargeant makes clear, that the relation between jazz rhythms and those of music composed in the western European tradition is "so slight as to be negligible." In other respects, of course, jazz has been strongly influenced by the cultivated tradition. Both its scalar and harmonic structure are largely borrowed or adapted from western European sources, though even in these aspects jazz has developed certain peculiarities—notably the "barbershop" or "close" harmony which it shares with other types of American music including that of the cowboys and the hill-billies.[6] But rhythmically jazz is a distinctive phenomenon.

The source of jazz polyrhythm is almost certainly to be found in the Afro-American folk music of the Southern Negroes. But from the point of view of our discussion, the important fact is that almost all American popular music, the commercial "sweet" as well as the hot variety, has whole-heartedly adopted both polyrhythm and syncopation, *and that both of these are devices for upsetting expected patterns.* In other words this music which originated in America and spread from there to the rest of the world depends for its distinctive quality upon two rhythmic devices which contribute to a single effect: the interruption of an established pattern of alternation between stressed and un-stressed beats.

This interruption of rhythmic regularity in jazz is perhaps most clearly exemplified by the so-called "break" or "hot lick"— the improvised solo bridge passage of two or four measures which frequently fills the interval between two melodic phrases. During the break the fundamental four-four beat is silenced and the solo goes off on its independent rhythmic and melodic tangents, until suddenly the band picks up the basic four-four beat again right where it would have been if it had never been interrupted. The effect is brilliantly described in the following paragraph from Winthrop Sargeant's book:

[6] Sargeant makes a convincing case for the idea that this barbershop harmony is not an echo of the post-Wagnerian chromatic effects of Euro-pean music, but was developed from the structural characteristics of ac-companying instruments like the guitar and banjo. It merely uses the chords you get by sliding the hand up and down the neck of the instrument while holding the fingers in the same relative position. Cf. *Jazz: Hot and Hybrid,* pp. 198-200.

In this process the fundamental rhythm is not really destroyed. The perceptive listener holds in his mind a continuation of its regular pulse even though the orchestra has stopped marking it. . . . The situation during the silent pulses is one that challenges the listener to hold his bearings. . . . If he does not feel the challenge, or is perfectly content to lose himself, then he is one of those who will never understand the appeal of jazz. The challenge is backed up by the chaotic behavior of the solo instrument playing the break. It does everything possible to throw the listener off his guard. It syncopates; it accents everything *but* the normal pulse of the fundamental rhythm. . . . The listener feels all the exhilaration of a battle.

It is essentially this same sort of battle between unexpected, challenging melodic rhythms and the regularity of the fundamental beat which characterizes all jazz. In hot jazz, when almost all the players are improvising all the time and nobody really knows what anybody is going to do next, the exhilaration is more intense than in rehearsed performances spiced with improvised solos and breaks. But the difference is one of degree, not of kind.

Now a musical form which exploits and encourages this kind of free-for-all might logically be expected to be chaotic and disorderly in the extreme. As Louis Armstrong once wrote, you would think "that if every man in a big sixteen-piece band had his own way and could play as he wanted, all you would get would be a lot of jumbled up, crazy noise." And with ordinary performers that is exactly what you would get—which is why most orchestras play from scores in which, with varying degrees of success, an arranger has incorporated hot phrasing. But, as Armstrong concludes, when you have "a real bunch of swing players" they can pick up and follow one another's improvisations "all by ear and sheer musical instinct." It is the essence of good jazz performance to be able to cut loose from the score, and to know—or feel—"just when to leave it and when to get back on it."

Benny Goodman, explaining the basis of organization for

the famous band he got together in 1934, put the matter thus: what he wanted was, first of all, "a good rhythm section that would kick out, or jump, or rock or swing," and secondly, musical arrangements that would be adequate vehicles for such a rhythmic section and at the same time would "give the men a chance to play solos and express the music in their own individual way." In other words, Goodman intuitively recognized that it is the rhythmic structure of jazz which reconciles the demands of group performance (the arrangement) and individual expression (the solos).

What we have here, then, is an art form which within its own well-recognized limits comes closer than any other we have devised to reconciling the conflict which Emerson long ago recognized as the fundamental problem in modern civilization—the conflict between the claims of the individual and of the group. Everybody in a first-class jazz band seems to be—and has all the satisfaction of feeling that he is—going his own way, uninhibited by a prescribed musical pattern, and at the same time all are performing in a dazzlingly precise creative unison. The thing that holds them together is the very thing they are all so busy flouting: the fundamental four-four beat. In this one artistic form, if nowhere else, Americans have found a way to give expression to the Emersonian ideal of a union which is perfect only "when all the uniters are isolated."

By its resolution of this basic conflict jazz relates itself intimately with the industrial society out of which it evolved. The problems with which Armstrong and Goodman are concerned have much less to do with the problems of the artist, in the traditional sense, than with those of industrial organization. It is not in traditional art criticism that we will find comparable values expressed, but in passages like this from Frederick Winslow Taylor's *Principles of Scientific Management,* published just seven years before the first jazz recordings were issued:

The time is fast going by for the great personal or individual achievement of any one man standing alone and without the help of those around him. And the time is coming when all great things will be done by that type of cooperation in which each man performs the function for which he is best suited, each man preserves his own individuality and is supreme in his particular function, and each man at the same time loses none of his originality and proper personal initiative, and yet is controlled by and must work harmoniously with many other men.

In other ways, also, jazz relates itself to the vernacular tradition out of which it came. Like all the patterns which that tradition has created, it is basically a very simple form. Harmonically it is little more than the repetition of four or five extremely simple and rather monotonous chord sequences. Melodically, it consists of the repetition of extremely simple tunes which, however lovely or amusing they may often be, are not subject to elaborate development, as are the themes of western European music. They may be worried and fooled with in hot solos till they are practically dismantled, but they are not thematically developed. Finally, even in its rhythm, where jazz displays so much ingenuity, it is restricted to four-four or two-four time.

As a musical form, then, jazz is so simple as scarcely to be a form at all. The "piece" being played always has, of course, at least an elementary formal pattern—a beginning, middle, and end; but the jazz performance as such usually does not. It merely starts and then—after an interval which has probably been determined more by the duration of phonograph records than anything else—it stops. But this structural simplicity accords with the other vernacular characteristics that jazz displays. The polyrhythmic and syncopated flights of hot solos and breaks, with their abrupt, impulsive adjustments to ever-changing rhythmic situations, give jazz an extraordinary flexibility; but they could exist only in a simple, firmly established musical framework.

Similarly, it is the structural simplicity of jazz which makes it, like other vernacular forms and patterns, so suitable for mass participation and enjoyment and so universally available.

In these terms one can understand Le Corbusier's brilliantly perceptive observation that the skyscrapers of Manhattan are "hot jazz in stone and steel." Jazz and the skyscrapers! It is these two, and jazz in a "more advanced" form than the other, which to one of the world's greatest living architects and city planners "represent the forces of today." And both, as we have seen, are climactic achievements of the vernacular tradition in America. Neither implies anything resembling the cultivated tradition's negation of or contempt for the actualities of a civilization founded upon technology and shaped by democratic political and social institutions. (It is no mere coincidence that in Nazi Germany and Communist Russia, and wherever authoritarian regimes have existed, the men in power have attempted to discourage if they have not forbidden the performance of jazz.)

Let it be clear that in making these points we are not implying the aesthetic superiority of jazz over western European music or of Rockefeller Center and the McGraw-Hill Building over the cathedrals of Chartres and Salisbury. Such comparative valuations have no place in the context of this book, whether or not they have validity elsewhere. Judged strictly in its own terms, jazz is admittedly limited in its emotional range. Like other vernacular forms, notably journalism and radio serials, it is pretty much restricted to moods of humor, sentimental sadness, and sexual excitement; it is difficult to conceive of a jazz performance which would evoke the moods of tragedy, of awe, or of spiritual exaltation which are found in the masterpieces of western European music. Furthermore, there is some question whether jazz is capable of evolutionary development. To many critics it seems that jazz today is in all essential respects precisely what it was at the moment when it emerged from the New Orleans sporting houses to sweep the country. Others might agree with the present writer that works like George Gershwin's *An American in Paris* and parts of his score for *Porgy and Bess,* and more recent works like Robert McBride's *Quintet for Oboe and Strings,* give evidence of an evolutionary process whereby the vernacular jazz tradition interacts creatively with the cultivated tradition, losing none of the former's vitality and immediate relevance but greatly augmenting its expressive range.

Certainly skyscraper architecture at its best owes more than a little of its success to cultivated influences which have modified its vernacular qualities. But the essential fact is that both of these forms fully acknowledge their vernacular roots. Both are forms of artistic expression which have evolved out of patterns originally devised by people without conscious aesthetic purpose or cultivated preconceptions, in direct, empirical response to the conditions of their everyday environment.

It is clear that these vernacular forms and the others we have touched upon in this essay do not—by themselves—yet offer a medium of artistic expression adequate to all our needs. Forms inherited from an older tradition still must play an important role if we are not to be aesthetically starved, or at least undernourished. Opera and poetic drama, for example, may be as moribund as their most candid critics assert, but there will inevitably be periodic attempts to rejuvenate them. And such attempts will be made not only because of the cultural (and social) prestige which attaches to these and many other heirlooms of the cultivated tradition but also because we cannot yet afford to let them die.

Meanwhile the techniques and forms of the vernacular are rapidly attaining widespread influence and prestige, and their popularity throughout the world serves to remind us once again that it is not their specifically American quality, in any nationalistic sense, which gives them their fateful significance. The products of the vernacular in America do, of course, bear the stamp of the national character, just as the artistic achievements of other peoples display certain national characteristics. But these are superficial features. The important thing about the vernacular is that it possesses inherent qualities of vitality and adaptability, of organic as opposed to static form, of energy rather than repose, that are particularly appropriate to the civilization which, during the brief life span of the United States, has transformed the world. By an accident of historical development it was in America that this tradition had the greatest freedom to develop its distinctive characteristics. It should, however, temper any undue nationalistic pride which that fact might induce in us, to remind ourselves that people in other lands have sometimes been more ready than we to appreciate the human and aesthetic values of vernacular modes of expression. Foreign movies have, after all, frequently surpassed ours in creative realization of the cinema's potentialities, and European and South American architects sometimes seem to be more alive than our own to the expressive possibilities of vernacular construction.

As a nation we have often been hesitant and apologetic about whatever has been made in America in the vernacular tradition. Perhaps the time has come when more of us are ready to accept the challenge offered to the creative imagination by the techniques and forms which first arose among our own people in our own land.

STUDY QUESTIONS

1. What, exactly, do you think Kouwenhoven means by "vernacular forms"?
2. Why is he concerned about historians and critics who oppose popular culture?
3. Kouwenhoven cites Talbot Hamlin's argument that the need for economy "can itself become a means to new and beautiful architectural forms." What does this statement mean? How reasonable

is it? What insights does it help give you into the new vernacular arts?

4. Read Norbert Wiener's small book *The Human Use of Human Beings* (1950), and see if you can discover any connections between the enthusiastic interest that cybernation and automation have engendered and Kouwenhoven's idealization of the machine.

5. How, specifically, does jazz reveal "both the extent to which vernacular forms and techniques have succeeded in modifying older traditions and the degree to which the newer forms and techniques are still limited"?

6. How did phonographic recording and radio broadcasting affect jazz?

7. How important is rhythm in jazz? Why?

8. How does jazz "give expression to the Emersonian ideal of a union which is perfect only 'when all the uniters are isolated' "?

9. Does Kouwenhoven feel that jazz is aesthetically superior to western European music? What limitations does he see in jazz? What strengths? What do you think about its aesthetic significance?

10. What contrasts would you draw between the kitsch art that Gilbert Highet dislikes ("Kitsch," p. 185) and the vernacular art that Kouwenhoven praises?

WILLIAM H. WHYTE, JR.

> As an editor of *Fortune* magazine, William H. Whyte, Jr.
> (1917-   ), is in an excellent position to observe the
> structure and the values of the American business society.
> The following selection comes from his widely discussed
> study of American society, *The Organization Man* (1956).
> His major thesis in *The Organization Man* is that the
> organization society is founded on contradictory values:
> a practical acceptance of laissez-faire competitiveness, and
> a less realistic desire for paternalism on the part of the
> organization. In his analysis of organization fiction, he
> shows how writers frequently attempt to disguise the
> brutal competitiveness of big business beneath a surface
> appearance of humanitarianism and selflessness; he further
> shows that, although organization heroes frequently ap-
> pear to fight the organization, in reality they tend to ac-
> cept it.

Literature in an
Organization Society

CHAPTER 19
Love That System

If you wanted to put in fiction form the split between the Protestant Ethic and the Social Ethic of organization life, you might,
if you wanted to be extreme about it, come up with a plot situation something like this.

A middle-management executive is in a spot of trouble. He
finds that the small branch plant he's helping to run is very likely

to blow up. There is a way to save it: if he presses a certain button the explosion will be averted. Unfortunately, however, just as he's about to press a button his boss heaves into view. The boss is a scoundrel and a fool, and at this moment he's so scared he is almost incoherent. Don't press the button, he says.

The middle-management man is no rebel and he knows that the boss, stupid as he is, represents The Organization. Still, he would like to save everyone's life. Thus his dilemma: if he presses the button he will not be acting like a good organization man and the plant will be saved. If he doesn't press it he will be a good organization man and they will all be blown to smithereens.

A damn silly dilemma, you might say. Almost exactly this basic problem, however, is the core of the biggest-selling novel of the postwar period, Herman Wouk's *The Caine Mutiny*, and rarely has a novel so touched a contemporary nerve. Much of its success, of course, was due to the fact it is a rattling good tale, and even if the author had ended it differently it would still probably have been a success. But it is the moral overtones that have made it compelling. Here, raised to the nth degree, is the problem of the individual versus authority, and the problem is put so that no reader can duck it. There is no "Lady or the Tiger" ending. We must, with the author, make a choice, and a choice that is presented as an ultimately moral one.

The boldness of it makes *The Caine Mutiny* something of a landmark in the shift of American values. Popular fiction in general, as I will take up in the next chapter, has been going in the same direction for a long time, and *The Caine Mutiny* is merely evolutionary in this respect. But it is franker; unlike most popular fare, it does not sugar-coat the precept to adjustment by trapping it up with the words of individualism. It is explicit. Author Wouk puts his protagonist in a dilemma and, through rigorous plotting, eliminates any easy middle course. The protagonist must do what he thinks is right or do what the system thinks is right.

The man caught in the dilemma is one the reader can identify himself with. He is Lieutenant Maryk, the executive officer of the mine sweeper *Caine*. Maryk is no scoffer, but a stolid, hard-working man who just wants to do his job well. He likes the system and all his inclinations lead him to seek a career in the Regular navy.

Ordinarily he would lead an uneventful, productive life. The ship of which he is executive officer, however, is commanded by a psychopath named Queeg. At first Maryk stubbornly resists the warnings about Queeg voiced by Lieutenant Keefer, an ex-writer. But slowly the truth dawns on him, and in a series of preliminary incidents the author leaves no doubt in Maryk's—or the reader's —mind that Queeg is in fact a bully, a neurotic, a coward, and what is to be most important of all, an incompetent.

In many similar instances subordinates have found ways to protect themselves without overtly questioning the system—they can make requests for mass transfer and thereby discipline the superior, control him by mass blackmail, and the like. Wouk, however, proceeds to build a climax in which such reconciliations are impossible. He places the *Caine* in the midst of a typhoon.

Terrified, Queeg turns the ship south, so that it no longer heads into the wind. Maryk pleads with him to keep it headed into the wind as their only chance for survival. Queeg, now virtually jabbering with fear, refuses to turn the ship around into the wind. The ship is on the verge of foundering.

What shall Maryk do? If he does nothing he is certain that they are all lost. If he takes advantage of Article 184 in Navy Regulations and relieves Queeg temporarily of command for medical reasons, he is in for great trouble later.

Maryk makes his decision. With as much dignity as possible he relieves Queeg of command and turns the ship into the wind. The ship still yaws and plunges, but it stays afloat. As if to punctuate Maryk's feat, the *Caine* passes the upturned bottom of a destroyer that hadn't made it.

Eventually there is a court-martial for Maryk and his fellow officers. The defense lawyer, Barney Greenwald, makes what appears to be highly justified points about Queeg and, through skillful cross-examination, reveals him to the court as a neurotic coward. The court acquits Maryk. Queeg's career is finished.

Then the author pulls the switch. At a party afterward, lawyer Greenwald tells Maryk and the junior officers that *they*, not Queeg, were the true villains of the piece. Greenwald argues that Queeg was a regular officer, and that without regular officers there would be no going system for reserves to join later. In what must be the most irrelevant climax in contemporary fiction, Greenwald says that he is a Jew and that his grandmother was boiled down for soap in Germany and that thanks be to the Queegs who kept the ships going. He throws a glass of champagne at Keefer.

"I see that we were in the wrong," one of the junior officers writes later, with Wouk's blessing. "The idea is, once you get an incompetent ass of a skipper—and it's a chance of war—there's nothing to do but serve him as though he were the wisest and the best, cover his mistakes, keep the ship going, and bear up." *

Here, certainly, is an astounding denial of individual responsibility. The system is presented as having such a mystique that apparent evil becomes a kind of good. What would have happened if Maryk *hadn't* relieved Queeg? We are asked to accept the implied moral that it would have been better to let the ship and several hundred men perish rather than question authority —which does seem a hell of a way to keep a ship going. True, Wouk doesn't extend his premises to this blunt a point, and after it's all over suggests that somehow things would have worked out

* From *The Caine Mutiny*, by Herman Wouk. Copyright 1951 by Herman Wouk. Reprinted by permission of Doubleday & Company, Inc.—*Ed.*

all right even if Maryk hadn't turned the ship around. But the lesson is plain. It is not for the individual to question the system.

An extraordinary point of view, but did Americans gag on it? In the critical reception of the book most people got the point— and most of them agreed with it.* Partly this was a contemporary reaction to the spate of war books which in lazy anger personified the evil of war in officers and discipline. But the larger moral was not overlooked. *The Caine Mutiny* rationalized the impulse to belong and to accept what is as what should be. If we can be shown there is virtue in following a Queeg, how much more reason to welcome the less onerous sanctions of ordinary authority! The "smart" people who question things, who upset people —they are the wrong ones. It was Keefer, with his clever mind, his needling of authority, who led the ordinary people like Maryk astray. Barney Greenwald was too smart for his own good too, and to redeem himself he had to throw a glass of champagne in Keefer's dirty intellectual face.

It could be argued that the public's acquiescence was only apparent and if people had bothered to think about the moral they would have protested it. To get some idea of what would happen if people had to think about its implications, I tried a modest experiment. In co-operation with the authorities of a small preparatory school, I initiated an essay contest for the

---

* Save for a few articles in the smaller magazines, critical reaction has been overwhelmingly favorable, and, to judge by my sample of reviews, only a handful of critics caviled at the moral. Theater and movie critics, possibly because the three-year time lapse between the book and the screen and stage versions gave them time for a double take, entertained more doubts than book critics. (John Mason Brown in *The Saturday Review*: ". . . he suddenly asks us to forgive the Queeg he has proved beyond doubt unfit for command." Martin Dworkin in *The Progressive*: "Wouk wants us to think less and obey more. . . . There are voices stating this view more clearly than Wouk . . . he, at least, is still confused.") As in the case of the book reviewers, however, the majority applauded, including even such usually perceptive critics as Brooks Atkinson and Walter Kerr. (Kerr: ". . . we are exhilarated by a ringing, rousing, thoroughly intelligible statement in [Queeg's] defense.")

students. The subject would be *The Caine Mutiny*. Prize win-
ners would be chosen for the literary excellence of their essays
and not for their point of view, but it was the moral issue of *The
Caine Mutiny* that was their subject. Here are the ground rules
we announced:

> The essay, which should be between 500 and 1,000 words in
> length, should consider the following problems:
>   I. What is the central moral issue of *The Caine Mutiny?*
> II. How does the author, Herman Wouk, speaking through char-
>   acters in the book, regard the resolution of the moral issue?
> III. How do the resolution of the moral issue and the author's
>   judgment of that resolution accord with life as you know it?

At length the essays were finished, and when we sat down to
read them we were pleased to find how well they had grasped
the essential issue. In a sense, it was a highly nondirective test;
not surprisingly, they had gone to some effort previously to
cadge some hints from the teachers, and it was obvious they tried
hard to cadge hints from Wouk. How they felt about the muti-
neers depended considerably on how they thought he felt; and,
understandably, they were somewhat confused as to what side
they were meant to disapprove. On the whole, however, they did
grasp the essential issue at stake. Each interpreted its relevance
to his life somewhat differently, but most of them saw the problem as that of individual independence versus the system.

With one exception they favored the system. Collusion may
have fortified them in this, but their phrasing, and their puzzle-
ment over Wouk's position, left little doubt that their feeling was
genuine. Several disagreed with Wouk, but the grounds on which
they disagreed with him were that he was too easy on the muti-
neers. Here is a sampling of final paragraphs:

> In everything we do there are certain rules and regulations we
> have to abide by, and, like Willie Keith, the only way we will learn
> is through experience. We have to abide by the rules of our particu-
> lar society to gain any end whatsoever.

I cannot agree with the author in that I believe that one should obey orders no matter what the circumstances.

It seems that life in general is like a baseball game; everywhere there are rules and laws set up by many people for the ultimate benefit of all. Yet there are people who think as the young rookie that their actions should be directed by what they feel is right, not by what everyone else has determined. True, there may be partly extenuating circumstances; but unless the reason is more than subjective, the one who breaks society's laws will be punished by fine, jail, or even death.

This is another example of why a subordinate should not have the power to question authority.

Morally, however, the very act that Maryk committed is against the law.

The underlying causes of the *Caine* mutiny have their parallel in everyday life. . . . The teacher who allows personal dislike to enter into his grading; the politician who blames his mistakes on others; both of these are examples of fraudulency. . . . Greenwald, Maryk's lawyer, confused Queeg and twisted his words so that Queeg was made to look stupid.

Men have always been subjected to the whims of those in command; and so it will be in the future. This plan must exist or anarchy will be the result.

The student who dissented was not rebellious; like the others, he pointed out the necessity for codes and rules and regulations if society is to have any collective purpose. Unlike them, however, he put these points before, rather than after, the "but." "Is a man justified," he asks, "in doing what he truly thinks is right under any circumstances?" After pointing out the dangers of individual conscience, he comes to his conclusion: "A man must realize that a wrong decision, however sincere, will leave him open to criticism and to probable punishment. Nevertheless, and after weighing all the facts, it is his moral duty to act as he thinks best."

It is his moral duty to act as he thinks best. Has this become an anachronistic concept? Fifteen students against, to one for, constitute, let me concede, very few straws in the wind. Nor do they mark any sudden shift in values. Had the question about Queeg been asked in, say, 1939, my guess is that a higher proportion of students would have voted for Maryk than would today; but even then it is probable that a majority would have voted against him.

It is a long-term shift of emphasis that has been taking place. So far we have been talking of only one book and one decade, and, while this gives some sort of fix, it does not illuminate what our popular morality has changed *from*. To this end I would now like to take a look at popular fiction in general—as it used to be, and where it seems to be going.

CHAPTER 20

Society As Hero

I have been talking of one book and one decade. Now I would like to broaden the angle of view, for the *The Caine Mutiny* is only one more step in a development that has been going on for a long time. Let me at once concede that much of what seems contemporary in popular fiction is fairly timeless. Black has always been black and white has always been white, with few shades of gray in between; coincidence outrageous and the endings happy, or at least symbolic of a better world ahead. The very fact that fiction does tell people what they want to hear, however, does make it a fairly serviceable barometer. Whether fiction leads people or merely reflects them, it is an index of changes in popular belief that might be imperceptible at closer range.

If we pick up popular fiction around the 1870s, we find the Protestant Ethic in full flower. It was plain that the hero's victories over his competitors and his accumulation of money were synonymous with godliness. The hero was shown in struggle with the environment, and though good fortune was an indispensable assist, it was less an accident than a reward directed his way by a just providence. This didn't always go without saying, but it could. As late as the turn of the century the ethic remained so unquestioned that the moralizing could be left out entirely. Heroes were openly, exultantly materialistic, and if they married the boss's daughter or pushed anyone around on the way up, this was as it should be.

For a farewell look at this hero we have "Ottenhausen's Coup" by John Walker Harrington in *McClure's* magazine, March 1898 (several years before *McClure's* muckraking phase). Young Carl Ottenhausen is sent by his company to take charge of an iron furnace, where, it so happens, the boss's blue-eyed daughter is giving a house party at near-by Eagle's Nest, the boss's palatial summer house. After a brief brush with the daughter, Ottenhausen hears there is a crisis down at the furnace at the bottom of the hill. Some anarchist has gotten the men to revolt. Ottenhausen rushes down to the furnace, pulls out two guns, and advances on the workers. The surly devils cower before him. "The men of Laird's Furnace had met their match."

As Ottenhausen stands triumphant before the workers, the house party group comes down in evening clothes to see what's going on. The president is among them. The last paragraph of the story:

In the top of a tall building, in Columbus, there is a door bearing a porcelain label which reads, General Manager; behind that door sits Carl Ottenhausen, who now directs the destinies of the Mingo Coal and Iron Company. He owns a handsome house in the West End which puts Eagle's Nest to shame. There presides over that household a blue-eyed woman whose very look is merriment.

As time went on the materialism became more muted. Only a few years after "Ottenhausen's Coup," *McClure's* articles were roundly denouncing people like Ottenhausen for their avarice.

Fiction was much slower to respond to the changing temper, but once Veblen and Steffens and others had set to work, fiction heroes could not savor riches with the old innocence. By the twenties, money-conscious as they may have been, heroes who married the boss's daughter married a girl who *turned out* to be the boss's daughter. Not so many years later there wasn't much point even in that; and now, with the social changes of the last two decades, stories are just as apt to have the hero who marries someone who turns out *not* to be the boss's daughter. In a recent *Saturday Evening Post* story, for example, the hero falls in love with a rich heiress who owns a near-by boat. Actually, she's a secretary who is taking care of her boss's boat. A happy ending comes when the hero finds this out.

But this does not mean that our fiction has become fundamentally any less materialistic. It hasn't; it's just more hypocritical about it. Today's heroes don't lust for big riches, but they are positively greedy for the good life. This yen, furthermore, is customarily interpreted as a renunciation of materialism rather than as the embrace of it that it actually is. The usual hero of the postwar rash of "New York" novels, for example, is overweeningly spiritual on this score. After making his spurious choice between good and evil, the hero heads for the country, where, presumably, he is now to find real meaning in life. Just what this meaning will be is hard to see; in the new egalitarianism of the market place, his precipitous flight from the bitch goddess success will enable him to live a lot more comfortably than the ulcerated colleagues left behind, and in more than one sense, it's the latter who are the less materialistic. Our hero has left the battlefield where his real fight must be fought; by puttering at a country newspaper and patronizing himself into a native, he evades any conflict, and in the process manages to live reasonably high off the hog. There's no Cadillac, but the Hillman Minx does pretty well, the chickens are stacked high in the deep freeze, and no doubt there is a hi-fi set in the stable which he and his wife have converted. All this may be very sensible, but it's mighty comfortable for a hair shirt.

Of late, sanctimonious materialism has been taking a somewhat different tack. Writers have been affected by the era of good feeling too, and heroes are now apt to stick around the market place. But they still have it both ways. Ponder the message of *The Man in the Gray Flannel Suit*. In this story of a man "heroically reconverting" to civilian life, hero Tom Rath is offered a big-money job by his boss. Tom turns it down; indeed, as we heard earlier, he virtually scolds the boss for so much as offering it to him. He'd have to work too hard and he wants to be with his family. Sacrifice? Blessed indeed are the acquiescent. The boss says he will give Tom a good job which won't ask so much, and grandmother's estate Tom inherited, it also transpires, can be chopped up into a development that will make lots of the money that Tom and Betsy so patently covet. ("One of the rare books of recent vintage," an ad quotes a grateful reader, "leaving one with a feeling of pride to be a member of the human race.")

In *Patterns,* another, equally curious business tale, the hero doesn't mind work so much but he is similarly sanctimonious. He is appalled by the ruthless tactics of an industrial buccaneer. When the buccaneer offers him a top spot the hero says he wants no part of it. He is a moral man and he gives the boss a tongue-lashing. Having thereby saved his soul, he takes the job (at twice the salary). In a masterpiece of the have-your-cake-and-eat-it finale, he tells the boss he'll punch his face if he doesn't act right.

Not in the materialism of heroes but in their attitude toward society is where the change has taken place. In older fiction there was some element of conflict between the individual and his environment; no matter how much assisted by coincidence, the hero had to *do* something—or at least seem to do something—before he got his reward. Rarely now. Society is so benevolent that there is no conflict left in it for anyone to be rebellious about. The hero only *thinks* there is.

Stories must have at least the appearance of a conflict if they are to be stories, but contemporary writers get around this by taking a chunk of environment and then in some fashion disguising its true goodness from the hero. Since this means that the hero's troubles stem from a false image of life, the climax is easily resolved. The author simply tears the veil away. It was really okay all along only the hero didn't know it. Relieved, the hero learns the wisdom of accepting what probably would have happened anyway.

We have the small-town girl planning to marry good, safe old Joe, or already married to him. Just about the time she's getting bored with Joe and the small-town life, an actor or celebrity of some kind comes to town from the city for a short stay. He gives her a mild rush, and she dreams of a glamorous life with him. Then some minor crisis comes up. Who rises to it? Surprisingly, safe old Joe. We leave her as she gazes at Joe, with his briar pipe and his lovable idiosyncracies and his calm, quiet strength. She would be stuck with him in any event, but now she is swept by a deep inner peace to boot.

It is a churlish critic who would gainsay people the solace of fairy tales. But good fairy tales frankly tell the reader that he is about to enter the land of make-believe and to relax as we go back once upon a time. Current slick fiction stories do not do this; the tales are not presented as make-believe; by the use of detail, by the flagrant plainness of their characters, they proclaim themselves realistic slices of life. They are much like the "situation" magazine covers and the pictures of American family life featured in ads like the "Beer belongs—enjoy it" series. The verisimilitude is superb—from the frayed cord on the bridge lamp to the askew hair of the young mother, the detail is almost photographically faithful to middle-class reality. But it is all sheer romance nonetheless; whether the scene is taking the first picture of the baby, a neighborly contretemps over shoveling snow, or a family reunion of one kind or another, the little humorous squabbles merely serve to high-light how lovable and conflict-less is the status quo beneath.

Let me detour a moment to nonfiction, for it shows the same change of emphasis. Take, for example, that American staple, the self-improvement book. A half-century ago the usual self-improvement book bore down heavily on the theme of individual effort to surmount obstacles. It was a sort of everyman's Protestant Ethic; you too, went the message, can become rich and powerful. This buoyant doctrine reached its apotheosis in the "New Thought" movement, which, by conceiving the individual mind as an emanation of God, confidently asserted that "anything is yours if you only want it hard enough." Typical book titles tell the story: *The Conquest of Poverty, Your Forces and How to Use Them, Mastery of Fate, Pushing to the Front,* or *Success under Difficulty, The Victorious Attitude.**

This theme has by no means disappeared. Best-selling books for salesmen preach the same message, and with a gusto that seems downright anachronistic. Frank Bettger's *How I Raised Myself from Failure to Success in Selling,* for example, could, save for a few topical references, have been written in 1910. There is nothing that our old friend Henry Clews would not have

* I am indebted to Reinhard Bendix's analysis of the New Thought movement. In his excellent study, *Work and Authority in Industry* (N.Y. 1956), Bendix points out the dilemma the Protestant Ethic had forced upon the middle class. In the older version there was a sharp division between the haves and have-nots, with very little comfortable middle ground in between. Only a few could be successful; the rest would have to accept their station as an indication of lack of necessary personal qualities. As N. C. Fowler wrote in 1902 in *The Boy, How to Help Him Succeed:* "Many a man is entirely incapable of assuming responsibility. . . . He lacks the courage of willingness to assume responsibility and the ability of handling others. He was born for a salaried man, and a salaried man he had better remain." This, as Bendix points out, was much too harsh a doctrine and the New Thought movement, which denied such exclusiveness to success, furnished a badly needed modification.

subscribed to—and, like him, Bettger winds up with the maxims of Benjamin Franklin. (If I may add a somewhat extraneous comment, the comparative anachronism of this viewpoint helps explain why selling has fallen into such low esteem. The beliefs of the salesmanship ideal remain unchanged—in a world where everything else has changed.

But the general run of current self-improvement books shows a rather sharp divergence from the old tradition. On the surface they do not seem to, and their titles promise the old fare. Essentially, however, what they tell you to do is to adjust to the situation rather than change it. They are full of ambiguities, to be sure, and many still borrow heavily from the mental-power concept of the New Thought movement. But for all this the picture they present is one of an essentially benevolent society, and the peace of mind or the positive thinking extolled is a kind of resignation to it.

"What should a person do," a puzzled man asks Norman Vincent Peale, "who is unhappy and bored in his job after twenty years but who earns a nice salary and hasn't the nerve to leave? He'll never go any higher in salary and position but will always have a job." Peale, one of the few who can preach the Social Ethic and the Protestant Ethic at one and the same time, answers thus: "The trouble here seems to be the tragedy of treadmill thoughts. This individual has gone stale, dull and dead in his thinking. He needs an intellectual rebirth. That job of his is filled with possibilities he never sees, with opportunities he hasn't realized. Tell him to wake up mentally and strive for some understanding of what he can accomplish in his present position." ("Norman Vincent Peale Answers Your Questions," *Look*, March 6, 1955.)

Life, as it is, is beautiful enough, and one could easily gather from current reading that God is so merged with society that the two are just about indistinguishable. In an advertisement for the movie, *A Man Called Peter*, there is a picture of a man walking up a hill through some dry-ice mist. In his white shirt and four-in-hand tie, he looks uncommonly like a thoughtful young executive, but we find that he is a minister: *"He was a first-name kind of guy. . . . He was everybody's kind of guy. . . .* He un-pomped the pompous, played baseball with kids, turned a two-hour leave into a honeymoon for a sailor and his girl, and gave voice to all the longings in a man's soul. . . . *He was a lovin' kind of guy. . . .* Every woman secretly had her eyes on him, but he had eyes for only one—Catherine—who learned from him what a wonderful thing it was to be a woman—and wrote this story that topped the nation's best-seller list for 128 weeks. . . . *He was God's kind of guy."*

This profanity, for that is what it is, is bold, even for the popular press, but it is characteristic. God likes regular people—people who play baseball, like movie nuns. He smiles on society, and his message is a relaxing one. He does not scold you; he does not demand of you. He is a gregarious God and he can be found in the smiling, happy people of the society about you. As the advertisements put it, religion can be fun.

Oddly, the only time popular culture gives us a momentary glimpse of the beast in the jungle is when it reverses the usual process and masquerades reality as a fairy tale. Through the thin convention of animals, the animated cartoons show man in conflict with unabashed sadism, and with vicarious enjoyment people roar as human beings gotten up as cats and pigs torture and kill one another. In some television programs, the tradition of the two-reel comedies is perpetuated; here the environment is capricious and sardonic and the protagonist is not merely beset but defeated by the unglamorous impedimenta of everyday life—leeching friends, in-laws, icy sidewalks, stupid waiters, mean superiors. Perhaps it is for the same reason that people still seek out the old W. C. Fields pictures; through the sanction of laughter they can surreptitiously enjoy his detestation for little children, motherhood, and mankind.

Since 1900, to recapitulate, the vision of life presented in popular fare has been one in which conflict has slowly been giving way to adjustment. But there is more to this change than mere degree, and I would now like to take up a further development.

For many years most writers of popular fiction have portrayed society amenably enough, but once they were guileless in this respect, and now they have lost their innocence. Instead of merely showing people not masters of their destiny—and leaving the moral latent—there now seems a disposition to go out of the way to show that people cannot be. Society is no longer merely an agreeable setting in which they place their subjects; it is becoming almost the central subject itself.

Fiction heroes and heroines, as we have seen, have been remarkably passive for some time. It is not enough, however, to show that they are not masters of their own destiny; there now seems to be a growing disposition on the part of writers to go out of their way to show that they *cannot* be. To what degree one can be is of course a matter for deep debate, and many of the best novels of the last decade have been concerned with the impotence of man against society. But where these books deplore, slick fiction seems to rejoice. The new society, it says—often quite forcefully—is such that the hero does not have to wrestle with external forces. He may mistakenly believe this for a while, but eventually he is shown how unnecessary it is.

Society itself becomes the *deus ex machina*. In such cases one of the characters is a sort of accredited spokesman for the system in which the protagonists operate. The system, with an assist from its spokesman, resolves the hero's apparent dilemma, and lest the point be lost on the hero, the spokesman usually has a few sententious words at the end.

In a *Saturday Evening Post* story we see how the system solves the problem of a baffled couple. An Army captain and his wife have gotten in trouble by adopting a Japanese child while they are serving in a regiment stationed in Japan. A mean major and his wife spend most of their time making life miserable for the couple and the child. The captain feels he cannot buck the system by strife with the major; the only way out that he can see is to give up the struggle entirely, resign his commission, and take his wife and the child back to the United States.

Then the wife of the colonel comes to tea. She is especially gracious to the little Japanese girl and thus tacitly announces to all that the little girl is now part of the system. The villainous major is not punished. He and his wife remain just as mean underneath, but they are members of the system too, and thus, we gather, will now be nice to the little girl. The story ends with the captain and his wife happily ascending the stairs to their bedroom.

In a sort of ultimate example of the system spokesman, another *Saturday Evening Post* story rings in the President himself. ("Unexpected Hero," by Paul Horgan, March 26, 1955.) A lawyer is trying to convince a widow to marry him, but her little boy stands in the way; the boy idolizes too much the memory of his war-hero father. One day the lawyer takes him to look at the sights in Washington. The boy is unimpressed. At length, the two stop by the White House where the lawyer runs across an old acquaintance. Suddenly, a presence comes into the room. He puts his arm on the little boy's shoulders, and from above, to judge by the full-page illustration, a luminous light encircles him. After a long, and what would seem to a taxpayer needlessly garrulous, conversation, the President recognizes the lawyer from the war days in Europe. Wasn't he at the Rhine crossing near Wesel in March 1945? The President recalls the details of the then major's fine work and how he had put him in for the Legion of Merit. The little boy now admires the lawyer and the two go back home, happy.

Sometimes society is personified by an animal or by an inanimate object. In his study of *Saturday Evening Post* fiction, Robert

Brustein was struck by the religious overtones writers invoked. "The theme is adoption. A powerful person experiences a difficulty which is resolved through the generous impulse of someone weaker; by his own considerable power or through mysterious intimacy with 'higher-ups,' the stronger then rewards the weaker, and the weaker is subsequently adopted. It is the weaker character—the adoptee—who is the central hero with whom the reader is meant to identify, and his face is featureless so that the reader can substitute his own." ("The New Faith of the *Saturday Evening Post*," Robert Brustein, *Commentary*, October 1953.)

Popular culture is not monolithic in this counseling of resignation, nor is the audience in accepting it. It too is rife with ambiguity, and just as the executive confuses himself by paying homage to mutually incompatible precepts, so the audience still responds to themes directly contrary to the usual fare. *High Noon*, one of the most successful movies in years, was a clear throwback to the Protestant Ethic. In this morality play the sheriff, who is the hero, starts out as a team player; when he is confronted by evil he diligently seeks the co-operation of the townspeople for a group effort to combat the killers who are coming to town. But the group fails him and the hero is left alone—and afraid. But he conquers his fear and he conquers the killers. The townspeople come out of hiding and congratulate him, but, contemptuous, he spurns them and rides off with his wife, unforgiving. When I saw the movie the audience applauded when the hero told off the townspeople. Conceivably, the same people cheered just as much when Barney Greenwald told off Keefer for questioning the system, but the point is that they can still do both.*

In any treatment of man's isolation and his need to belong,

* *High Noon* seems to be susceptible to some much more involved interpretations. In "The Olympian Cowboy" (*The American Scholar*, Summer 1955, Vol. 24, No. 3) a Swedish critic named Harry Schein manages to interpret it as a piece of American propaganda. He writes: "I see *High*

diagnosis does not have to lead to precept. In *From Here to Eternity* Prewitt cannot exist outside the cocoon of the Regular Army, but the author presents this as a fact of life and a rather harsh one at that. In many recent books, however, there is an unmistakable note of approval; J. P. Marquand's protagonists, for example, are etched with great detachment yet they are impelled to peace through acceptance, and though there is no exaltation over their acquiescence, neither is there a sense of tragedy. When Sid Skelton, the successful commentator in *Melville Goodwin USA*, goes to a cocktail party for Army brass, the reader braces himself for some sharp comment on Army life. He gets none; Skelton, prototype of the Connecticut suburbanite made miserable by success, envies too much the Army people's sense of belonging and their rootedness in a firm system. He is the man on the outside looking in.

For all the ambiguities and cross currents the dominant strain in popular culture does seem to be adjustment to the system. To what degree this is conscious direction on the part of authors is, of course, impossible to determine. On any one story critics could long split hairs as to whether the author was resolving for or against the system, and perhaps the author might be in some doubt himself. Nonetheless, there does seem to be a sense of direction, and whether it is conscious or not, popular writers are showing an increasing affinity for it.

One way to chart the direction would be to provide a cross section of slick fiction writers with a new plot situation, let each of them make what he will of it, and then do a follow-up study

---

Noon as having an urgent political message. The little community seems to be crippled with fear before the approaching villains; seems to be timid, neutral, and halfhearted, like the United Nations before the Soviet Union, China, and North Korea; moral courage is apparent only in the very American sheriff. . . . *High Noon*, artistically, is the most convincing and, likewise, certainly the most honest explanation of American foreign policy."

of the results to see how they played back the material. By accident, I found myself involved in what was in effect, if not in design, an almost controlled experiment along these lines, and I would like to present the results in evidence for my thesis.

The plot situation came out of a study my colleagues and I did of the tensions in the life of corporation wives and their families. One article, essentially reportorial, described the growing domination of the family by the corporation and the active "wife programs" some large corporations were instituting to make the domination more absolute. The other article went into the wives' attitudes toward all this. I thought this the more important, for the interviews indicated that most wives agreed with the corporation; they too felt that the good wife is the wife who adjusts graciously to the system, curbs open intellectualism or the desire to be alone. There were exceptions, and they were significant ones, but the majority view was so depressingly strong, particularly among the younger wives, that we felt compelled to add a special editorial "In Praise of Ornery Wives." In some small way, we hoped, the articles would be a counter-irritant.

We were soon inundated with letters. Many readers were furious at the conformity described, and so furious they blamed us for it. This wasn't so bad, but the praise was something else again. Soon articles began to appear in trade journals and the women's pages of newspapers on "the wife problem." Congratulations to *Fortune,* they said, for breaking the ice and showing how wrong was the old hands-off policy. The rules of the game we had paraphrased tongue-in-cheek were reprinted verbatim as psychologically sound guides for peace of mind in corporate life; worse yet, the examples of company wife programs we had described were stimulating other companies into devising even more stringently controlled programs.*

---

* *Sales Management,* January 15, 1952, describes how U.S. Machine Corporation saw the problem: "All too often, so often in fact that it becomes almost a common situation, a sort of 'love triangle' develops in the

At length the fiction began to appear, and by the end of the year there was hardly a women's magazine that hadn't printed a story along the lines of "I Was a Company Wife," "Management Bride." On first glance, the stories would appear to be heartening omens of protest. The pictures in the opening layout were of women deeply troubled and apparently in some kind of bondage. As one caption asked, How is a wife to fight when an intangible force comes between her and her husband? But this was only the come-on. No praise of ornery wives; by the end of the story both the heroine and the reader learn that the good wife, as corporations said all along, is highly gregarious and highly adaptable.

In one story, to cite a typical example of the genre, an inexperienced company wife is trying to figure out how to make the next promotion go to her husband instead of the husband of a somewhat older friend down the street. Since the boss and his wife will be making the decision when they come to town for a week's stay, the heroine decides to throw a fancy dinner with caviar and all the trimmings. Her friend, she correctly estimates, will probably serve a much plainer dinner.

The day arrives. The boss and his gracious wife—boss's wives are usually gracious in today's fiction—come to dinner. Too late, our heroine realizes that she has made herself seem pretentious, and, sure enough, the other couple get the job. As with the colonel's wife, however, the system the boss's wife personifies is a warm one, and so she stops by for a friendly chat. Delicately she tells the heroine that it would have been better if she had served a plainer meal, but not to worry, her chance will come again.

----

lives of salesmen. The three sides of the triangle are salesman, wife, company. The wife sees the company robbing her of her husband's time and companionship, becoming a rival, she feels, for his affection. At first she is slightly resentful. In time she may become openly jealous. This, unless brought under control, can end up in irreparable damage to the salesman's worth to his employer."

I found one ostensible exception. It was a story called "Fireworks for Michelle," a complete-in-one-issue novel in the *Ladies' Home Journal*, May 1953. Michelle and her husband are enslaved to a particularly noxious company. The personnel people use all of the many different devices noted in our study and a couple we hadn't heard of yet. The boss tells Michelle's tousled-haired husband, Garry, how Michelle should dress, who her friends should be, and what decoration scheme she should use. Garry doesn't altogether like this, but he's a good corporation man and passes the word along to Michelle. Michelle, apparently made of stronger stuff than her husband, decides that she has had it. She and Garry invite the top executives and their wives for dinner. At dessert they turn and insult their guests.

"Well, ladies and gentlemen," Garry said, "I'm through racing after your mechanical rabbit. I'm not going to climb any further up your blasted ladder. This is where I get off."

She got up somehow on wobbly knees and went to meet him between the tables. His strong arm held her close against his chest.

"To love and to cherish," he said softly.

"To love and to cherish," she repeated.

A soul-searing decision? Not a bit of it; just in time for this bravura scene, it seems, old Grandpa Fitch died and left them a prospering farm.

Phony as this revolt was, most protagonists are not allowed so much as the appearance of one, and if the husbands have a common denominator it is acceptance. The movie *Woman's World* is a particularly good example. The gist is the idea of a company president selecting between men on the basis of their wives. No moral was intended—the writers didn't use the ending of the original magazine story (which antedated our study) and evidently had some trouble settling on the winner. As to the ethics of the whole business, however, they admirably reflect the current climate; they hardly bother to raise an eyebrow over the appalling tactics of the boss (cast as Clifton Webb); they playfully accuse him of being a bit of a torturer, but they make his tactics seem reasonable enough. He needs a general manager, *ergo* he must bring three men and their wives to New York for several days of scrutiny to see which couple should get the job.

Why any of this sorry crew should be considered at all is difficult to understand. One contending couple, Katie and Bill, consists of a juvenile and an equally juvenile wife who is interested chiefly in staying home and being dowdy. Another contender, Sid, is an ambitious fool who has forgotten how to be a husband to his wife; at length he and his wife revisit one of those quaint Italian restaurants with a comic-dialect proprietor (Tomaso, by name), and the emotional hang-over of this experience helps the wife reform him out of his ambition.

This leaves only one man fit for the job. He is Jerry Talbot, a hard-working husband with a sexy, ambitious wife. In terms of the values of the world depicted in the film, she's the only worthwhile person in the bunch. Unlike the others, busily sabotaging their husbands, she's actually trying to do something for her husband, albeit a little too pushily. She has the same zest for manipulation as the top man, and her ambition will provide her husband just the same economic motivation companies are so keen on. By the curious morality of popular fiction, however, she is too materialistic. Openly, she savors the idea of high life in New York. The movie does too—that's what its "production values" are all about—but, like the biblical movies, it must in the end smite that which it has exploited. She has to go. Some ten minutes before the dinner at which the boss has promised to award the prize, the husband viciously tells her to get packing. He won't even let her eat supper with the others. He gets the job. The boss explains that by ditching a person inimical to the team the man has shown his true mettle. To quote from the shooting script:

GIFFORD: Talbot, I think you have that . . .
"X plus" . . . that makes a big man big.
(pause)
But there was something that made me
doubt that you could ever function
successfully as a general manager—
a handicap—and frankly it caused me to
decide against you.

I was convinced you were not aware of
this handicap and I wanted to call it
to your attention. I found an opportunity that gave me a chance to do so.
I can only guess at the details, but
this much I know: that suddenly you
did become aware of it and had the
courage to get rid of it—and just
as suddenly I'd found my new general
manager! Congratulations!

Jerry looks up at Gifford, dazed, and it is a moment before he can grasp the hand that is offered him. Liz turns quickly to Sid and when she sees the unutterable relief in his eyes her own are suddenly filled with tears. Sid reaches for her hand.

And now his arms are around Liz and she presses against him with a warmth he hasn't felt in years. And next to them Katie and Bill are hugging each other ecstatically.

Hardly a morality tale. Nor are most such stories, singly. Taken together, however, they constitute a sort of ever continuing serial, and innocent of thought as any one story may be, cumulatively they have a message. And for all the fluff, what a dismal one it is! *Accept*.

To compare it with the theme George Orwell tackled in *1984* might seem to be freighting popular fiction with more portent than it deserves; Orwell was writing of totalitarianism, specifically Communism, and because he makes the leaders of society so villainous, the terrible world he sketched would seem far remote, a hell to our heaven. Yet in the final paragraph there is a scene which is hauntingly similar to the endings of our current fiction. As the erstwhile rebel Winston sits idly at a café, he gazes up at a picture of Big Brother. He begins to babble incoherently. Tears of gratitude well up in his eyes. At last, as the officers of the *Caine* had learned to love Queeg, he had won the victory over himself. He had learned to love Big Brother.

STUDY QUESTIONS

1. Judging from this selection, what do you think Whyte means by "the organization ideal"?

2. In the novels Whyte discusses, what traditional values do the heroes sacrifice to conform to the organization ideal? How do the heroes justify their sacrifice? Why do the authors of these novels consider conformity to organization values heroic? Why does the sacrifice of traditional values to the organization ideal disturb Whyte?

3. In what ways do modern novels, movies, or TV programs about big business—such as *Executive Suite* (novel, 1952; movie, 1954), *Room at the Top* (novel, 1957; movie, 1958), and *Patterns* (TV program, 1955; movie, 1956; play, 1959)—uphold the organization ideal, even though they seem to be critical of it? Are there any significant differences between the novel and the film or TV versions of any of these?

4. To what extent are doctor heroes on television, such as Ben Casey and Dr. Kildare, actually organization men? In what ways do the doctor heroes seem to be incompatible with the organization ideal? Why? How does, say, the *Ben Casey* series (1961) handle this incompatibility? Who generally wins, the doctor or the organization?

5. From your own experience, do you feel that stories in slick magazines—*Good Housekeeping, Look, Saturday Evening Post,* for instance—tend to define the good life in terms of the organization ideal? On what details do you base your conclusion?

6. Cowboy heroes are an obvious exception to the organization ideal. Why do they not conform to it? How does John Williams' " 'The Western': Definition of the Myth" (p. 98) help to explain this exception?

7. Does Robert Warshow's "The Gangster as Tragic Hero" (p. 155) suggest any reasons why the organization ideal should appeal so strongly to modern Americans?

NORMAN PODHORETZ

Norman Podhoretz (1929-   ), the editor of *Commentary*, is one of the most outspoken young critics in the United States today. Although he has dealt successfully with established writers such as Faulkner and Fitzgerald, he is particularly interested in newer writers and popular arts. He believes that the popular arts should be taken seriously; for, as he says in the following essay, "We may be looking in the wrong place for the achievements of the creative literary imagination when we look for them only where they were last seen—in novels and poems and plays." This essay indicates the real seriousness with which Podhoretz views television drama. He is concerned with the moral softness of drama which pretends to deal significantly with significant problems. His analysis of the cowardice implicit in many television plays will suggest many other places in which this same kind of cowardice is found in the popular arts.

Our Changing Ideals, as Seen on TV

At least fifty plays are produced on television every week. About a third of these are detective and mystery stories; another large slice is devoted to whimsical tales with surprise endings. But the remainder constitutes a genre peculiar to television. It has de-

This article originally appeared in *Commentary*, XVI (December, 1953), 534-540. Reprinted by permission of *Commentary* and the author.

veloped its own style, its own conventions, and to some extent its own subject matter.

These TV plays are theatrical rather than cinematic, taking their cue from Broadway, not Hollywood. Movie stars rarely appear in them, though prominent Broadway figures often do; the casts consist of extremely competent actors most of whom, I imagine, consider themselves theater people. The direction almost always betrays the influence of men like Kazan—which is to say that it tries to combine realism of surface with self-conscious, sometimes arty, arrangements, movement, and overtones. Both dialogue and acting are more sophisticated than is usual in the movies. In general the productions are on a surprisingly high level, considering the number of plays turned out every week.

The tendency is toward low-key drama, a kind of domestic realism whose effect derives from its accuracy in reflecting the ordinary man's conceptions of the world. The very style of the acting—always plausible, always controlled, never permitting itself the least intimation of hamminess, rarely even admitting that it is artifice rather than actual conversation—restricts the drama to that level of reality which is easily accessible to common sense. A whole play may be based on a very trivial incident, chosen because everyone in the audience will have experienced something similar. For example, a teen-age boy takes the family car without his father's permission, gets involved in a minor accident, and doesn't come home until three in the morning. His parents wait up for him, anxiety-ridden, and when he finally returns, all is forgiven and the whole family goes to bed with the sense of having got through another crisis. This play is "true to life" in a way that popular culture seldom is: the audience has never had the stuff of its daily existence taken so seriously, and it responds with a new feeling of self-importance and dignity. Unlike the soap operas, which betray a masochistic relish in minor troubles, the point here is the relief people feel in being able to resume their usual routine: trouble teaches gratitude for the humdrum.

Depending for its effectiveness on its ability to remain content with the world perceived and comprehended by common sense, this kind of drama must resist appealing either to escapist fantasy or to the critical intelligence, never wandering above or below the staples of experience. Nowadays, to be sure, that can include a great deal of surprising matter. In a play about the relation between a mother and her son, suggestions of an Oedipus complex are offered in much the same way as characters appear wearing clothes: the writer, the director, the actors, take it completely for granted as an ordinary element in the family. It isn't a mysterious, sinister force (as it tends to be in the movies) but a tangible factor existing almost wholly on the surface and demanding to be observed. This means, of course, that it needn't have consequences; in this particular instance, it counted for nothing in the plot. That a son should be in love with his mother is an index of his normality, not of his monstrousness. This must imply, I suppose, that the audience has been trained to regard it thus, or is well on its way to doing so.

Life in these plays, then, is non-heroic: a world governed by common sense is a world where "everyone has his faults and his good points." No insuperable moral problems are recognized, for, in a universe ruled exclusively by forces visible to the common-sense eye, there can be no dilemma which resists the touch of good will and a spirit of compromise. Often a play will open with a situation in which right seems to conflict with right, but in the end someone is proved wrong or neurotic or misguided, and the difficulty immediately resolves *itself*. A common-sense ethos must always hack its way through to the simple truths which are supposed to lie buried beneath the ugly and delusory overgrowths of experience.

Though everyone in these plays has weaknesses as well as virtues, we find the weaknesses far less in evidence. If a man sins, he does so almost accidentally, for sin is something that happens to people, not something they do. They make errors of judgment all the time, but they generally know nothing of pure or gratuitous malice. Only their virtues are essential to them; their sins are somehow external, reefs against which they have blundered in the fog. (The TV crime plays, on the other hand, become a repository of much that is omitted from domestic drama: crime is a violation of common-sense living, and therefore results in the criminal's exclusion from the sphere in which all slips can be made good.)

One would expect that a world made by common sense, ruled by common sense, and upheld by common sense, would be a pleasant world to live in. In many ways it is. It produces people whose passions are under control, who are well-bred, well-mannered, open, friendly, helpful, and above all, reasonable. More than anything else, they want to get along, they will do nearly anything to keep the peace.

And yet the optimism we find here is gray rather than flaming; it is overcast with a sadness that seems a new element in American popular culture. There is a distinct feeling that life is tough even for those who aren't harassed by the landlord and the grocer; and there is a shade of disillusion over the discovery that human possibility is not infinite—reverberations of Korea are in the air. The mood is more sober than what used to be called American optimism, and, as we shall see, far more honest.

Before the dislocations caused by 3D, Hollywood had been gravitating in several full-dress productions toward a similar form of drama (see Robert Warshow's "The Movie Camera and the American" in *Commentary*, March 1952). But the features characterizing the new genre—an insistent interest in domestic life, a *dramatis personae* entirely composed of ordinary people, a strict fidelity to the appearance of things, a quiet tone (everything is underplayed), a paucity of plot, and much discussion and debate—made it apparent that its real home was in television. Going to the movies is still more or less an occasion for most people, and an occasion demands something extraordinary. Even the size of the cinema screen insures that the movie world shall be larger than life (indeed, in answer to the small television screen, movie screens have become larger); perhaps for this reason, movies reproduced on television lose their bite. Watching television, on the other hand, has become an integral part of domestic routine, and the new genre serves an impulse to make the program a relevant and appropriate presence in the living room.

The living room, in fact, is the favorite setting of these plays, just as the favorite cast is a family. It is a middle-class family, neither unusually happy nor (as in the soap operas) continually besieged with trouble. Its most remarkable quality as a group is a negative one—fear is absent from the relations of its members and power thus becomes a corollary of love: it can only be had by free consent. The father guides and administers his household; he does not rule it. The plot always turns on some crisis that has suddenly developed, often in the family relations themselves: as in any family, its members are continually in the process of losing their illusions about one another, and the effort at readjustment is constant. Ultimately they emerge from their difficulties as more of a family, having restored a workable balance of power.

Almost always the father comes through as a sharper figure than the mother, who is supposed to have her being in and through her husband and children. A good woman is not so much *by* as *on* the side of her husband. If she asserts her personality too forcefully, we may be sure that calamity will result. Evil, when it makes one of its rare visits to these plays, is likely to come in the shape of a domineering wife or an overly possessive mother. As for the father, he is an earnest man, but his earnestness is mellow compared with the fierce unyielding grimness of his children or his wife's firm, uncritical loyalty to her feelings. Soft-spoken, controlled, never glamorous-looking, but always carrying himself with great dignity and self-assurance, he exhibits the palpable scars of a long combat with life. His humility, patience, and sadness are the products of many frustrations, and he is thus extremely skeptical of any comprehensive schemes or over-ambitious plans. Sometimes he is portrayed as a great disappointment to his children—for we live in an era where parents rather than children are perennially on trial—and in such cases the guilt and bitterness he feels are tempered by his pity for the son who will soon learn that all human beings are disappointing to those who make excessive demands on them.

We practically never see this new American father (as we used to in the movies and as we still do in television soap operas) involved in the big business deal, or embroiled in the problems of earning money: a comfortable income is taken for granted, while his career is merely a shadowy presence in the background. The great reality of his life, the sphere in which things happen to him, is his family. He carries his responsibilities willingly, without a sense of oppression, and the fact that they occupy him so fully, challenging all his resources of character and mind, never allowing him to get bored, is his most powerful proof to his son that the ordinary life is worth living. For this is the great lesson he is intent upon teaching. We find him telling his daughter that marriage, children, and love are far more important than fame and wealth; we find him insisting to his son that there is no disgrace in compromise. He represents reasonableness, tolerance, and good will: the image of American maturity.

Preserving the family from disruption is the role he is most often called upon to play. One species of disruption is conflict with his children. The conflict never takes the form of youth's rebellion against parental authority because the father's authority over his children is not given in the nature of things. Since he is a constitutional leader rather than an absolute monarch, his authority must constantly be reaffirmed at the polls. Nor can he assert it forcefully or arbitrarily: he must win the right to participate in his son's problems by making himself sufficiently attractive in the boy's eyes—good "public relations" is essential to his position. Interference with his son's private affairs being a matter of the greatest delicacy, he only presumes to speak in crucial matters. Otherwise he is there, looking on, setting an example, communicating through the silent power of his personality.

In an encounter with his children, he confronts them with a flexibility that often seems to be weakness but in reality turns out to be a wisdom based on the knowledge that human beings cannot afford to be too hard either on themselves or others. One play (already mentioned above) was about a young man of twenty who discovers his mother committing adultery while his father is away on a business trip. After wandering around the streets all night, the son staggers into his house, dishevelled, distraught, and looking a little drunk; to his amazement, he finds his father waiting for him. "Now listen, son, I know everything; your mother wired me and I took the next plane back. She told me the whole story." * The boy covers his face with his hands, unable to speak. "What are you going to do?" asks his father. "What do you mean, what am *I* going to do? What are *you* going to do?" "Well, what do you expect me to do—leave your mother and break up our home because she made a mistake?" At this suggestion that his father wants to forget the whole thing,

---

* I quote from memory throughout this article.

the boy stares at him incredulously; it's impossible to go on living with an immoral mother and a weak-kneed father. Patiently and sympathetically, the father persists in trying to convince his son that their family is too important to be destroyed by a mistake. His wife, he explains, is going through a difficult phase; her son is grown up, she has nothing left to do, she thinks she isn't needed. Now she's upstairs suffering more than her son would believe, terrified that he may turn away from her. "Our job is to help her, not to kill her. I've got to be more loving, you've got to show that you understand her side of things. Will you do it?" And, of course, the play ends with the boy going upstairs to comfort his mother. This is an atmosphere in which adultery and betrayal breed not hatred, but new responsibility. Yet all this understanding disturbs one: is there no breaking point?

Occasionally there is, as when the father's worldliness becomes irrelevant (or worse) to his son's problems. A young man, caught violating the Honor System in his pregraduation exams at college, is about to be expelled by a committee of his peers, when he offers to turn in the names of the others who had cheated with him. The list of names is confided to the chairman of the committee, a brilliant student who is planning to marry a sweet young classmate and go into his father's business. On the list he finds his fiancée's name. Should he, before handing it in to the Dean, strike off her name? His father, guessing the boy's trouble, persuades him to do so: "You're going out into a tough world where nobody will care about you and your interests. You have to look out for yourself and the people you love. This is a small town, son; they never forget a scandal, they'll never let you forget that your wife was once expelled from college for cheating. Everybody cheats; the only difference between a respectable man and a cheater is that the cheater has been caught. Son, don't let your 'principles' destroy your happiness. Use your head, boy!" At first the boy takes this advice, but later, to the consternation of his father, confesses while delivering his valedictory address, and proclaims his own expulsion. The two young people leave the small university town together to begin a new life.

Though repudiated, the father in this play is not unsympathetically portrayed. He realizes that the Honor System places too great a burden on young people, and that there is something absurd—something that violates common sense—in allowing a trivial matter to ruin a life. He does not, as his own father might have done, advise his son to give up this girl who will disgrace him: the highest value is still preservation of the family, even if it hasn't quite been formed yet. And in this play the idea of family takes on a special significance. The world outside is assumed to be hostile (like the outraged student body demanding the expulsion of the cheaters), or, like the kindly Dean, helpless in the face of circumstances and the Rules. The world outside is mechanical, rigid, governed by cold standards of no one's making: even the Dean can't protect the students he would like to forgive. Within the family, however, a man has resources, for the family rests on love and reasonableness, and it is in the nature of love to persist despite circumstance, while reasonableness provides flexibility to liberate the spirit from the tyranny of Rules. A person is most a person to those who love him; otherwise he is judged and disposed of.

That understanding and flexibility should be the father's greatest qualities is not surprising. What does surprise us, however, is that he rarely feels ambition for his children, merely wishing them to lead normal, contented lives. The only ambitious father I remember seeing is the one in the play just discussed, and he is also the only father who comes off badly in the end—as if ambitiousness were an act of *hubris* to be avenged. The drive for extraordinary achievement has always been considered notoriously American. An identity is something that must be earned, not inherited, and once earned it remains precarious and must be vigilantly maintained: if you lose your money, you also lose your name. This compulsion to prove that we are "saved" is probably a consequence of being born into a Puritan culture—many marks of status in America are simply secularized versions of what once were the symptoms of grace.

We seem, however, under the influence of psychoanalysis, to have reached a point where the most important mark of status has become not money, power, or fame, but a reasonably happy family life. Play after play insists that everyone is saved, that all are granted grace if they are but willing to accept it: adjustment is supposed to be available to all.

The way to justify the space you take up in the world is— as one father puts it—not to be *somebody*, but just to *be*. An adaptation of Dos Passos' *The Big Money* is used as a vehicle for showing the disastrous consequences of the pursuit of wealth; a young boxer who had been a foundling realizes that he needn't be compulsive about becoming a champion in order to give his infant son a "name"; a great soprano feigns the loss of her voice because she has learned that happiness lies in raising children and being supported by a responsible husband; a distinguished (divorced) actress gives up her career because she falls in love with a man who teaches her that what she really wants is a husband and family; a potentially great pianist is forced to admit that he is incapable of performing on the concert stage, and finds that being released from an immature ambition allows him for the first time to feel content in his marriage.

A particularly interesting example is a play about a widower, father of a fifteen-year-old daughter, who falls in love with a formerly great concert pianist. We are given to understand that some sort of illness interrupted her career, but now she is working steadily to stage a comeback. The woman is in her thirties, completely dedicated to music, living in a room which is stuffed with busts of great composers and that suggests the atmosphere of a mausoleum. Pressured into a date with the widower by a friendly neighbor, she reveals herself as socially inept. Her behavior is awkward, she can't dance, and she commits the great crime of being a kill-joy by leaving the country club at midnight. ("I'm so sorry to have ruined your evening," she apologizes pathetically. "I knew I shouldn't have come. I'm just no good at this sort of thing. And now I have to get some sleep, because I have a long day of practice ahead of me.") The widower was an extremely good representative of his type: equable, quiet, observant (the camera kept finding excuses for giving us close-ups of his intently serious eyes), sensible, understanding, and completely at his ease in the many different situations the play showed him in. We soon discover that the widower's young daughter fancies herself a pianist too. Against the tactful urging of her father, she breaks a date for the junior prom in order to prepare for a high-school concert. Eventually, of course, the daughter and the ex-concert pianist become great friends. Father is disturbed, but for the moment does nothing, allowing her to study with the older woman. As soon as the high-school concert is over, he intends to be firm. The night before the concert, however, he is horrified to learn that great plans are being made for his daughter. "She reminds me so much of what I was like at her age. And she has talent. You can't stand in her way. I've sent for the Great Maestro to hear her tomorrow night. He'll convince you." After the concert, the Great Maestro tells his ex-pupil that her protegé is extremely talented, but that she'll never be anything more than a competent performer: the divine spark is missing. Father is pleased, but the woman refuses to accept this judgment as final. "There are other teachers. We'll get them to hear her. I *know* she has talent. She'll work hard, oh it will be very hard, but she'll make it, I know she will." The father shakes his head sadly. "Why did you stop giving concerts?" "Because I was ill." "No, you weren't ill. I know because I looked up the reviews. They said you had lost your genius, that you were a great child prodigy who never developed." "No, no, it's not true!" "But it *is* true, my darling. Why can't you face reality? Why won't you move out of this tomb and live?" Through her tears she whimpers, "But don't you understand? I have to be somebody." Then comes the clinching line of the play: "Why do you have to be *somebody?* Why can't you just *be?*" And she collapses into his arms. In the last act, the young girl tells her idol that she has to be somebody, but the redeemed artist repeats father's epigram, adding that "there are so many things in life for you. There's your first dance, and the first time you fall in love, and marriage and children." The child weeps hysterically and rushes out of the room, but father and stepmother-to-be embrace. "Don't worry. She'll be all right now."

The play hardly entertains the suggestion that there are circumstances in which a normal life is worth sacrificing, nor does the writer admit that there may be more than one way of finding happiness, or that there may be other forms of the good life which take place outside the family circle. All this is typical of serious television drama. It would be a mistake, however, to think that "conformity" is being urged, if we mean by that imposing a specific model of behavior. On the assumption that everyone really wants the same kind of things out of life, these plays argue, quite plausibly, that only childishness or neurosis (both of which are characterized by the excessive demands they foster) will prevent people from taking advantage of their inalienable right to pursue happiness. Nor is there any uncertainty about the content of happiness; the only problem is finding the surest, swiftest, and safest means to a predetermined end.

Yet, curiously enough, the most salient feature of this ethos remains its sadness. It presents itself as making a modest demand upon life, a demand so modest that life would be guilty of the cruelest perversity to deny it. Bearing in its countenance the lines and wrinkles of maturity, it is always opposed to the presumptuous, enthusiastic "idealism" of youth. Yet what could be more optimistic than the belief that contentment and security are within everyone's reach? When success is measured by money or fame, failure can be chalked up to bad luck; the whole man is rarely in the balance, for a certain distinction will be maintained between the private and public selves: the private self is there to fall back upon if the other turns out treacherous. But when success is conceived as an attribute of the personality rather than of the wallet, failure becomes the tenth circle of Hell. A new fortune can be made, but a man's personality is his essence— personality, in fact, is the modern word for soul—and if that proves befouled, then no good can come of it. In these plays personality itself figures as the goal of all striving; the object of ambition becomes not success but "successful living." The type of all failures is the neurotic, pictured writhing under his burdens like one of the damned; and appropriately so, for in this view of things, a failure of the personality is the last and most refined torture of the Devil. Perhaps some perception of this accounts for the resignation that overcomes the intrinsic cheeriness of the new ethos.

It would be foolish at this point to make any simple judgments of television drama as a whole. Its most notable achievements, I think, are the sharpness with which it has distinguished itself from the movies, the effort it has made to be honest, the success with which it has managed to be serious without being objectionably pretentious. Most important, perhaps, it gives pleasure as so many "serious" movies have failed to do—Hollywood's great fault is its inability to see any connection between "entertainment" and "significance." Apart from a few comic strips, television drama seems the only area of American popular culture that refuses to distinguish finally between the two. Because it isn't imitative, it gives a picture of American life whose accuracy may be difficult to measure but whose honesty is sometimes astonishing: there was a time when the play about the mother's adultery would have ended with the discovery that she hadn't really committed adultery at all.

It may be that this drama reflects the values and aspirations of the newly emerged middle class, now large enough to constitute a mass audience and powerful enough to set the stamp of its attitudes on an important segment of popular culture. Formed by psychoanalysis and nourished by the concepts of social work, this class shows a conspicuous distaste for violence and a remarkable lack of interest in the ungovernable passions of young love. It puts a very high value on the family, though not in order to retreat from the community. The family here is an expanding rather than a restrictive entity, the nucleus of community; it comes to mean all decent, sensible, and understanding people, "people like us," people, that is, who act *as* people and not as "forces." The retreat to the home, then, means a retreat from "environment"—from the competitive world of business and politics, which menaces amiable human relations and does not yield easily to compromise and good will.

Finally, this drama has contributed a new figure to the popular imagination. Attractive and disturbing as he is, the father may turn out to be a summation of the postwar ethos. In his benign firmness, in his mature sobriety, in his sad but determined sense of responsibility, in his unceasing efforts to keep the peace, we can detect the traces of the contemporary political climate. He reflects the feeling that the only safe oasis in a dangerous, cold-war world is our own home, a home which, though it may once have been taken lightly, must now be preserved at all costs if the battle is not to be lost everywhere. And in the long series of plays which turn on a rediscovery of the father by his son, we find, perhaps, the mark of a generation which has moved out of rebellion and skepticism into a patient and humble acquiescence; and we may here discover the role the new middle class seems to have marked out for its own.

STUDY QUESTIONS

1. In what ways does the common-sense world of television that Podhoretz discusses oversimplify experience?
2. Why do you think this common-sense world of television is more sober than movies used to be in the 1940's?
3. Podhoretz says that the new genre of common-sense television plays is better suited to television than to the movies. Why? Sketch the beginnings of what might be called "a TV aesthetic" from Podhoretz' scattered remarks about the characteristics of television.
4. How does the constant "effort at readjustment" that Podhoretz sees as the main struggle going on in the new television plays relate to what William Whyte says about literature dedicated to the organization ideal ("Literature in an Organization Society," p. 50)? Are the ideals of organization and adjustment similar?
5. Compare the "image of American maturity" that Podhoretz sees in these television plays with the image of maturity expressed in some recent novels you have read. Compare it with the kind of maturity Hemingway, Faulkner, Cozzens, or Camus seems to want.
6. Why is Podhoretz disturbed by the great emphasis in the new television plays on understanding?
7. What does Podhoretz mean when he says that these plays do not urge conformity, at least in the usual sense of that term? What kind of conformity do they urge?
8. What does he mean when he says that "in these plays personality itself figures as the goal of all striving"? How does this goal of

personality relate to our current educational emphasis on objective personality tests? Why does personality seem to Podhoretz a limited goal?

9. Why does he say that television drama refuses to distinguish finally between entertainment and significance?

10. Podhoretz wrote his article in 1953. Is "the patient and humble acquiescence" he saw then still reflected in television drama? Do you see any new signs of "rebellion and skepticism"?

11. Podhoretz is talking primarily about television drama. Do you find any evidence of acquiescence to popular ideals in news reporting and television documentaries?

JACQUES BARZUN

Jacques Barzun (1907-   ) has, for many years, enjoyed a considerable reputation in many fields—as a music critic, a man of letters, a philosopher, an educator, and above all, a leading exponent of the humanist position in American education. He is especially well known for his attacks on teacher education in America. Perhaps part of his insight into the peculiarities of Americans comes from his background. Barzun was born in France and received part of his early education in French schools. Although the remainder of his education was in the United States, his early experience with French schools served to sharpen his awareness of the contradictory attitudes toward education and the life of the mind which he encountered in the U.S. His entire career has served to shape this native sensitivity into clearly developed and articulated insights about contemporary culture. He has spent much of his professional life on the faculty of Columbia University, where he is now dean and where he works actively with problems of American education. His books include *The Pleasures of Music* (1951), *God's Country and Mine* (1954), *The Energies of Art* (1956), and *Classic, Romantic, and Modern* (1961). This selection, from *House of Intellect* (1959), is intended by the author as an illustration of the popularly accepted idea that intellectual activity is opposed to and less desirable than the natural or primitive activities of man. The selection touches on not only some of the attitudes evident in the photographic exhibition *The Family of Man*, but also some of the attitudes widely current in American society; and it suggests some of the reasons that popular arts frequently lack intellectual content or subject matter.

Primitivism in
The Family of Man

In 1955 there appeared among the publications of the Museum
of Modern Art a catalogue of 192 pages entitled *The Family of
Man*. It reproduced an exhibition of five hundred photographs
gathered from sixty-eight nations to represent the multifarious
activities of the species. Quotations from James Joyce, Tom
Paine, and others put into words the fraternal outlook implied in
the title. The volume enjoyed an unusual popularity.* It was
seen and talked of in many places outside artistic circles and always, as it seemed to me, with that warmth of praise which
greets the objectification of strong contemporary feelings.

Presumably, then, *The Family of Man* gave visual pleasure
coupled with the confirmation of a philosophy of life. The ground
of that philosophy is best indicated by the cant phrase 'the human condition,' † and its setting forth in *The Family of Man* is
seen in the many variations played on but a few themes—those
of sexual love, misery, poverty, and the innocence of childhood.
Also emphatically represented are: birth, death, motherhood,
toil, music, and dancing.

One may of course take these scenes as direct evidence of
what is. Yet it is hard to resist the impression of sentimental bias
that they create by repetition, which one suspects is not ex-

---

* It has now been reissued as a small paperback at fifty cents.
† Its originator, Montaigne, would undoubtedly repudiate the intention
that the phrase almost always carries today—that of 'the detestable human
condition.' Montaigne knew the wretchedness of man's lot as well as anyone,
but strength of intellect kept him from infatuation with misery.

clusively the work of the local editors. Photography is a minor art, but it readily transmits—this is no frivolous play on words— the views of the photographer. And in this portfolio the views disclose a worldwide concentration on the helplessness of man, and on its excuse and anodyne—his animal needs and sensual pleasures.

The book opens with a rather tendentious female nude, prone amid the ferns of a forest glade. This is followed by episodes of kissing and caresses in public places. Next, in the middle of a black page, is a small square transom through which one sees a shoulder, face, and hand belonging to a couple making love. The vignette is printed horizontally so that there shall be no mistaking the subject. The theme of copulation is frequently repeated, notably as a restorative after the half-dozen pages devoted to schoolwork. The only other image of man that receives comparable insistence is that of suffering, as shown by faces of misery, worn limbs, and postures of dejection.

The rare views more or less related to Intellect are almost all of effort, chiefly by the young. Accomplishment and embodied power as they might be shown by the faces of great men and women are absent—except for a small snapshot of Albert Einstein, looking innocent and bewildered, and a truly magnificent full-page portrait of Judge Learned Hand. Here Intellect shines out for one five-hundredth of the kaleidoscope, though from its placing and its anonymity one surmises that the portrait is intended to represent not so much Mind as The Law.

Yet the law in action, a model of articulate precision, is also skimped, and government as well. Except for a view of the United Nations Assembly—the least of governments—one would scarcely know that man had fashioned the state and that it had value. The pictures that allude to it are of riots and mass deportations. An isolated sentence from Jefferson suggests that only the unorganized people are trustworthy, and a passage from the diary of Anne Frank asserts that they are all good.

Elsewhere, the extracts from the Bhagavad-Gita and from Sioux, Kwakiutl, Maori, and other folk literatures stress the simplicities. Primitivism is preferred. There are superb views of aboriginal nature, including a pair of nebulas as frontispiece; there are none of architecture as such. The book ends with yet another group of small children at play.

Whatever is formed and constituted (the work seems to say), whatever is adult, whatever exerts power, whatever is characteristically Western, whatever is unique or has a name, or embodies the complexity of thought, is of less interest and worth than what is native, common, and sensual; what is weak and confused; what is unhappy, anonymous, and elemental.

The rhythmic return of the main themes makes it evident that questioning the proportions of the work would be met by the statistical argument—there is in the world more fornication than philosophy; and by the documentary argument—all facts are created equal. Science, or a hankering for it, shows why it seems important to record the facial expression and gripping fingers of a woman during sexual intercourse. And art, that is, the works of the last half-century, have put us in the mood for this and all other primitivisms by giving us a peepshow as deceptive as the dark little square on page thirteen.

The pictorial art of the volume, which Carl Sandburg in his Prologue calls 'a camera testament,' has the ambiguity of photography itself. Message and composition do not always jibe, and at times one suspects that the exhibitors, bewildered by 'over two million photographs,' forgot one of their aims. For on the cover we are told to expect 'the greatest photographic exhibition of all time,' which promises a mainly aesthetic criterion. But inside, the purpose turns sociological, not to say philanthropic, as appears from the chief editor's absent-minded jargon: 'the gamut of life from birth to death with emphasis on the daily relationships of man to himself, to his family, to the community, and to the world we live in . . . Photographs of lovers . . . of the

family unit . . . of the home in all its warmth and magnificence.
. . . of the individual and the family unit in its reactions to the
beginnings of life and continuing on through death and burial.
. . . Photographs concerned with man in relation to his environment . . . the good and the great things, the stupid and the
destructive things. . . .' [6]

It is easy to believe that *The Family of Man* has been 'created in a passionate spirit of devoted love and faith in man,' [7]
but one may be permitted to ask whether that love was not
blind—blind to whole ranges of man's life, blind to the effect of
certain iterations, blind to the requirements of sense and manly
pride, blind to the discretion which judgment owes to even the
sincerest faith.

STUDY QUESTIONS

1. Barzun believes that the exhibition *The Family of Man* reveals the
   underlying anti-intellectualism of American culture. Do you see
   any of this same anti-intellectualism revealed in other aspects of
   popular arts? For example, what about the top-rated hillbilly
   shows? To what extent do the popular western programs share this
   anti-intellectualism? With what are the daytime soap operas concerned?

2. What popular stereotypes do you find to back up Barzun's con-
   tention that intellectual activity is of comparatively little value to
   most people?

3. In what ways are intellectual heroes treated to make them acceptable to the popular audience? How successful are these populari-
   zations?

4. Do you see any evidence (for instance, the rapid growth of the

---

[6] Edward Steichen, *op. cit.* [in *Toynbee and History,* ed. M. F. Ashley
Montagu (Boston, 1956)], 4-5.
   [7] *Ibid.*

market for academic paperbacks) that a regard for intellectual activities has changed? Or does your answer to this question depend in part on the way in which you define "intellectualism"?

5. Can you think of any reasons besides anti-intellectualism that a photographic exhibition might stress primitivism? Is there anything about the nature of the medium that would explain in part this stress? Is there anything about the nature of modern art that would influence the selection of material for this exhibition?

JOHN WILLIAMS

John Williams (1922-) is professor of English at the
University of Denver and editor of the *University of
Denver Quarterly*. His publications include two novels entitled *Butcher's Crossing* (1960) and *Stoner* (1965). The
following essay on the western hero is, in some ways,
closely related to Gilbert Highet's comments in "History
on the Silver Screen" (p. 225) on the uses of history in
epics. Both essays are concerned with the ways in which
facts may best be used artistically. But where Highet is
concerned with Hollywood's habit of overlooking the
dramatic potential of historical facts, Williams is concerned with the way in which western writers attempt to
push historical facts into inappropriate literary forms.
Williams examines the historical and social facts connected
with the myth of the western hero and then explains why
these facts do not easily lend themselves to epic or tragic
use, which most serious writers of westerns have attempted
to make of them.

The "Western":
Definition of the Myth

Given the dense history of the American West, nearly unexplored in its most fundamental aspects and potentially the richest of American myths, why has there not emerged a modern
novelist of the first rank to deal adequately with the subject?
Why has the West not produced its equivalent of New England's Melville or Hawthorne—or, in modern times, of the South's
Faulkner or Warren?

The question has been asked before, but the answers usually given are somewhat too easy. It is true that the Western subject has had the curious fate to be exploited, cheapened and sentimentalized before it had a chance to enrich itself naturally, through the slow accretion of history and change. It is true that the subject of the West has undergone a process of mindless stereotyping by a line of literary racketeers that extends from the hired hacks of a hundred years ago who composed Erastus Beadle's Dime Novels to such contemporary pulp writers as Nelson Nye and Luke Short—men contemptuous of the stories they have to tell, of the people who animate them and of the settings upon which they are played. It is true that the history of the West has been nearly taken over by the romantic regionalist, almost always an amateur historian with an obsessive but sentimental concern for Western objects and history, a concern which is consistently a means of escaping significance rather than a means of confronting it.

But the real reason that the Western theme remains inadequately explored is more fundamental. It concerns a misunderstanding of the nature of the subject out of which the theme emerges and hence a misunderstanding of its implications, literary and otherwise.

There are, broadly speaking, two kinds of uses to which the Western myth has been put in modern fiction—the first and more familiar is found in the conventional "Western"; the second is found in the serious treatment of the Western theme by such novelists as Walter van Tilburg Clark, A. B. Guthrie and Frederick Manfred. At first glance, it might seem that these two uses have as little in common as have the two sets of authors who employ them. But I believe that if they are examined with some care it will become clear that they do have failings in common, and that an understanding of both the uses and their failures will suggest an answer to the question with which I began this note.

In its simplest form, the conventional Western involves an elemental conflict between the personified forces of Good and Evil, as these are variously represented by cowboy and rustler, cowboy and Indian, the marshal and the bank robber, or (in a later and more socially conscious version of the formula) by the conflict between the squatter and the landowner. Complications may enter—the marshal may be beset with worldly temptations; the landowner, imperfectly evil, may enlist our sympathies for a moment; and in curious neo-classic variations, passion may set itself against honor.

It is tempting to dismiss such familiar manipulation of the myth; but the formula persists, and with a disturbing vigor. However cheaply it may be presented, however superficially exploited, its persistence demonstrates the evocation of a deep response in the consciousness of the people. The response is real; but though it may have been widely identified as such, it is not, I believe, really a response to the *Western* myth. It is, rather, a response to another habit of mind, deeply rooted and essentially American in its tone and application.

That is the New England Calvinist habit of mind, whose influence upon American culture has been both pervasive and profound. The early Calvinists saw experience as a never-ending contest between Good and Evil. Though fundamentally corrupt, man might receive, through the grace of God, a state of salvation. Of this inner state of Grace man can never be fully sure, but he may suspect its presence by such outward signs as wealth, power or worldly success. Since this state is the choice of God, the elect tend to be absolutely good; and the more numerous damned tend to be absolutely evil. This affair is wholly predetermined; man's will avails him only the illusion of choice; and the world is only a stage upon which mankind acts out a drama in which Good will ultimately prevail and in which Evil will inevitably be destroyed. In the very simplicity and inadequacy of this world view lies its essentially dramatic nature. All experience is finally allegorical, and its meaning is determined by something outside itself.

The relationship between this habit of mind and the typically primitive Western is immediately apparent. The hero is inexplicably and essentially good. His virtue does not depend upon the "good deeds" he performs; rather, such deeds operate as outward signs of inward grace. Similarly, the villain is by his nature villainous, and not made so by choice, circumstances or environment; more often than not these are identical to those of the hero. And even in those instances, relatively infrequent today, when the villain is Indian or Mexican, the uses of racial origin are not so conventionally bigoted as they might appear. Racial backgrounds are not explanations of villainy; they are merely outward signs of inward damnation. In the curiously primitive nature of this drama, it is necessary that we know at every moment the figure in whom Evil is concentrated and that we be constantly assured that it is doomed to destruction. Beneath the gunplay, the pounding hooves and the crashing stagecoaches, there is a curious, slow, ritualistic movement that is essentially religious.

There are, to be sure, more sophisticated variations upon this allegorical formula, though even the variations have inescapable connections with the original Calvinistic base. For example, in Owen Wister's *The Virginian,* though the hidden base is Calvinistic, certain recognizable Emersonian revisions upon the doctrine emerge. In the Emersonian formula, the Natural Man (i.e., the man who places his faith in his instinct rather than in his reason) replaces the Elect of God. In either formula, the end is a state of Grace, but in the Emersonian version the reliance upon instinct may come about either accidentally out of ignorance or by an initial act of the will whereby one chooses to re-

linquish the will. The Virginian, the Natural Man, is good by virtue of his "naturalness"; Trampas is evil in the older, more purely
Calvinistic sense; and the schoolteacher, Mary Wood, is the figure
of Emersonian compromise, the neither-good-nor-evil, code-pro-
duced human being whose salvation lies in the surrender of the
intellect.

If, viewed in this manner, *The Virginian* seems a grotesque
echo of Henry James's formula (the "natural," crude, innocent
American versus the "unnatural," sensitive, cultured European),
we should not be surprised. Calvinism, as it manifests itself in
literary art, is most likely to move toward allegory, as does the
primitive Western; but when the more serious artist can no
longer sustain the religious faith necessary for allegory, then the
transformed Calvinist habit of mind is likely to move toward
the novel of manners. Henry James, a Calvinist out of the Emersonian transformation, was a novelist of manners less from choice
than from necessity; he perceived that "essences" of tremendous
complexity lay in human character, and that these essences
existed mysteriously, obscurely. The only way to get at them was
by an examination of their outward manifestations, which were
most precisely discoverable in the manners of individuals, classes,
or even nations. To put it baldly, the novel of allegory depends
upon a rigid and simple religious or philosophical system; the
novel of manners depends upon a stable and numerous society,
one in which the moral code can in some way be externalized in
the more or less predictable details of daily life.

It seems obvious, then, that the Western landscape and subject, especially in their historic beginnings, are not really appropriate to the Calvinistic formula which has most frequently
enclosed them. What has been widely accepted as the "Western"
myth is really a habit of mind emerging from the geography
and history of New England and applied uncritically to another
place and time.

If the popular Western mechanically and irrelevantly furnishes forth perfunctory details, using stories so stereotyped and empty that they have become independent of human beings, and therefore contemptuous of them, what of the serious novel that would make use of the Western theme and subject?

Because of their integrity and talent, one might wish to exempt such novelists as Walter van Tilburg Clark, Frederick Manfred and even A. B. Guthrie from a charge even remotely similar to the one leveled against the legion of hacks who have done so much to cheapen the Western theme. But with the possible exception of Clark, each of these novelists is, in his own way, guilty of mistaking the real nature of his subject and of imprecisely adjusting his form to the demands of that subject. It is not that they have hit upon the wrong myth, but that they have failed to recognize in the first place that their subject is mythic. Moment by moment, the good novelist is confronted by the necessities and implications of his matter; the worth of his novel will in many respects be dependent upon his success in adjusting form to subject.

Novelists have used, singly or in combination, four forms: the tragic, the comic, the epic and the mythic.

The details which formalize the tragic subject are most often historical and "true," either in fact or effect; thus tragedy has the advantage of seeming inevitable. So that they may have great powers of generalization, its characters are usually of high rank, most often functionaries of the state; the province of tragedy is public life, and hence the feeling that it evokes is public feeling. It is a requisite of tragedy that its outcome be unfortunate, because its theme is the cost of disorder in an ordered universe.

Comedy, on the other hand, is non-historical and invented; the characters are of low or moderate estate—or if they are not, the novelist's focus is upon the non-public aspects of their lives; the conflicts which turn the plot and impel the characters are relatively trivial; the field in which they exist is that of private experience. Thus, the subject of comedy is most often domestic or social; and the outcome, if not always joyful, is at least ironic and mixed. Comedy has been profoundly influential upon the development of the novel; from its near-beginnings in Madame de LaFayette, Defoe and Fielding, and through its development in Jane Austen, Henry James and Ford Madox Ford, it has achieved most of its distinction as a form by exploring the comic subject.

The epic was a form most meaningful to primitive cultures seeking unification of scattered strengths and cultural resources; it has been used imperfectly and with relative infrequency in the last two or three hundred years. Since its central character embodies the most primitive nationalistic aspirations of a people, its plot, though embedded in a kind of history, is really an accretion of fantastic and superhuman adventures. Because its intention is relatively simple, its structure is sequential and repetitive. Unlike the tragic character, the epic character tends to be one-dimensional, flat and not particularly distinguished by intellectual or moral powers. His virtues are the simple ones of physical courage and strength, singleness of purpose and blind endurance. Again, unlike tragedy, the outcome of the epic is always fortunate for the real subject, the people—though the hero may sacrifice himself to make that outcome possible. Its tone is triumphant; its rhetoric is inflated, extreme; as a form that embodies an intention prior to that of tragedy, it is a movement through those conflicts that must be overcome to establish order in the first place. It does not move among the conflicts that threaten an order long established.

It is upon this epic subject, or more exactly upon the form and manner which is an outgrowth of the subject, that the novelist who would put to serious use the Western theme has most frequently and unfortunately stumbled.

Superficially, the Western adventure seems typically epic, compounded as it is of individual acts of bravery; of strength

and endurance before dreadful hardships; of treks across unknown lands; of enemies subjugated and wild beasts slain; of
heroes whose names have come down with legendary force.
But despite its appearance, the adventure is not epical, and it is
not so essentially.

What gives the epic its unique force and what finally justifies
and sustains both its rhetoric and repetitive structure, is its fundamentally nationalistic nature. The heroism, the bloodletting,
the superhuman bravery, the terrible mutilations—these are
given point and intensity only by the nationalistic impulse that
lies behind them. Without that impulse, the adventure (handled
epically) is empty, is bombast, is violence without rage.

Myth bears certain resemblances to the other forms and subjects I have mentioned; but these are in the main superficial. As
in tragedy, the mythic subject rises from the enveloping action
of history, but the events that detail that subject are invented.
For example, in *Moby Dick* we are at all times profoundly aware
of the social, economic, religious and political forces that impel
the *Pequod* and its crew upon their journey, and we believe in
those forces as a matter of course. But the events and characters
which specify the quest are intensely symbolic and they compel
belief on a level different from that of historical reality. Like
the tragic character, the mythic character is designed to generalize the subject; but whereas the tragic character gets his
generalizing power from his high rank (ideally, as the function-
ary of the state, he is a perfect and inclusive type whose fate is
inextricably tied to that of his subjects), the mythic character
gets his generalizing power from his archetypal nature. The
mythic subject typically involves a quest—one that is essentially
inner, however externally it may disclose itself. Thus its feeling
is neither public in the large and impersonal sense that tragic
feeling must be, nor private in the small and domestic sense that
comic feeling must be. It is that feeling which comes with an
awareness of the cost of insight, the exaction of the human spirit

by the terror of truth. The outcome of myth is always mixed; its quest is for an order of the self that is gained at the expense of knowing at last the essential chaos of the universe.

The pure critic or anthropologist might wish to separate myth from its historic base; but in the twentieth century the practicing novelist cannot do so. By his nature, he is not "pure"; and since in the main his imagination is historical, he cannot commit himself seriously to localities, times and subjects that he cannot feel in his bones; therefore the habitation of myth is of great importance to him. In the history of the Western landscape, and in its relation to human character, he may find that habitation, and I know of no other place from which the myth might so richly proceed.

But if the myth is to emerge with some meaning, the novelist must consider the implications of its history.

The history of the West is in some respects the record of its exploitation. Its early exploitation by the Spanish moving up from Mexico was clearly nationalistic, for the open purpose of strengthening an already powerful nation and church. But the American frontiersman, who came from the East through Kentucky and Tennessee and out of St. Louis, was a lone human being who went upon plain and mountain, who subjugated nature on his own terms, and who exploited the land for his own benefit. There was no precise ideological motive for his exploitation, and because of that lack of external motive the adventure became all the more private and intense. Removed from a social structure of some stability, imbued to some degree with a New England-Calvinist-Emersonian tradition that afforded him an abstract view of the nature of his experience, he suddenly found himself in the midst of a few desperate and concrete facts, primary among which was the necessity for survival in a universe whose brutality he had theretofore but dimly suspected. And whether he wished to or not, he was forced to reconsider those ideas he held about the nature of himself and the world in which he lived, ideas that had once, since they sprang from the very social and economic structure they explained, served him quite adequately.

The Western adventure, then, is not really epical; no national force stronger than himself pushed the American frontiersman beyond the bounds of his known experience into the chaos of a new land, into the unknown. His voyage into the wilderness was most meaningfully a voyage into the self, experimental, private and sometimes obscure.

We may now turn to those novelists, whom I mentioned earlier, who have chosen to deal with the Western adventure but who have mistaken the nature of their subject and who have, consciously or unconsciously, imposed epic strategies upon mythic subjects.

The first (and the best of them) is Walter van Tilburg Clark; the novels with which I am concerned are *The Oxbow Incident* and *The Track of the Cat.* I deal with Clark first in order to get him out of the way, since he has managed to escape the trap into which the others have fallen. He has managed to escape for reasons that may be technically described as accidental, though of course the escape is really a solution and in art there are no accidents. Both of these novels are essentially morality plays, but of a pronounced human subtlety and complexity; and though both make use of the Western landscape, it is not really necessary to either of them. Insofar as these matters can be pinned down, Clark seems to have gathered most of his technical resources from a study of the French novel, particularly the Flaubertian novel, with its concern for locked structure, restrained prose and physical detail raised to symbolic import. Thus, the precisely located scene of his novels is more nearly a necessity demanded by his technique than a genuine use of scene as an aspect of subject. Clark certainly has imposed no epic strategies upon his work, but neither has he availed himself of the Western myth. Which is to say that he is not an essentially *Western* novelist in the sense that I have been using that word. I hardly need to add that there is no reason why he should be.

The Big Sky was A. B. Guthrie's first serious novel, and it remains his best. Guthrie began as a writer of popular fiction, and even in his more serious work he is primarily concerned with the feelings that rise from his subjects rather than with their meanings. In this accidental respect, and on a less intense level, his intention is similar to that of the writer of epic. Moreover, the structure of *The Big Sky* is fundamentally epic; it is sequential, accretive and repetitive, and its primary purpose is to display the epical virtues of physical strength, courage and endurance in its chief characters. But no very vital purpose animates the adventures of the characters; they are flat and typical in the most limited sense of that word; and because of their purposelessness and flatness, the impact of experience upon them is curiously unreal and almost totally visual. We finally see that both plot and character are merely the means whereby we "experience" the landscape, which is the real subject of the novel. This suggests, perhaps, that Guthrie's novel has no true subject. It is an apparatus designed with some elaboration for the rather simple purpose of expressing a few vague and romantic feelings about the land itself. It is unsatisfactory as a work of art; its epical structure and character depiction are irrelevant, if not misleading, since they spring from an imprecise feeling about the subject rather than from an understanding of it. And though a wake of feeling ripples after it, the novel itself is curiously unmemorable.

Frederick Manfred in *Lord Grizzly* displays that ability without which no novelist can long endure—the instinct to choose a good subject. *Lord Grizzly* deals with one of the most potentially rich myths of the West, and one which has the advantage of being firmly embedded in historical fact. It is the story of Hugh Glass, the old hunter who, attacked and terribly wounded by a grizzly, and armed only with a hunting knife, yet manages to slay the bear. Left by his two companions to die, he survives. Without weapons or food, he crawls two hundred miles to take revenge upon the men who abandoned him. Out of history we know that he found them, yet took no revenge; out of myth we reconstruct the meaning he earned which made the exaction of revenge impossible.

But again, upon the mythic subject has been imposed those devices and techniques which derive from the epic intention. Although the structure of *Lord Grizzly* is not so loose and anecdotal as that of *The Big Sky*, it nevertheless has some of that expansiveness and irrelevance of detail endemic to the epic. In the primitive epic, the unused detail is present, we feel, because of a childlike wonder at its mere existence; but in the literary epic, the only kind possible today, the same detail seems ornamental, artificial and strangely jarring. Moreover, Manfred has chosen a rhetoric derived from the Homeric epic, the Old Testament and folk speech which tends to inflate the subject where it needs constriction and to deflate it where it needs elevation—a rhetoric, in short, which falsifies the subject. Only occasionally does the detail manage to emerge genuinely from the style; but when it does, we can measure the loss achieved by Manfred's choice of certain epical techniques which, imposed upon an unwilling detail, falsify the value of the subject rather than reveal and judge it for what it might be.

It is not surprising that the commercial exploiters of the Western theme have so mistaken the nature of their subject that, unaware, they have imposed upon it a fundamentally alien New England-Calvinistic world view; it is both surprising and disturbing that such talented novelists as Guthrie and Manfred have made a parallel mistake about the nature and implications of their subjects.

The nineteenth- and early twentieth-century adventure of

the American West is essentially mythic. It is not tragic; there is no order to be disturbed, its heroes are not of high rank, and the feeling that emerges from the adventure is not public, in the tragic sense of the word. It is not comic: no elaborate social structure furnishes the details of manners, and the difficulties are neither slight nor trivial. Nor is it epic. Except in the Indian wars, its field of action is neither nationalistic nor political.

The mythic subject is one that has not yet found its proper form. I believe that the most usable and authentic myth available to us may be discovered in the adventure of the American West. Viewed in a certain way, the American frontiersman—whether he was hunter, guide, scout, explorer or adventurer—becomes an archetypal figure, and begins to extend beyond his location in history. He is nineteenth-century man moving into the twentieth century; he is European man moving into a new continent; he is man moving into the unknown, into potentiality, and by that move profoundly changing his own nature. He and the land into which he moves may have their counterparts in both *Sir Gawaine and the Green Knight* and in *Moby Dick*—which is to say that, though the myth which embodies him has its locality and time, it is confined by neither. He walks in his time and through his adventure, out of history and into myth. He is an adventurer in chaos, searching for meaning there. He is, in short, ourselves.

STUDY QUESTIONS

1. Williams says that most western writers have exploited the western myth by treating it in the tradition of the New England Puritan. What does he mean by this? How has this tradition been used in the western myth? What kind of popular literature has resulted?
2. To what extent do current western films and television plays utilize the traditional Puritan version of the western myth? Do you

see any attempts by producers and writers to escape from these simple versions of the western? How successful are these attempts? Do they represent new concepts of what a western should be or simply overlays of modern sophistication in the western myth?

3. Williams says that the western myth is not epic. What does he think is essential to the epic? What qualities that are essential to the epic are missing in the western? Can you think of any attempts to produce epic western films? To what degree have they been successful? What basic elements of good literature have been missing?

4. Williams also dismisses the possibility that the western can be tragic. What qualities necessary to tragedy are missing in the western myth? Can you think of any films, novels, or television plays that attempt to create western tragedy? How would you evaluate them?

5. What, then, are the essential qualities of the western myth that the writer should utilize? Why? To what extent do contemporary film and television producers attempt to utilize these elements? Does a film like *High Noon* (1952) succeed in capturing those elements that Williams feels are essential?

6. Williams says that writers of western fiction, like Luke Short, have a contempt both for their subjects and for their audiences. What does he mean? Do you find a similar contempt present in other uses of the western myth in popular arts?

7. Williams defines a number of common literary forms and discards them all as unsuited to the western myth. Can you think of any other literary forms that have been tried? (For example, what about Stephen Crane's story "The Bride Comes to Yellow Sky" [1898]?) To what extent does the television series *Gunsmoke* (1955) appear to explore new possibilities for the western? How successful is it? How does it fail, and why?

8. A great deal of modern literature is based on psychological explanations of reality. From what Williams has said, do you think that the western hero could easily be explained psychologically?

REUEL DENNEY

Reuel Denney (1913-) is both a poet and a social scientist. He received a national award from *Poetry* magazine in 1954 and is a professor of social science at the University of Chicago. He is co-author, with David Riesman and Nathan Glazer, of *The Lonely Crowd* (1953). A perceptive critic of the popular arts, he analyzes in the following essay the literary form of contemporary science fiction, shows his reader the literary tradition from which science fiction springs, and uses his knowledge of the literary tradition to help the reader understand the kinds of values that are actually expressed and reflected in science fiction.

Reactors of the Imagination

THE ASTRONAUTS

What's play for the man is work for the child. Kids who come home in the late afternoon from ducking ray-gun fire in every interstellar empty lot are almost pleased when they are told that their faces are dirty go wash before dinner. Organized bands of space patrollers, after struggling all day to keep the Seventh-Grade Martians from reaching the water-fountain button (whose touch will blow up the world), are glad to enjoy the overnight truce until next day's recess. These minions of cosmic law and lawlessness have left on the apartment houses a chalk trail that seems to glow at twilight. "This is Planet X and it isn't here." The adepts, exhausted by their playground argument over topics that sound strangely like the theory of limits, have, from sheer fatigue, lost their Moebius strips on the way home. Even a few cowboys and Indians who have not yet learned to trade in their lariats for space suits are glad the day is over. It is time for the children to rest from building the future and time for the adults to begin. The pages of *Arcturus* magazine begin to turn. . . .

In these pages is to be found a product that bears little resemblance to the weird pieces published a generation ago by an editor-publisher named Hugo Gernsback. His publications featured little more than the electronic evaporation of monsters and blondes. Today the readership of a magazine such as *Astounding Science Fiction* includes about 47 per cent college graduates, a percentage much higher than in the total United States population and in most magazine readership. About one out of four of its readers belongs to the engineering occupations, with chemical and electrical engineers leading the list; teachers, executives, and mechanical and building tradesmen are among the other frequent readers of the magazine. Three out of four of its readers are under thirty-five years of age, and their average monthly income is roughly twice as high as the average income of the employed person in the United States. What are they finding in their favorite genre? First of all, it seems, a sort of cosmology.

The Egyptians were fond of referring to the Nile Valley as "the world" and felt that the sun's efforts were patriotically Egyptian. The Yurok Indians of the west coast of North America imagined the universe to be an economy-size version of the Columbia Valley. They also imagined, in order to get some Yuroks into the picture, that both the Columbia Valley and the cosmos were built on the model of man's physiology. The salmon descending and ascending the visceral river in their annual migration sometimes seemed a symbol, as well as a fact, in the nutritional system of the world; and they sometimes seemed a symbol, as well as a fact, in the sexual system of the world. No one thinks it strange that in our world of split atoms, non-Euclidean geometries, and dynamic psychologies we feel a queasy affinity for the farthest spaces and the most distant pasts and futures. Nor that a group of rather entertaining writers are busy populating these unstaked areas of possibility with human and non-human creatures.

It may be that science-fiction writers are special kinds of people. It is noticeable that although many women write detective stories, and write them very well, almost all science-fiction writers are men. Someone has said that women will always be a little more interested in whodunits than in far planets. And when the talk moves from movies and mobiles to space opera, the women's faces do not light up. Is it possible that they don't want the science, don't need the fantasy, and are already more accomplished in the possibilities of fiction? Perhaps science fiction is essentially a boys' dormitory commodity, like the western story, and is produced most congenially by men. In any event, whatever science-fiction writers are like as social animals rather than as writers, the purpose of this chapter is to emphasize neither the writers nor the readers of the product but the product itself.

Science-fiction, if we hyphenate it for a moment, reminds us that the worlds of wish and the worlds of matter—if that separation is still viable—have been married in other ways before. Some people think that John Donne wrote a kind of science-poetry. Other people will tell you that Jonathan Edwards tried to write a kind of science-theology. And the historian Leopold von Ranke claimed that he was writing science-history. Considering the intellectual ambitions involved in those undertakings, why shouldn't someone named Murray Leinster or Fritz Leiber write science-fiction? Considering the names that have been associated with the very approaches of science-fiction itself —Plato, Lucian, More, and the mythmakers who thought of

Daedalus and Icarus—why shouldn't science-fiction writers of today be read respectfully?

The sample of science fiction discussed in this chapter is significant for several reasons. First, it permits us to test more concretely the guess (shared by the author and Seymour Krim) that current science fiction is a late and crucial reincarnation of the great literary tradition of naturalism—perhaps its last stand. Second, it permits us to see how science fiction, apart from naturalism, contains some of the fantasy that has been driven out of other forms. The heroic quests and confrontations that previous generations found in detective fiction now seem to be found in science fiction. Finally, it helps us to identify science fiction as a vehicle for the apt exposition of utopian and anti-utopian attitudes toward society. Perhaps themes debased from higher forms may be discovered in the folk literature of the pulps.

It is true enough that some of our past pioneers in science fiction missed the rocket after having bought tickets. In *The Tempest* Shakespeare toyed with teleportation and sleep-teaching but settled for a story about a duke in five acts of blank verse. Milton in *Paradise Lost* displayed a Clausewitzian grasp of war in space but left the manual of tactics to the authors of *Space Cadets*. Perhaps these references seem to beg the question: What is science fiction? They are not meant to. One way to define it is to make it include much of the "marvelous" that survives into an age of rationality after an age of myth; and by these lights the Alexandrian romancers who followed Euripides and made some of the naïve wonders of mythology at home in the cosmopolitan environment, by converting them, skeptically enough, into the apparatus of adventure stories, were forerunners of science fiction.

A SAMPLE OF UNIVERSES

Is science fiction merely fantasy masked by self-conscious "realism about the future"? Is it utopianism disguised as a prophecy of doom? Is it the only kind of literature displayed in country drugstores in which young readers are invited to cast off their ethnocentrism and consider the possibility that there are alternative hypotheses about human nature and society? Does it lack manifest sexuality because so much latent sexuality is stored in it? Is it self-concealing secularization of essentially "religious" concerns? Does its current popularity coincide in more than an accidental way with the shortage of physicists, chemists, and engineers? Is it an advance view of the consumer-goods and personality market of the future, and, as such, does it function for its technologically intense readers as a kind of cross-my-fingers prayer about the spiritual presumption that goes into invention? Is it a literary genre that should be associated with the hard-boiled detective story, the realistic children's story, and *True Comics*? And are these all after-products generated by the shattering of the aesthetic atom of naturalism in the cyclotron of popular culture?

Science-fiction writers are careful to expound the physical, social, and psychological principles on which their imaginary kingdoms in space and time are based. Different worlds, different principles. We should take the same precautions when entering the universe of criticism of science fiction. Our voyage cannot carry us through that universe; therefore let us examine the work of two of its prominent citizens, Fredric Brown and Ray Bradbury. Where Brown is deft and clear with plot, Bradbury is potent in the invention of situation and theme.

To speak first of their similarities, it is important to say that in their diction—and diction is the point of first contact between the reader and the writer—they are both smooth workmen. Brown writes in the linotypical fashion of the better pulp writer, knocking out sizable slugs of phrases and clauses in the idiomatic vocabulary of a newspaper feature writer. He is anxious to get there, clearly and quickly, and he does get there. Bradbury writes in the manner of a man who, when he has completed a sentence, stands back to take in the view of it. He has a chromatic vocabulary of adjectives of color and texture and light that gives to his space scenes the oddly appropriate effect of being painted in luminescent pigment. He is anxious to set a visual scene with symbolic overtones as a basis for his narrative effects. As in most science-fiction stories, the prose surface wrought by Brown and Bradbury is not employed to any great degree to achieve understatement or overstatement, types of irony, or other counterpoints between matter and manner.

This is not to say that science fiction lacks the technique to shift narrative viewpoint within a given story, but there seems to be a tendency on the part of science-fiction writers to standardize on third-person modes of narration. In the nineteenth century, science fiction was often presented, as in Poe, in the form of a story related by a first-person narrator. At least part of the intended effect was to exploit the journalistic documentary "I-was-there" quality of such a narrative. In a few earlier instances, the "I" narrative was plainly intended to hoax people into thinking that the story was not fiction but journalistic truth. It is understandable that present-day science-fiction writers should lean over backward to avoid such mechanisms. They prefer not to exploit these spurious claims to realism. On the other hand, the distrust of the "I" narrator probably reduces the technical armory of science-fiction writers. Certain fictional effects that could contribute to science fiction depend absolutely on the ambiguities about reality and illusion created for the reader by having the story recounted by an "I" narrator with a gradually disclosed viewpoint and system of knowledge. This is evident enough in some of the "fantasy" of Henry James.

Bradbury generally rests his story on the premise of interplanetary travel and, in many cases, on the possibility of hallucination or other interferences with mental process by some marvelous means. He writes about people who seem to come from a wide range of social classes; and he writes a great share of his stories about people who, while they might come from either the upper-middle or lower-upper class, do not clearly belong to either of the two. His characters are generally engaged in responding to some highly defined problem of group relations, such as racial conflict, industrial teamwork, class differences. Most of his characters are shown in some sort of antagonism toward each other. These characters are generally presented in stories that emphasize tragic, macabre, sardonic, or even allegorical formulations. The major principle of organization that he employs is to focus the reader's attention on a character and the consequences of a character's orientation. Somewhat less often, he appeals to the reader's interest in the ideas of the characters. A frequent focus in his work is the tension between parents and children. Here are some of Bradbury's tales.

Parents, alarmed at the African scenes conjured up in the "mentalistic" nursery of their children, who think that life in their automatized house should consist of nothing but nursery fantasy, decide to close the house and go back to normal living. The children beg for a final "three-dimension fantasy" in their nursery. When a friend of the family comes, they have already fed their parents to the lions they have learned how to materialize out of their nursery walls.

Rocket men, scattered out of a broken rocket in space, keep talking to and baiting each other via radio while they are whirled away from each other in their space suits, heading toward different deaths. Hollis, the one who was captain and is falling toward earth, hears the others killed or cut off or taken away by meteor swarms. He wonders if anyone will see him when he reaches earth's atmosphere. A boy in the country sees a "falling star." Says his mother: "Make a wish."

Braling, a gentleman who has had a marionette of himself made so that he can leave the marionette with his wife while he runs off to Rio for a vacation, tells his friend Smith about these wonderful duplicates that can be bought for only $10,000.

Smith, planning to have one made, comes home only to discover that his sleeping wife goes tick-tick-tick. At the same time, Braling returns to his house only to find that his marionette, Braling Two, has fallen in love with Mrs. Braling. Braling Two packs Braling One away in the marionette box and leaves for Rio with Mrs. Braling.

The wife and son of a spaceman, after his last fatal trip, sleep all day and walk only in the rain—because he died by falling into the sun.

Fredric Brown writes about people who give evidence of belonging to what C. Wright Mills calls the "New Middle Class." By this term, Mills means the salesmen, teachers, professionals, and specialists in our society who comprise a skilled group—the white-collar class from its lower to its higher levels, and especially the salaried groups with relatively intense occupational training. These characters in Brown's work are generally to be found in situations involving interplanetary travel or some sort of body-mind problem. They show a great deal of solidarity with each other, but their dominating emotional tone is one of hostility toward, and uncertainty about, each other. Brown's characters are assigned class status by their occupation, which is always noted. By contrast, Bradbury gives away the social status of his characters, not by occupation, which is rarely referred to except in the case of space pilots, but by significant details revealing the life-style, ideology, type of home maintained, and attitudes toward children. Brown's handling of tone ranges from a dominantly sardonic toward a comic and farcical treatment. Where he is satirical, his satire is lighter and less punitive than Bradbury's. His major formal appeal to the reader is that he generally gives his audience a complicated plot of some sort and generally succeeds in providing a tidy denouement. Here are some of Brown's yarns.

Astronomers of 1987 discover that the stars are developing a "proper motion" faster than the speed of light and that all the old constellations, such as the Big Dipper, are going out of business. The stars suddenly spell "Snively's Soap." It is later discovered that this apparent shift of the stars' position has been electronically contrived by a soap millionaire whose sales went up 915 per cent during the period before his apparatus was smashed and the appearance of the constellations returned to normal.

The last man on earth waits for a knock on the door of his dwelling, knowing in advance that it will be, if she has decided to come back and do some repopulating, the last girl.

Napoleon's psyche, rediscovering itself in the body of an American newspaper reporter, keeps itself a secret which is never challenged until the day the reporter is asked to enter an insane asylum to make a special investigation under the disguise of a madman who *thinks* he is Napoleon. The reporter cannot figure out whether his employer thinks he is Napoleon or whether, indeed, he is or not. An extra-planetary voice reassures him that he is and that this knowledge will, of course, make him regarded as a madman. He goes mad, receives shock treatment, forgets he is Napoleon, and is released from the asylum as his reporter self. His delusion that he was the reporter squared with the delusions of all the others around him at the office and in the asylum.

The work of Brown and Bradbury generally delivers shock in reasonable proportions. The major differences between the two authors can be suggested by saying that Bradbury often tries to deliver catharsis in place of shock and fails, while Brown, rarely trying to deliver catharsis, sometimes does so. One reason is that many of Bradbury's stories have a quasi-tragic framework suggesting to readers that they ought to be judged with some of the attention that a "serious" craftsman of the short story sometimes calls for. The trouble is that they cannot stand that test, and one feels that it would be more comfortable if they were not in that predicament. Brown's stories, on the other hand, ask to be taken as comedy of stereotypical types of character and are sometimes sustained by brilliant plotting. When these two elements come together, as in his story of the criminologist who protects criminals from the lie detector by a hypnosis-amnesia which also then deprives them of their criminal drive, "Crisis, 1999," the results are truly comic; and the effect on the reader is a sense of emotional relief and resolution proportionate to his emotional commitment to the yarn.

The suggestion here is that Bradbury, looking more often toward the higher seriousness, aims at a star he cannot reach, while Brown, who is content with a jitney to the moon, sets himself a somewhat more attainable goal. Still another way of suggesting this, in literary terms, is to notice that Bradbury attempts to use a wide range of genres (tragedy, social realism, comedy, parable, the macabre, the sardonic) and therefore invites comparison with those who have been specialists and masters in each of these fields. Brown, on the other hand, sticks to a narrower and shallower range of genres (emphasizing the comic, the farcical, the slapstick, and the facetious) and essentially invites comparison with other popular writers. Both Brown and Bradbury, like other science-fiction writers, find that the plasticity of scene and character in science fiction is a burden on, as well as a spur to, fictional invention.

THE DISAPPEARING ACT

We should remind ourselves here that it may be necessary in theoretical physics to hold, as Bohr suggests, two contradictory but complementary notions of the same process. Analogies to this exist in literary criticism. Notice that the comments above are haunted by a similar air of paradox. At times they seem to suggest that the stories by these two writers are, by and large, comparable because they are in the same "form." They are all "stories." They are, as some scientists say it, isomorphic. At times, however, the foregoing comments take care to suggest that the stories of these two writers are distinct from each other, individually and en masse, because they appeal to different principles of form. Some are "parables," and others are "comic," and one of the writers is distinct from the other in the frequency of his appeal to such subforms. In this light, the work of these two men is, as the scientists say it, allomorphic. Perhaps the two writers use distinct forms to embody distinctly different intentions; and perhaps the foregoing remarks favor Brown's intentions at the expense of Bradbury's.

Suppose then, alternatively, we set us a different set of expectations. We assume, for example, that science fiction is a folktale type and that it takes as its hero a specific kind of man, the type called Faustian. In his American-engineer form, as a stereotype, he is the man who loves the world as an object of inquiry. He is surrounded by other types, the Natural Man (Tarzan, for example), the Tyrant, the Woman (outdoor, dangerous, or little), and others. Assume also that the characteristic actions and passions of these types are myths generated by our own culture and psychology. For example, you might consider the theory that the emphasis on teleportations, hallucinations, and hallucinations materialized is connected with the American Fantasy of Disappearance from Society. (Vanishing was what many young children wanted most, according to their answers some years ago to the questions asked about their wishes by an inquiring psychologist. Vanishing has become a theme in journalistic literature, as in Geoffrey Hellman's "How To Disappear for an Hour.")

Suppose also that you attribute this theme to a tendency on the part of Americans to sense themselves pressured into social conformity so that it satisfies them to involve themselves in fantasies of beating the world by vanishing from it. Suppose further you assume that these themes, along with others, are built into American child-rearing so that they are widespread foci of familial anxiety. Then, in comparing Bradbury and Brown, you might well prefer Bradbury on the ground that he is a symbolic psychologist, sociologist, and moralist for the current scene. You would argue for Bradbury's greater interest on the ground that although he uses the form of a "story," he achieves interest because he is actually making an "argument" and writing "symbolic history." To people who argue that his effects are mere shock, you answer, "Yes, the shock of a kind of recognition of a truth."

With this critical alternative in mind, we would be forced, finally, to the suspicion that, besides catharsis and shock, other effects may be attained by science fiction of some sorts. We would begin to suspect that some fiction, much as it seems to invite us to enjoy an extended suspicion of belief, appeals to us as a morality play, an allegory, a parable. We would notice, too, that the development of the story is often such that it creates a spectral dialogue between the reader and the writer and between both of those and the characters; and this spectral dialogue, although it may change its terms as it goes along, is asking for a definition of the real. "Is this watch controlled by a troll?" asks one character. The other answers: "What a question! What would it be like to know what it would be *like* to have a watch controlled by a troll?"

It may be that with Bradbury the question is little more than "What profits a natural man if he developeth a technology?" To this question the rejoinders can be made: "What is a natural man? What is technology? Isn't the very concept of a natural man a cultural product, like a technology?" The difficulty is that these rejoinders are not anticipated by the texture of Bradbury's work. Nevertheless, the current run of American science fiction is often implicitly, and not necessarily incorrectly, theological. Indeed, it often reminds us, perhaps much more than it intends to, of the reaction against modern life and industrialism found, for example, in Edgar Allan Poe.

THE HAUNTED PALACE

"Man," wrote Poe, "because he could not but acknowledge the majesty of Nature, fell into childish exultation at his acquired and still increasing dominion over her elements. Even while he stalked a God in his own fancy, an infantile imbecility came over him. . . . Meantime, huge smoking cities rose, innumerable. . . ." For Poe, Nature, in some Wordsworthian sense, is a palace haunted by the evil possibilities of applied science and industrialism. He was one of the first to touch on a theme that became tremendously important to mass culture: the Faustian theme of the irrationality of too intensely applied reason. As Americans shifted their attention from the businessman to the scientist as the promoter of social change, science as a devil was diffused down the class scale into the mass-culture horror story. Poe's reaction against the inhumanity of industrialism expressed for his generation a conservatism akin to Ray Bradbury's in our day.

Poe's contribution to a popular American image of science was considerable, and it is necessary to get some sense of his own concept of science. His stories appear to group themselves into classes. First, there are the stories of scientific wonders, such as the transmutation of gold in "Von Kempelen's Discovery"; second, there are the stories of criminological reasoning, as in "The Purloined Letter." Each of these types has its own rules of construction and its own characteristic manner or mood. All of them, including the stories of criminological detection, are shrewdly constructed machines for extracting a thrill out of the macabre aspects of scientific activity.

The more one considers Poe's stories of detection, the more one is likely to notice two important elements of these stories that depend on the rise of an industrial and urban order and that anticipate modern science-fiction rather than detective-story themes. The first is the tendency of the later Industrial Revolution to make every state a police state in a sense that it did not approach this form before. We tend to forget that private police have grown about as fast, sometimes faster, than public police in the Western industrial community. In this sense, the disinterested amateur in detection, created originally by Poe and then developed in the portraits of Sergeant Cuff by Wilkie Collins and of Sherlock Holmes by Conan Doyle, is in part a sublimation of the private police of industrial societies. The fact that the private detective is often a knight-errant or a Robin Hood does not detract from his private-force identification with the Pinkertons.

The crux here is that the detection of crime, in an industrial state, becomes a part of the general industrial discipline and develops an appropriately scientific method: the object of the detective is to know more about the city, from a certain point of view, than anyone else. The difficulties of early urban policing are suggested in "The Murders in the Rue Morgue"; French police find it impossible to imagine what actually happened: that the killer was an ape brought off a ship by a sailor. The ape's presence in Paris might be said to represent the sheer improbability of many patterns of crime that appeared in the stages of early industrialization. The bureaucratization of the police in the nineteenth century was a result of the recognition that law and lawlessness were engaged in working out new relationships with each other: easygoing relations between sheriffs and robbers were disrupted by big-city life, and middle-class demands for property protection brought about a new division of labor in which whole new classes of fences and stool-pigeons arose, just as new classes of police officials appeared.

It will help us to see the "anti-utopian" theme in Poe if we recall that large-city life in the United States presents problems in law enforcement different from the problems of the small community, especially the Puritan community, where public opinion was strong enough to be far stronger than the law. The emphasis on punishment rather than detection in the criminological thinking of the Colonial statute books has a double meaning: it means, on the one hand, that detection was easy; on the other, that the very conditions of private snooping, gossip, and word-of-mouth policing in the community built up such a strong pressure that the emotional process of punishment itself became highly charged for the punishers. If an individual reacted so strongly against such a tight web of the mores that he became criminal, what punishment could be heavy enough for him? Scientific law enforcement, appearing in a period when the mores were breaking up under the impact of city life, correlated with a liberalizing change in attitude toward punishment, since it shifted its focus away from punishment in order to focus the better on the detection and the deterrence of crime.

The texture of Poe's fiction often suggests that he was aware of changes like this going on in the United States of his time. The citizen whose attitudes are dominated by the customary law of the personalized country or small town wants the law of both country and city to think in terms of moralities and punishment; the police of the impersonalized city, faced with a breakdown of customary behavior, want to think about it in terms of information and control. In our own history, the moralizing of the countryside, culminating in the Prohibition laws of the 1920's, produced a situation in which the police were forced to act against the very social nature of the city. This, in turn, brings about a breakdown of the city law-enforcement fabric, which in turn is blamed upon the city by the moralists and the country folk. Poe's narratives of crime detection hint at the literary discovery of the law-man so rationalistically interested in the motivation for crime as an element in his pattern of detection that he can, in cosmopolitan fashion, leave obsessions with moralizing and with punishment behind him.

Poe's amateur detective, to be sure, also appears on the scene because the failure of the official police to solve their problems is an aspect of the emotional blocks in their administration which result either from their implication in the crime itself or from their sociopsychological obtuseness. Correspondingly, the success of the amateur detective is an aspect of his clinical disinterestedness in the scene: he is able to uncover the sources of wrongdoing in the industrialized society in a methodical and objective way because, as a gentleman of the older social order, he has not acquired the cultural pattern of the new society, and he can therefore look objectively at its culturally patterned vices and virtues. We have seen the degree to which this clinical aspect of the detective has been developed as a white-collar trait of modern legal bureaucracy in the Jack Webb portrait of Joe Friday.

As we see now, Poe's criminological yarns show a concern for the way in which the scientific method, especially in psychology and secondarily in sociology, begins to assert itself as a mode of social control. The ratiocinative genius of the gentleman specialist is necessary, in the new urban and industrial order, to pierce the web of criminal circumstance. Criminals are defined as superindividuals let loose in an anomic society; they can be caught up with only by a Cartesian mentality that can identify with the "mechanisms" of their aberrant humanity. Deviance is fundamentally systematic—"Vice and virtue are products like vitriol and sugar," Taine said—and it can be controlled, not by feudal bailiffs and sheriffs, but by men wise in the ways of modernity.

In all of this we see Poe employing the generalized scene of the big city and the impersonal society in a way that resembles some current science-fiction writers' use of an imaginary Martian landscape and its "controlled society." Thus the link between current science fiction, which emphasizes manipulation of individuals by a new social pattern and its managers, and the fiction of Poe is a link that connects more strongly with his detective fiction than with his exercises in fantasy. It is his detective fiction that expresses disillusionment with a technological society. He has had a long-run influence on the more popular mass-cultural forms of American fiction.

Poe's almost mechanical and obsessive conservatism is a reminder that one's general point of view toward life may occasionally interrupt the enjoyment of a science-fiction adventure. If you are not especially Kantian in your views, you may get tired of all the excitement in science fiction over the split between the theoretical and the practical reason. If you are not a monist, you may get tired of the reduction of the cosmos to physicalistic models. If you are aware of some of the problems of the behaviorist, you may get tired of the stimulus-response simplicities of some of science fiction's neomentalistic creatures. If you reject Descartes, you may be bored by the mind-body dichotomist. If you follow Wittgenstein into his later phase, you may find that his "book with the blue covers" (as I heard a positivist say) "contains more universes than a science fiction convention." It seems fair to say that science fiction is as philosophically sophisticated as semantics, which isn't much, and as culturally sophisticated as Herbert Spencer or technocracy, which never was much. At the same time, this may be of no relevance at all to the scientist reader of science fiction who, working from nonverbal models of behavior in a way that other readers do not, finds symbolic structures in science fiction that others of us do not find at all. The average reader of science fiction is of course merely revealing his taste for cosmic cowboy thrillers. What he shares with more sophisticated readers is not ideology but fantasy.

The fantasy theme, therefore, raises again the question suggested by Rosalie Moore and Anthony Boucher: Why is it that the *same* stories will sell better, and perhaps even be enjoyed more, if they are bound in a cover presenting neo-technological fantasy scenes rather than any other kind of fantasy scenes? For one pervasive reason, we might guess. The dream content of the science-fiction story is expressed in manifest symbols that are the stock-in-trade of the daydreams of the scientist. When the scientist carries out some of the same dreamwork that the rest of us carry out by representation of landscapes, blondes, tones, and colors, he is representing similar fantasies in new cosmogonies, fancies about biological mutation, and so on. In this manner the twentieth-century scientist wraps up his play in his work; and his influence is such that the style of his dreamwork becomes an acceptable stylistic norm for the dreamwork of many other people.

Just those considerations may make it appropriate for the fan to read science fiction as symbolic journalism of today's world, as prophecy, as occupational guidance, as social theory— as the dialogue of the hypnotic master criminal, Nature, with the somewhat less masterful, telepathist-detective, Man. A general debate about the status of good, evil, culture, history, progress, psyche, and human freedom is as native to science fiction as rectilinear motion was to the atoms of Democritus. Correspondingly, it compels people to debate whether it is pessimistic or optimistic. Pessimistic or optimistic about what?

Pessimism about human society as a whole, toward which American science fiction tends, may seem to be less gloomy than doubt about the nature of man as such, toward which it does not tend. Pessimism about the values of a specific cultural setting, limited in time and place, toward which science fiction tends, is less threatening than pessimism about the nature of culture itself, a formula toward which it does not tend. Pessimism about rational intervention in historical change, toward which science fiction often tends, is less oppressive than doubts about the very nature of history itself, toward which it does not tend. In their choice of Noble Lies, Americans betray their very hopes in a willingness to include an indeterminate Tomorrow within the scope of their despairs.

1. Reuel Denney believes that modern science fiction derives from the nineteenth-century tales of Edgar Allan Poe. Why does he believe that the tradition passes from Poe to science fiction rather than to modern detective fiction? What characteristics have Poe's detectives and villains in common with the heroes and the villains of modern science fiction? What significant differences are there between them? Can you think of any modern attitudes toward either science or law enforcement that would account for the way in which the tradition, begun by Poe, has developed?

2. Denney believes that science fiction reveals a deep distrust of the intellectual. Can you think of other kinds of popular fiction that reveal this same distrust? How, for instance, is the lawyer frequently treated in popular fiction? To what extent is our attitude ambiguous, that is, one of mixed admiration and distrust? Do you find indications of this ambiguity in a television series like *The Trials of O'Brien* (1965)? What about *Perry Mason* (1957) at one extreme, and *The Defenders* (1961) at the other?

3. Are we equally ambiguous in our treatment of doctors in popular fiction and drama? Are there any factors other than anti-intellectualism which would intensify our ambiguity toward doctors?

4. Denney says that frequently the appeal of science fiction lies in the writer's ability to take an incredible situation and follow it through. Does his analysis seem valid for a series such as *The Twilight Zone* (1959)? How does a series such as *Bewitched* (1964) take advantage of this appeal? What are the limitations of this approach to fiction and drama? How seriously can you take a novel or a play based upon an impossible situation?

5. William Golding's *Lord of the Flies* (1945) might, at first glance, seem to employ the same dependence on an incredible situation as much science fiction does. What are the differences between Golding's plot situation and that of the science fiction writer?

6. According to Denney, science fiction writers frequently show great concern over the moral problems that might occur in a scientifi-

cally run society. Do these writers seem to you to present the problems with maturity and imagination? In what ways do they sometimes seem to fall short of dealing realistically with the problems they present?

7. How are the moral problems presented in science fiction similar to those that plague the writers of organization fiction (see William H. Whyte, Jr.'s "Literature in an Organization Society," p. 50)? What connections do you see among the problems of an organization society, those of a scientifically run society, and our current concern with automation and cybernation?

WILLIAM O. AYDELOTTE

William O. Aydelotte (1910-   ) has been chairman of the department of history at the University of Iowa since 1947. As a historian he has specialized in British and European history of the nineteenth century. In the following selection he examines the detective story from an unusual perspective: "What," he asks, "would the historian discover about contemporary American society from an examination of the form and values embodied in the detective story?" He then analyzes the plot structure of the detective story, the nature of the modern detective hero, and the similarity between the hero of the detective story and its villain. In the process, he destroys a number of common misconceptions about the detective story and offers a disquieting theory about the reasons for its great popularity in the United States.

The Detective Story
as a Historical Source

One would hardly go to the detective story for an accurate picture of modern life. If a historian five hundred years hence were to base a reconstruction of our twentieth-century civilization solely on the evidence contained in detective stories, he might reach strange conclusions. He would probably infer that the most prominent features of our culture were inefficient or corrupt police forces, a multitude of private detectives, sometimes urbane and sometimes hard-boiled, and a constant series of domestic crimes occurring principally in large country houses and committed exclusively by people of the most harmless and respectable outward appearance. What little realism detective stories possess lies on the surface and does not extend to the characters or to the action. The notion that they give a literal representation of modern society may be rejected at the outset. Far from being realistic, they constitute one of the most conventionalized of literary forms, being exceeded in this respect perhaps only by the comic strip.

This does not argue, however, that detective novels are completely dissociated from the age in which they are written. On the contrary, their immense popularity—it is alleged that one out of every four new works of fiction published in the English language belongs to this category—suggests that they are an impressive portent of our culture. Their popularity is not likely to be accidental. If we can ascertain the reason for it, we may be able to grasp the link between detective literature and the society of which it forms a part.

I suggest that the widespread and sustained popularity of detective stories is principally due to the very elements which make them unrealistic, to their conventions. These conventions (which will be analysed at length in the course of this essay) have been fairly constant in the century-long history of the *genre*, amid all the variations of setting and technique. A substantial number of them appear even in the stories of Poe. The long persistence and regular recurrence of these stereotypes afford at least a presumption that they are essential to the detective story's continued vogue. Their role is of course clear. They are wish-fulfilment fantasies designed to produce certain agreeable sensations in the reader, to foist upon him illusions he wants to entertain and which he goes to this literature to find.

The charm of detective stories lies neither in originality nor in artistic merit, though they may possess both these qualities. It consists rather in the repetition of a formula that through trial and error has been found pleasing. We read these books, not to have a new experience, but to repeat in slightly different form an experience we have had already. Thus, for example, the "surprise" ending is not really a surprise. It is the ending we expect and demand, and we would feel outraged if any other kind of ending were offered to us. It is true that many of these works introduce elements of novelty in the background and setting, and that the best of them unquestionably show considerable skill in writing and construction. Such amenities, however, serve not so much to change the formula as to render it more palatable to the highbrow. The educated part of the detective-story audience shows no unwillingness to accept the formula but merely a fastidious distaste for its cruder expressions.

The interest of detective stories to the historian is that they shed light on the people who read them. By studying the fantasies contained in this literature, one may gather a description of its readers, in terms of their unsatisfied motivational drives. Thus these books are the more illuminating the more unrealistic and inaccurate they are. It is precisely by their inaccuracies that they reveal attitudes and emotions of the audience to which they cater. To the historian concerned with popular opinion, this audience is of particular interest for two reasons. In the first place it is large—the detective story is a mass medium—and in the second place it is extremely varied. Detective novels appeal to different types of readers, highbrows as well as lowbrows. They are read with avidity by intellectuals who despise soap operas and are repelled by the success stories in popular magazines. Some critics even assert that they are written primarily for intellectuals, a claim which is of course invalid in view of the breadth and extent of their circulation. The reading of this literature is, rather, a widespread habit to which the educated also adhere.

The extent and variety of the detective-story audience argue a surprising degree of unity in our culture, at least in respect to the demand for the particular fantasies which this literature purveys. Since these books appeal, not only to many people, but to many different kinds of people, they presumably reflect attitudes and needs that are widely distributed. A study of the stereotypes in the detective story may, therefore, reveal to us attitudes and opinions which, if not universal, at least occur in our age with significant frequency.

Primarily, the detective story presents a view of life which is agreeable and reassuring. By ingenious and long-tested devices, it persuades the reader that the world it describes is simple and understandable, that it is meaningful, and that it is secure.

(1) In place of the complex issues of modern existence, people in a detective story have very simple problems. Life goes along well except for the single point that some crime, usually, in modern stories, a murder, has been committed. (There are some exceptions, particularly among the Sherlock Holmes stories, which are not wholly typical of the modern form of the *genre:* many of these contain no murder, and some involve no crime at all, merely a puzzle.) From this act follow most of the troubles which the sympathetic characters must endure: they may, for example, come under temporary suspicion of murder, or they may have a misunderstanding with their loved ones. Troubles are objectively caused by an external circumstance, the murder, which can and will be resolved, whereupon the troubles will disappear. Once the solution has been reached, most of the other difficulties are ended and the characters go away happy, never apparently to be vexed by the minor worries and neuroses of modern man. The mess, confusion, and frustration of life have been reduced to a simple issue between good and evil, virtue and wickedness. And virtue triumphs.

To carry the argument to the next stage, the simplification of the problem is matched by a corresponding simplification of the solution. Here we come to one of the most universal conventions in the *genre,* the essential clue, the unique significant detail that unlocks the mystery. The detective story makes a distinction between essential and non-essential facts. As Sherlock Holmes puts it, "It is of the highest importance in the art of detection to be able to recognize, out of a number of facts, which are incidental and which vital. Otherwise your energy and attention must be dissipated instead of being concentrated." ("The Reigate Puzzle.") In the unreal world of the detective story, we depart from the intricate currents of causation in life as we know it, and find instead that a whole elaborate plot may be unravelled by discovering the one relevant detail. Furthermore, the factual nature of this detail lends an air of concreteness to the solution: we are led to feel it is the only solution, inevitable, unique, completely certain.

(2) By other commonly used devices the detective story makes life more meaningful and endows the events it describes with significance, even with glamor. To say that detective stories provide a thrill which compensates for the dullness of their readers' lives is only the beginning of the story. It is true that they offer the excitement of adventure, and also capitalize on popular indignations or fetishes in the manner of other types of sensation literature. But they do more than this. In many subtle ways they help their readers to believe in the existence of a richer and fuller world.

Even the sordid surroundings of crime make their contribution to the atmosphere of richness and meaning. As G. K. Chesterton says, this form of literature succeeds often in getting the romance and poetry of the city, and "the investigator crosses London with something of the loneliness and liberty of a prince in a tale of elfland."

Comparable effects are achieved in other ways. Consider, for example, the following quotation, in which Sherlock Holmes is explaining one of his solutions: "I am only, of course, giving you the leading results now of my examination of the paper. There were twenty-three other deductions which would be of more interest to experts than to you." ("The Reigate Puzzle.")

This is one of many passages in which Conan Doyle contrives to suggest there is a great world of intellectual phenomena, beyond the range of the average man, but really existent for all that and within the competence of the superior mind. Thus, for other illustrations, Holmes deduces a whole life-history from the appearance of a hat or a watch. ("The Blue Carbuncle," "The Sign of Four.") The implication is that life is not the simple and drab affair we ordinarily encounter, but something more extensive and more interesting.

To add further to the reader's sense of new frontiers of meaning and significance, the detective story manages in various ways to cast a glamor on its characters and to convey to the reader that these people count, that they matter in the world. Such an illusion is achieved, for example, when the action takes place in the classical setting of the large English country-house with its atmosphere of butlers and scullery maids, lawns and shrubberies, French windows and guest-wings, and large house parties of elegant guests.

(3) Finally, the detective story introduces us to a secure universe. We find here an ordered world obedient to fixed laws. The outcome is certain and the criminal will without fail be beaten by the detective. In this world man has power to control his own affairs and the problems of life can be mastered by human agency.

Even the handling of the theme of death contributes to this feeling of security. One might not at first expect a form of literature which deals with death by violence to have the cheerful and encouraging effect I have attributed to the detective story. Yet murder is an almost universal feature of these books. From the point of view of literary construction, of course, a murder is useful for the plot and provides the suitable starting-point for an investigation. But there is another reason for including it.

This is that the detective story, by its peculiar treatment of death, contrives to minimize the fear of it. Death is always presented in a rather special way. It is something that happens to somebody else, not to anyone we like or identify ourselves with. The victim, though he is ultimately avenged, is not allowed to be a sympathetic character. The reader's emotions must not become engaged on his behalf. At the least the victim is killed off before his personality has been developed far enough for the reader to take an interest in him or to like him. More often the victim is clearly unattractive, a man who has been injuring the lives of a number of the other characters (which also helps the plot by increasing the list of possible suspects), and his death is good riddance. In many cases, the murder turns out to be the best thing that could have happened. After everything has been straightened out, the lovers, if any, are brought together, the detective has had a chance to prove his worth, all the other characters are now freed from the burden of the late victim's persecution of them, and also purged from the guilt of his murder, since this guilt has now been thrown on an acceptable scapegoat, and everyone is set for a cheerful future.

The detective story uses crime not to make life more horrible but to make it more cheerful. The despair and horror it seems to offer the reader are presented in a very manageable form and really subserve, not a pessimistic view of life, but a view that is exactly the opposite. Its concern with crime and the seamy side of life misleads the observer as to its true impact. Its message is essentially agreeable, almost to the point of being saccharine.

The agreeable view of life presented in the detective story is deepened and enlarged by the actions of its two most important characters, the criminal and the detective. Each plays a standardized role that affords a special kind of satisfaction to the reader. We will consider the criminal first.

The criminal is a scapegoat. He is the cause of and can justly be blamed for all the troubles of the detective-story world, the murder and everything that follows from it. The detective story evades the complex issues of life and saves us the effort of analysing the sources of our difficulties and frustrations by presenting every problem as one of personal morality. The criminal therefore must be a single individual, who can eventually be identified. A detective novel where the murder was due to "conditions" of some sort, and where no individual was responsible, would be quite unsatisfactory.

But the criminal is not only a scapegoat, he is also something more deeply gratifying, a scapegoat that can be beaten. His great charm is that he is conquerable and will infallibly be conquered. He appears for most of the story as a colossus, formidable in his cunning and power. But his strength, though great, is futile, only sham strength. His position is actually unreal, for he has no place nor meaning in an ordered world. If you look closely, the criminal is a miserable creature. He can do little ultimately against organized society which is rapidly closing in on him. If we are terrified of him for a while, because of his apparent cunning and dexterity, that simply enhances the relief we feel when he gets beaten, and also the satisfaction we have in knowing all the time, in our inmost hearts, that he is going to be beaten.

Besides this, I believe the criminal also fulfils another and more subtle purpose. He relieves our feelings of aggression, not only by becoming an object of them himself, but also in a second and quite different way, by committing the murder. As I tried to show earlier, it not infrequently happens that the murder is a good thing; the victim is a menace to the sympathetic characters and the murder starts off the train of events that leads finally to the happy ending. In novels where this is the case, the criminal, by killing the victim, performs a service to society, a service we would not wish, however, to have performed by any sympathetic character because of the penalty that must ensue. The criminal, though he is made to act from selfish and unworthy motives and must therefore be punished, still gratifies us by committing the act we are glad to see done. He shares something of the ambiguous character of the scapegoat of mythology who is both a friend and enemy to society, who commits the act of sin or disobedience that helps us all and then removes the taint or penalty attached thereto by himself undergoing the punishment, a punishment that is occasionally even inflicted by the beneficiaries.

Perhaps the most gratifying function of the detective story, and one that is also achieved through the agency of the criminal, is the illusion the reader obtains of being released from guilt and dissociated from the murderer. This illusion is achieved by bringing a number of the most prominent characters, including any with whom the reader might perhaps identify himself, temporarily under suspicion. For this purpose, the criminal must be a member of the closed circle, the small group affected by or concerned with the crime, so that the possibility of an outside murderer will be excluded and any member of this little society may therefore conceivably be guilty. (Here again the Holmes stories constitute a partial exception to the convention that has crystallized in our own day: in very few cases are there several suspects, and in some cases the criminal is an outsider who does not appear till caught.) The criminal must also be the least likely person, revealed only in the surprise ending, so that, since the identity of the murderer is kept a secret until the end, no single character in the closed circle can be assumed to be assuredly free from guilt. By such means the fear of guilt is temporarily intensified and the reader's relief at the identification of the criminal is increased.

Once the criminal is discovered, everyone else is at once freed from the burden of possible guilt. The suspicious actions of the other characters now turn out to have a perfectly innocent explanation. Yet the temporary suspicion directed against them was in a sense justified, for many of them benefited from the crime and would perhaps have liked to commit it if they could have escaped the consequences. For that reason, their relief is the greater. The satisfaction of the "innocent" characters and the reader at being released from guilt is all the more poignant because they do not deserve it; in thought and feeling, if not in action, they are also guilty. Therefore our gratification when the murder is committed does not conflict with our satisfaction at being ultimately freed from guilt, but on the contrary enhances it.

Besides all this, the criminal has one additional function. He contributes to the illusion of the power of the detective. His crime is thought out in great detail, is indeed perfect except for the single flaw discernible only to the detective's penetrating eye. The botched crime of real life is unknown to the detective story. The criminal shows incredible self-possession and address, and conducts himself with such poise and assurance that he is not suspected until the end. In all this he is a worthy antagonist and gives the detective full scope to demonstrate his talents. However, though the crime is so difficult that it can be solved only by the detective, the detective almost invariably does succeed in solving it. He always has the particular bit of esoteric knowledge or the particular type of intuition that turns out to be just what is needed, the one and only thing that will clear up this particular mystery. The point, as we may now perceive, is that the crime is tailored to fit the detective. It finally proves to be exactly the kind of crime that is best suited to his peculiar and unique talents. The criminal actually serves the detective by offering him just the kind of problem that he is best equipped to deal with. Though a skilful writer seeks to maintain the illusion, the crime is really a setup, and the detective solves it because the author has contrived everything to that end.

The detective contributes even more than the criminal to the good view of life set forth in these books. He makes the world simple, comprehensible, and orderly by discovering the essential clue and solving the murder. He understands the meanings and possibilities of life and reveals its vistas to us. He gives us security, certainty and protection. By unearthing the criminal he sets in motion the scapegoat mechanism which shifts the burden of guilt from our shoulders. He can do all these things because he has control over the world we know and the destinies of men in it.

The most prominent feature of the detective is his power and strength. The fact that he is also represented as an intellectual need not lead us astray about this. He is not the feckless intellectual of popular culture, the absent-minded professor, the man who is cloistered, impractical and ineffective. On the contrary, his talents are used for a concrete practical end, the apprehension of the murderer. Intellect is for him simply a path to power, a means of controlling the external world.

Furthermore, his power is not solely intellectual. There is a tradition that he must be physically as well as mentally competent. Detectives in American stories of the hard-boiled school are supposed to be handy with their fists. Sherlock Holmes, though to some extent a recluse and at times a drug-addict, is an expert singlestick player, boxer, and swordsman. Peter Wimsey, no he-man, is still a famous athlete whose proficiency as a cricketer gives away his identity in "Murder Must Advertise." Even the effeminate Poirot shows a courage and alertness in ticklish situations which fit him a little bit into the type of the hero of adventure. Besides this, the detective works not just by intellect and logic but also by intuition. He often senses something wrong in a situation, and this sense prevents him from acting mistakenly or making a fool of himself, even though the whole truth is not yet revealed to his intellect. He plays his hunches, and they are apt to be right.

To make the detective appear a figure of power the police, like the criminal, are drummed into his service. By their very inadequacy or opposition to him they do more to display his qualities than they could by giving him the most efficient cooperation. The convention of the inept police force helps to establish the unique excellence of the detective, his ability to do things nobody else can do. Thus the superiority of the detective to the police has been a common feature of detective literature from Poe's Dupin to Gardner's Perry Mason. It has become especially prominent in recent books, especially American ones such as those of Geoffrey Homes or Dashiell Hammett. Despite some notable exceptions like Inspector Alleyn or Inspector French, there have been relatively few policeman-heroes, and a substantial number of these are police officers only in name who in practice perform something like the role of a private detective. Ellery Queen plays a lone hand and summons in his father's cohorts only for special tasks; the solution is his work and not theirs. Maigret, too, works mostly alone and excites the enmity or disapproval of his colleagues. In one of the latest of the series, he has retired from the *Sûreté*.

Since our present interest in the detective story is its impact on the reader, the important question to ask about the detective is what kind of fantasy he evokes in the reader's mind. At first glance the issue might seem to be whether the reader's relation to the detective is one of identification or dependence. We might attempt, as Louise Bogan suggests would be possible, to divide detective stories into those written for sadists and those written for masochists. Yet this first and most obvious way of putting the question does violence to the complexity of the reader's emotions and reactions, which for any book are likely to be not simple but ambiguous and multiple. As a matter of fact, identification and dependence do not exclude each other; each refers to a different aspect of the reader's reaction, and both are possible at the same time.

I suggest that the reader probably does identify himself with the detective, make the detective an extension of his ego, but only in very general terms. The detective is on our side. His actions are beneficial to us, and we feel ourselves in some degree represented in them. On the other hand, this representation occurs at a distance. The reader may identify himself with the detective to the extent that he gets a vicarious thrill of power when the detective solves the mystery. But I doubt that he identifies himself with the detective to the larger extent of trying to solve the murder himself. The reader is audience. He is like the spectator at a football game, identifying himself with his team, feeling a personal triumph if they win, yet always aware that it is the players and not himself who do the work on which his satisfaction is based. Though the reader both identifies and depends, the emphasis is on the latter, the significant relationship is dependence.

I would argue, to support this, that the reader does not generally compete intellectually with the detective. A detective story is not an invitation to intellectual exercise or exertion, not a puzzle to which the reader must guess the answer. On the contrary, the claim of detective stories to be puzzle literature is in large part a fraud, and the reader, far from attempting to solve the mystery himself, depends on the detective to do it for him.

This is an extremely controversial point. Many detective stories claim to put all the clues in the reader's hands, to show him everything the detective sees, so that the reader has an equal chance to make something out of it. This is the so-called "gentlemen's agreement," the supposedly best modern practice, according to which, says Miss Sayers, readers demand to be put "on an equal footing with the detective himself, as regards all clues and discoveries." Mr. R. Austin Freeman, who also insists that the satisfaction a detective story offers the reader is primarily an intellectual one, argues that the principal connoisseurs of this literature are theologians, scholars and lawyers. To please this audience of subtle and skilled dialecticians, he thinks a good detective story must have above all two things: accuracy as to external facts, and freedom from fallacies of reasoning.

Unfortunately many detective stories, including some of the best-known ones, have neither one nor the other. Critics have amused themselves for some time now by pointing out errors of fact and deduction in the Sherlock Holmes tales. And the same weaknesses can be found in many other works. If we applied to detective stories the critical attention we give to serious literature, we would find a surprising number that simply do not hang together intellectually. This point is the theme of an important article by Raymond Chandler in the December, 1944, issue of the "Atlantic." Mr. Chandler examines a number of the most famous detective novels of all time, "The Red House Mystery," "Trent's Last Case," "Busman's Honeymoon," "Murder in the Calais Coach," and demonstrates conclusively that none of them is free from important fallacies of reasoning, and that they will not stand up for a moment under strict analysis.

The point should not, however, be pushed too far, for there is a certain amount to be said on the other side. It might be argued that the four stories selected by Mr. Chandler for comment are not a fair sample of the best writing in the *genre*. Furthermore, the very fact that the detective story is popularly regarded as puzzle literature has no doubt influenced writers to try to create puzzles that are fair. Some of these books, particularly including Mr. Freeman's, are well written and articulated, and in fact detective literature at its best demands a good deal in the way of strict construction and technical proficiency, and is not easy to write. Also, I have found a number of readers who insist that they read detective stories as puzzles, and are often able to determine the identity of the murderer in the middle of the story by logical deduction from the clues. And yet, without going into the question of the extent to which these readers may be deceiving themselves, I would doubt that the majority of readers discover the murderer by logical processes of thought before the denouement, and I would doubt that this is even possible in a large number, perhaps the majority, of detective stories.

Any writer of detective fiction who tries to adhere to the

"gentlemen's agreement" faces the problem well put by Miss Sayers, "How can we at the same time show the reader everything and yet legitimately obfuscate him as to its meaning?" I submit that what this "legitimate obfuscation" often amounts to is that either the clues are *not* all given to the reader, or, if they are, this is not done in a significant way that will enable him to determine their meaning.

The reader, if he guesses correctly at all, does so not by reasoning from the evidence, but rather by selecting the least probable character, the person the evidence does not point to. The reader's solution is a guess and not a deduction. It is on the level of the speculations of the woman in the Thurber story who knew that, whoever might have murdered Duncan, the deed could not possibly have been done by Macbeth because he was too obvious a suspect, a patent red herring.

For a detective story to have a solution that could readily be guessed by the majority of readers would go clean against the whole nature and character of the *genre*. The solution has to come as a surprise. A story has no punch when the reader can guess the murderer before the denouement. Furthermore, the purpose of the detective novel, as we saw from other evidence, is to comfort the reader, create agreeable illusions for him. If these books described themselves primarily as tests of the reader's intelligence, which the reader would flunk if he did not guess the murderer before the end, many readers would scarcely find detective stories comforting. For, if the puzzles are so difficult that they can be worked out by the most intelligent readers only with some effort, they would be far beyond the less intelligent but more numerous remainder of the audience.

Detective stories are not a test of the reader's intelligence but, at the most, a means of creating in the reader a delusion that he is intelligent and that, by following the steps in the analysis, he has somehow displayed intellectual proficiency. All too often, the "gentlemen's agreement" means in practice nothing more than that the *appearance* of fair play is to be maintained. The good writing, if any, helps to create and maintain this illusion.

This effort to maintain the illusion of the reader's intelligence is simply a device to keep decently concealed what I consider to be the basic feature of the detective story, the reader's dependence on the detective. Our attitude toward dependence is apt to be ambivalent: we may need it, and at the same time resent having to confess this need or having it called to our attention. The pretense that the detective story is an intellectual puzzle helps to hide the feeling of dependence which the reader goes to these books to find but which he hates to acknowledge.

In any case, there seems little doubt about the dependence of the reader, as of all the characters in the story, upon the detective-hero. The attraction of this literature is that, though the problem may be beyond the powers of the reader or of any of the characters in the story, we can always depend on the detective to step in and solve it. We get satisfaction from seeing him do this even before we know how he is going to bring it off, for the interest lies not in the steps of the analysis but in the certainty of the solution. Thus the reader may get a little bored in the middle of the book when one theory after another is tried and discarded, but when Dr. Fell says he now pretty well knows who the murderer was, when Poirot says he of course identified the murderer two days ago and is only waiting to settle the details, when Holmes says the crime is simple and obvious and presents no points of difficulty—the reader's interest is quickened by a thrill of excitement.

The characters in the book, like the reader, prove to be passive under the detective's control. By the end they sometimes become his puppets, doing what he planned without knowing he meant them to. In the denouement scene, a character will make an important statement, or act in a particular manner, or even commit suicide, and after it is all over people will realize that the detective planned it just that way. The detective's interference with the lives of the other characters is almost as self-confident and arbitrary as that of a deity, and the reader is supposed to love it.

The passiveness of the reader is underlined by one of the most famous devices of all, the narration of the story by a confidant, a foil to the detective, of which Dr. Watson is the outstanding example. The reader sees the story through the eyes of Watson or Hastings or whoever it may be, and also shares the confidant's sense of security and stability which comes from his dependence on the detective.

The confidant, though he may be of various types, is generally somewhat stupid, inferior to the detective, and the detective pokes fun at his blunders and obtuseness. But the confidant doesn't object to this. Even Dr. Watson, though he does at times rebel against Holmes' superior manner, shows an almost masochistic streak. He doesn't mind being ordered around by Holmes without explanation; in fact, he gets a thrill out of it. He is delighted to be proved wrong and to have his stupidity shown up For all this enhances his belief in the infallibility of the detective. The detective becomes a kind of father-image to whom the narrator is occasionally opposed but in general submissive. The Watson-Holmes relationship gives an opening for the instincts of hero-worship.

But what is the historical importance of this? How can such a description as I have attempted here of fantasies and the motivations to which they correspond, even if it is made much more accurate and extensive, be translated into terms of society and politics? The answer to this question, suggested at the beginning of this paper, may now be given more fully. The point of all I have been saying is that the detective story is hokum, a means of arousing in the reader a belief in contrary-to-fact conditions, an opiate and a drug, which protects the reader from the facts of life by covering him with veils upon veils of illusions. The historical value of the detective story is that it describes daydreams, and describes them with a wealth of documentation extending into innumerable volumes. A knowledge of people's day-dreams may enable us to progress to an understanding of their desires. In this way, a careful study of literature of this kind may reveal popular attitudes which shed a flood of light on the motivation behind political, social, and economic history.

The method can be illustrated on the basis of the preliminary survey attempted here, and I will now, finally, indicate by a couple of suggestions how it might work. To take a negative point first, even this cursory examination will enable us to dismiss as uncritical and altogether false the thesis, which has been hazarded by not a few writers, that the detective story is in some fashion a flower of democracy and an embodiment of the democratic way of life. The argument used to support this view is that these books have appeared almost exclusively in democratic countries, chiefly England and America, while by contrast the writings of Agatha Christie and Edgar Wallace were banned by Hitler as "decadent." The reason alleged is that this kind of literature can flourish only in a society where there is due process of law, a non-faulty procedure for handling evidence, public sympathy on the side of order, and an effective police dedicated to finding the truth by objective means.

This argument, in the light of what has so far been said, is obviously nonsense. It is not true, incidentally, that detective literature has appeared solely in democratic societies, for Vidocq published his "Memoirs" in the age of Louis Philippe and Gaboriau wrote mostly under the Second Empire. Nor does the development of effective police forces seem relevant, since the fictional detective works separately from or even against the police, who are represented as anything but effective.

Even if we grant, what is for the most part true, that the *genre* has flourished mainly in England and the United States, it does not follow that it is an illustration of democratic sentiment or a symbol of democratic culture. Our analysis of the detective story would lead to a somewhat less reassuring view. The whole tenor of these books appears to be that they show an enormous demand for gratification, on the level of fantasy, of basic drives which apparently cannot be satisfied in our western society on the level of ordinary reality, and which have an application going rather beyond democratic institutions. The resemblance of the fantasies of dependence and aggression in the detective novel to the two principal political figures of totalitarianism, the dictator and the scapegoat, has been pointed out before this.

Though the detective story appears non-political on the surface, the roles of its two protagonists are saturated with political meanings. The criminal, by the very fact that he is the least likely person, justifies the reader's suspicion that all men, including those who appear most innocent, are really his potential enemies. The reader gets a tremendous vicarious satisfaction when the criminal is identified, for this denouement confirms to the reader that he is right to suspect everybody. The criminal is a fantasy developing out of a competitive, uncohesive society. He is a personalization of our grievances, as we like to personalize them in the atmosphere of political or social crisis in real life. We have toward the criminal the same or comparable feelings that we have toward any one of the commonly accepted scapegoats of our day, the Jew, the labor agitator, Wall Street, the "radical," the capitalist, or whatever other image we have formed the habit of using. And we like to attribute to these bogeymen, as we do to the criminal, sham strength instead of real strength, and to think of them as major threats which, however, we will somehow always be able to counter.

The detective, on the other hand, has many characteristics in common with the modern political leader or agitator. He simplifies life, makes sense out of it and gives it meaning. His strength is real, unlike the criminal's pseudo-strength, for it is based not just on externals but on intuition and a sense of community with the right things in the universe. Like the agitator in Professor Lowenthal's article (in "The Public Opinion Quarterly," Fall, 1948), he is conservative and objects not to the system but to certain people, the criminal or criminals, who seem to be endangering it. And yet the detective is not really a part of the established framework of society, for he neither belongs to the police, the official guardians of the law, nor is he a member of the closed circle or group within which the plot develops. Thus, though he moves in an ordered universe, the order is not that of the police or other regular authorities, but an order that is discovered and imposed by him. The detective may have a kind of democratic aura, for he frequently rises from the ranks and is not distinguished by birth, and although he moves unperturbed among the highly placed he is not one of them. Yet he is indispensable, for he alone can solve the riddle. Therefore the authorities (the family or the police) perforce surrender the controls to him, sometimes reluctantly and occasionally with sharp protest. One could argue that all these qualities add up to a dictator, that the detective is the extra-legal superman who is called in to accomplish by extraordinary measures what is impossible within the traditional organization of society.

Thus a case could be made to show that the detective story is no monument to the strength of democracy but rather a symptom revealing its weaknesses, the insupportable burdens it places on the individual. The detective story does not reflect order, but expresses on the fantasy level a yearning for order; it suggests, then, a disordered world, and its roots are to be sought in social disintegration rather than in social cohesion.

All this is not to suggest that the impulses catered to in this literature made their first appearance in history in the nineteenth century, and never existed before. On the contrary, the fantasies of the detective story appear in recognizable form in the popular culture of other ages, in folklore for example, and the drives they reveal are therefore by no means recent in origin but might rather be regarded as traditional elements of the human character as it has developed in our civilization. Nostalgia for the dependent relationships of childhood is hardly a novelty of our own age. The significant thing is rather that so many people of our age, roughly the era of democratic liberalism, have seemingly come to depend on an enormous literature for the development and even the artificial stimulation of these fantasies. This literature offers disturbing evidence of psychological tensions, and of the prevalence in our modern western culture of elements of character-structure which do not provide adequate support for democratic institutions. The hypothesis toward which a study of these books might tend is that the political arrangements in a democracy, in contrast to the political arrangements in more authoritarian types of government, are simply not adequate to take up this strain.

But perhaps we should beware of taking evidence of this sort too tragically, or of deducing from detective stories nothing but a pessimistic moral. The condemnation of detective stories as drugs or cheap escapism may be pedantic. For, if they are a symptom, they can also be a cure. If we credit the Freudian view that socially dangerous impulses can be got rid of by removing them to the level of fantasy, then detective stories could be described as a harmless safety valve, a wholesome therapy serving a desirable social purpose. And yet one may wonder if this commonly accepted view is entirely correct, if fantasy and real life are actually so unrelated. To some extent we may build our real life around our fantasy and, if this is so, sensation literature may not so much rid us of dangerous drives as reinforce and reshape them.

In any case, if detective stories are not so sinister as they at first appear from analysis, neither are they as frivolous as some critics have judged them. The drives they cater to are compelling and basic, and relate ultimately to the struggle for self-preservation. It is the universal nature of their theme which explains the size and variety of their reading audience. The intellectual, who scorns the cheap fantasies of the popular magazines, is not likely to be able to forgo the fantasies which give him hope for his survival in an alien world. Detective stories deal, in their own way and on their own level, with the most essential and urgent problems in the human situation.

STUDY QUESTIONS

1. Aydelotte believes that the detective story depends for its popularity on its ability to make the reader feel that the world is actually logical and predictable (and, hence, secure) rather than mysterious and unpredictable (and uncertain). To what extent would the recent popularity of heroes like James Bond of Ian Fleming's novels tend to support his conclusion?

2. To what extent is Aydelotte's description of the detective hero applicable to the "James Bond" heroes (for example, Amos Burke of *Burke's Law*, the 1880's hero of the *Wild, Wild West*, *The Man from U.N.C.L.E.*)? Do you see any significant differences between Aydelotte's typical detective hero and these contemporary detective heroes?

3. In his book on the modern detective story, *The Simple Art of Murder* (1950), Raymond Chandler suggests that the essence of modern detective fiction lies in its attention to the details of violence rather than in the solution of a mystery or the apprehension of a criminal. To what extent would Chandler's thesis seem to contradict Aydelotte's theory about the "secure universe" of the detective story? Does Aydelotte show any ways in which the violent hero actually creates in the reader a sense of security?

4. Judging from your own reactions to detective heroes who resemble gangsters, how seriously do you think the reader takes these heroes? For instance, how seriously do you take the James Bond of *Goldfinger* (novel, 1959; movie, 1964)?

5. What are the differences between the attitude of intellectuals toward contemporary detective heroes and the attitude of the general public? Can you account for these differing attitudes?

6. To what extent do these contemporary detective heroes seem to satisfy the taste for pornography that Eric Larrabee deplores in "Pornography Is Not Enough" (p. 164)?

ROBERT WARSHOW

Robert Warshow (1917-1955) spent most of his short
professional life as an editor of *Commentary*. His interest
in popular arts sprang partly from his concern with contemporary culture, partly from his sense of his responsibilities as the father of a lively young son, partly from his
interest in art, and partly from his own awareness of the
delight he took in popular arts and the extent to which
they had influenced him. Despite the fact that many
scholars in New York regarded popular arts as nonsense,
Warshow's criticism earned him their respect and affection. For Warshow cheerfully admitted that he took "all
that nonsense" seriously; not in the sense that he preached
for or against popular arts, but in the sense that he examined them on the basis of their artistic merits, without con-
descension or apology. Like the following essay, Warshow's criticism is distinguished for its objectivity, its
keenness of observation, the excellence of the scholarship
it brings to bear on critical problems, and above all, for
the balance, humor, and deep humanity embodied in his
comments.

The Gangster
as Tragic Hero

America, as a social and political organization, is committed to a
cheerful view of life. It could not be otherwise. The sense of
tragedy is a luxury of aristocratic societies, where the fate of the
individual is not conceived of as having a direct and legitimate
political importance, being determined by a fixed and supra-

political—that is, non-controversial—moral order or fate. Modern equalitarian societies, however, whether democratic or authoritarian in their political forms, always base themselves on the claim that they are making life happier; the avowed function of the modern state, at least in its ultimate terms, is not only to regulate social relations, but also to determine the quality and the possibilities of human life in general. Happiness thus becomes the chief political issue—in a sense, the only political issue—and for that reason it can never be treated as an issue at all. If an American or a Russian is unhappy, it implies a certain reprobation of his society, and therefore, by a logic of which we can all recognize the necessity, it becomes an obligation of citizenship to be cheerful; if the authorities find it necessary, the citizen may even be compelled to make a public display of his cheerfulness on important occasions, just as he may be conscripted into the army in time of war.

Naturally, this civic responsibility rests most strongly upon the organs of mass culture. The individual citizen may still be permitted his private unhappiness so long as it does not take on political significance, the extent of this tolerance being determined by how large an area of private life the society can accommodate. But every production of mass culture is a public act and must conform with accepted notions of the public good. Nobody seriously questions the principle that it is the function of mass culture to maintain public morale, and certainly nobody in the mass audience objects to having his morale maintained.* At a time when the normal condition of the citizen is a state of anxiety, euphoria spreads over our culture like the broad smile

* In her testimony before the House Committee on Un-American Activities, Mrs. Leila Rogers said that the movie *None But the Lonely Heart* was un-American because it was gloomy. Like so much else that was said during the unhappy investigation of Hollywood, this statement was at once stupid and illuminating. One knew immediately what Mrs. Rogers was talking about; she had simply been insensitive enough to carry her philistinism to its conclusion.

of an idiot. In terms of attitudes towards life, there is very little difference between a "happy" movie like *Good News,* which ignores death and suffering, and a "sad" movie like *A Tree Grows in Brooklyn,* which uses death and suffering as incidents in the service of a higher optimism.

But, whatever its effectiveness as a source of consolation and a means of pressure for maintaining "positive" social attitudes, this optimism is fundamentally satisfying to no one, not even to those who would be most disoriented without its support. Even within the area of mass culture, there always exists a current of opposition, seeking to express by whatever means are available to it that sense of desperation and inevitable failure which optimism itself helps to create. Most often, this opposition is confined to rudimentary or semi-literate forms: in mob politics and journalism, for example, or in certain kinds of religious enthusiasm. When it does enter the field of art, it is likely to be disguised or attenuated: in an unspecific form of expression like jazz, in the basically harmless nihilism of the Marx Brothers, in the continually reasserted strain of hopelessness that often seems to be the real meaning of the soap opera. The gangster film is remarkable in that it fills the need for disguise (though not sufficiently to avoid arousing uneasiness) without requiring any serious distortion. From its beginnings, it has been a consistent and astonishingly complete presentation of the modern sense of tragedy.*

In its initial character, the gangster film is simply one example of the movies' constant tendency to create fixed dramatic patterns that can be repeated indefinitely with a reasonable expectation of profit. One gangster film follows another as

---

* Efforts have been made from time to time to bring the gangster film into line with the prevailing optimism and social constructiveness of our culture; *Kiss of Death* is a recent example. These efforts are usually unsuccessful; the reasons for their lack of success are interesting in themselves, but I shall not be able to discuss them here.

one musical or one Western follows another. But this rigidity is not necessarily opposed to the requirements of art. There have been very successful types of art in the past which developed such specific and detailed conventions as almost to make individual examples of the type interchangeable. This is true, for example, of Elizabethan revenge tragedy and Restoration comedy.

For such a type to be successful means that its conventions have imposed themselves upon the general consciousness and become the accepted vehicles of a particular set of attitudes and a particular aesthetic effect. One goes to any individual example of the type with very definite expectations, and originality is to be welcomed only in the degree that it intensifies the expected experience without fundamentally altering it. Moreover, the relationship between the conventions which go to make up such a type and the real experience of its audience or the real facts of whatever situation it pretends to describe is of only secondary importance and does not determine its aesthetic force. It is only in an ultimate sense that the type appeals to its audience's experience of reality; much more immediately, it appeals to previous experience of the type itself: it creates its own field of reference.

Thus the importance of the gangster film, and the nature and intensity of its emotional and aesthetic impact, cannot be measured in terms of the place of the gangster himself or the importance of the problem of crime in American life. Those European movie-goers who think there is a gangster on every corner in New York are certainly deceived, but defenders of the "positive" side of American culture are equally deceived if they think it relevant to point out that most Americans have never seen a gangster. What matters is that the experience of the gangster *as an experience of art* is universal to Americans. There is almost nothing we understand better or react to more readily or with quicker intelligence. The Western film, though it seems never to

diminish in popularity, is for most of us no more than the folklore of the past, familiar and understandable only because it has
been repeated so often. The gangster film comes much closer.
In ways that we do not easily or willingly define, the gangster
speaks for us, expressing that part of the American psyche which
rejects the qualities and the demands of modern life, which rejects "Americanism" itself.

The gangster is the man of the city, with the city's language
and knowledge, with its queer and dishonest skills and its terrible daring, carrying his life in his hands like a placard, like a
club. For everyone else, there is at least the theoretical possibility of another world—in that happier American culture which
the gangster denies, the city does not really exist; it is only a
more crowded and more brightly lit country—but for the gangster there is only the city; he must inhabit it in order to personify
it: not the real city, but that dangerous and sad city of the
imagination which is so much more important, which is the modern world. And the gangster—though there are real gangsters—
is also, and primarily, a creature of the imagination. The real
city, one might say, produces only criminals; the imaginary city
produces the gangster: he is what we want to be and what we
are afraid we may become.

Thrown into the crowd without background or advantages,
with only those ambiguous skills which the rest of us—the real
people of the real city—can only pretend to have, the gangster
is required to make his way, to make his life and impose it on
others. Usually, when we come upon him, he has already made
his choice or the choice has already been made for him, it doesn't
matter which: we are not permitted to ask whether at some point
he could have chosen to be something else than what he is.

The gangster's activity is actually a form of rational enterprise, involving fairly definite goals and various techniques for
achieving them. But this rationality is usually no more than a
vague background; we know, perhaps, that the gangster sells

liquor or that he operates a numbers racket; often we are not given even that much information. So his activity becomes a kind of pure criminality: he hurts people. Certainly our response to the gangster film is most consistently and most universally a response to sadism; we gain the double satisfaction of participating vicariously in the gangster's sadism and then seeing it turned against the gangster himself.

But on another level the quality of irrational brutality and the quality of rational enterprise become one. Since we do not see the rational and routine aspects of the gangster's behavior, the practice of brutality—the quality of unmixed criminality— becomes the totality of his career. At the same time, we are always conscious that the whole meaning of this career is a drive for success: the typical gangster film presents a steady upward progress followed by a very precipitate fall. Thus brutality itself becomes at once the means to success and the content of success —a success that is defined in its most general terms, not as accomplishment or specific gain, but simply as the unlimited possibility of aggression. (In the same way, film presentations of businessmen tend to make it appear that they achieve their success by talking on the telephone and holding conferences and that success *is* talking on the telephone and holding conferences.)

From this point of view, the initial contact between the film and its audience is an agreed conception of human life: that man is a being with the possibilities of success or failure. This principle, too, belongs to the city; one must emerge from the crowd or else one is nothing. On that basis the necessity of the action is established, and it progresses by inalterable paths to the point where the gangster lies dead and the principle has been modified: there is really only one possibility—failure. The final meaning of the city is anonymity and death.

In the opening scene of *Scarface*, we are shown a successful man; we know he is successful because he has just given a party of opulent proportions and because he is called Big Louie.

Through some monstrous lack of caution, he permits himself to be alone for a few moments. We understand from this immediately that he is about to be killed. No convention of the gangster film is more strongly established than this: it is dangerous to be alone. And yet the very conditions of success make it impossible not to be alone, for success is always the establishment of an *individual* pre-eminence that must be imposed on others, in whom it automatically arouses hatred; the successful man is an outlaw. The gangster's whole life is an effort to assert himself as an individual, to draw himself out of the crowd, and he always dies *because* he is an individual; the final bullet thrusts him back, makes him, after all, a failure. "Mother of God," says the dying Little Caesar, "is this the end of Rico?"—speaking of himself thus in the third person because what has been brought low is not the undifferentiated *man*, but the individual with a name, the gangster, the success; even to himself he is a creature of the imagination. (T. S. Eliot has pointed out that a number of Shakespeare's tragic heroes have this trick of looking at themselves dramatically; their true identity, the thing that is destroyed when they die, is something outside themselves—not a man, but a style of life, a kind of meaning.)

At bottom, the gangster is doomed because he is under the obligation to succeed, not because the means he employs are unlawful. In the deeper layers of the modern consciousness, *all* means are unlawful, every attempt to succeed is an act of aggression, leaving one alone and guilty and defenseless among enemies: one is *punished* for success. This is our intolerable dilemma: that failure is a kind of death and success is evil and dangerous, is—ultimately—impossible. The effect of the gangster film is to embody this dilemma in the person of the gangster and resolve it by his death. The dilemma is resolved because it is *his* death, not ours. We are safe; for the moment, we can acquiesce in our failure, we can choose to fail.

(1948)

STUDY QUESTIONS

1. Warshow's article is based upon his observation that there is a discrepancy between our commonly expressed attitude toward gangsters and the attitude taken toward them in movies. Exactly what is this discrepancy? Can you cite examples of this apparent contradiction in popular arts other than the film?
2. According to Warshow, what is the basis for the apparently favorable treatment gangsters receive in films? Are there any qualities about the settings for gangster films that would tend to reinforce Warshow's interpretation? How does the usual *modus operandi* of the gangster in films tend to confirm Warshow's analysis? What about his social life?
3. What qualities of gangster figures tend to make them naturally more glamorous than the law-abiding heroes are? How have film makers treated the heroes to make them equally attractive? For example, how did the producers of the television series *The Untouchables* (1958) handle the problem? What about such law-abiding heroes as Peter Gunn? In current crime films, how easily can you tell the heroes from the villains? Why?
4. Warshow was thinking of gangster films of the thirties and the forties when he wrote this article. Has the treatment of gangsters changed any since that time? How does the treatment of juvenile delinquents, for example, tend to differ from the standard treatment of criminals in earlier years? Why have black leather jackets and motorcycles become so popular in the last ten years?
5. Recently, writers have often treated criminals as victims of society. How is this treatment actually similar to the earlier treatment of gangsters? Does this new treatment seem to offer any greater promise for writers who wish to treat gangsters realistically or artistically? Why or why not?
6. In "Literature in an Organization Society" (p. 50), William H. Whyte, Jr., describes our ambivalent attitudes toward success. How

does this ambivalence help to explain our contradictory feelings toward gangster heroes? What commonly accepted stereotypes of city life would tend to make us more tolerant of treating gangsters heroically?

ERIC LARRABEE

> Eric Larrabee (1922-   ) has been an editor of *Harper's Magazine,* of *American Heritage,* and of *Horizon,* and is currently a free-lance writer. He is also one of the President's advisors on the teaching of English in the United States. His books—*The Self-Conscious Society* (1960), *American Panorama* (1957), and *Mass Leisure* (1958)—are concerned with the relationship between popular culture and social values. In "Pornography Is Not Enough," Larrabee examines the question of whether perverted expressions of sex are any less objectionable than the kind of pornography against which court action is frequently taken. He asks a number of provocative questions about the moral health of a society which readily accepts sterile and sadistic literature but rejects art which contains overt and normal displays of sex.

Pornography Is Not Enough

Anyone who deliberately sets out to write about sex is taking his chances. The reader will immediately be alert for indications of immoderate interest in the subject, and the author will be under an implicit obligation to demonstrate that he has, at heart, a serene and untroubled spirit. There is after all a certain logic in taboo. While customs vary, even in the most undeveloped societies the emotional tension between male and female is commonly maintained by some form of restraint; and the state of primitive innocence, free from all sexual inhibition, is more likely to be a fantasy of the sophisticated than an existing fact. In March 1955 an Australian patrol in New Guinea came upon a tribe of 20,000

Papuans who had never before made contact with the outside world. "The men and women live in houses built on the tops of tree stumps, with separate entrances . . ." reported the New York *Herald Tribune*. "The men's and women's sections are divided by a central wall." [1]

Where sex is concerned, the imposition of partial curbs serves a double purpose: to stimulate and to hold back—never too much of either. A counterpoise to individual desires may also measure and reinforce their intensity, in such a way as to become virtually necessary to their existence. This is partly what the would-be censor means when he says that there has always been censorship, or that the social structure depends on preserving it. In that sense, we all "censor," internally, our own actions and those of others whom we influence. We define in our heads, as a matter of course, the range between what our contemporaries will and will not tolerate. We play between these definitions, stretching them now one way, now another. We live in a state of permanent conflict between our daring and our decency; and, though few go out of their way to say as much, few would have it otherwise.

Yet censorship, as we ordinarily know it, differs sharply from this internalized mechanism for enforcing communal assumptions. Of all forms of sex censorship, that of the individual psyche—which sees to it that some things simply cannot be said, even to oneself—is undoubtedly the most effective. It is truly effective, however, only for those tradition-bound societies in which sexual inhibitions are more or less uniformly shared. The modern world, where more than one set of assumptions exist about what is and is not to be allowed, can make sex censorship of literature and the arts a subject of heated dispute. Censorship as an issue, in other words, is almost inevitably a by-product of class rivalry. It arises along the shared boundaries between two or more antagonistic schools of thought; and in societies like our

[1] New York *Herald Tribune*, April 1, 1955, p. 3, col. 3.

own, where law has replaced the rule of universally accepted custom, it is eventually (though not always successfully) dealt with by law. The law underlines the vague sanctions of community disapproval with a tangible threat. It establishes certain minima of restriction and maxima of license, and, therefore, the limits of acceptable variation in erotic tone.

But the study of the law, case by case, tends to reduce the "problem" of obscenity to the problems posed in court proceedings of a rather specialized character, largely concerned with books and most often with books of a special kind—those that fall somewhere between the obvious trash and the invulnerable classic—whose publishers are sufficiently tenacious or self-confident to sustain litigation. Since the law offers apparently endless possibilities for reinterpretation, both parties to an obscenity dispute tend to regard it as a critical test—a step, in whichever direction, along the linear scale between total censorship and total liberality. Thus, a lawyer may see in Judge Woolsey's famous decision on *Ulysses* "a great stride forward, possibly a greater stride than in any previous single case," while a Congressional committee can see it as "the basis for excuse to print and circulate the filthiest, most obscene literature, without concurrent literary value to support it, ever known in history." [2] Both share the flattering illusion (for lawyers) that society takes its sexual cues from the bench.

The legal defense of literature against legal censorship, moreover, has had a somewhat confusing effect on debates over obscenity. It has focused attention on near-irrelevancies, such as the question of artistic merit or the number of equally objectionable passages in Shakespeare and the Bible, and distracted it from the much more important conflict "between the literati and the Philistines," as two scholars have put it, for jurisdiction over

---

[2] Morris L. Ernst and Alexander Lindey, *The Censor Marches On* (Doubleday; New York: 1940), p. 21. "Report of the Select Committee on Current Pornographic Materials," H.R. No. 2510, 82nd Congress, 2nd Session (1952), p. 6, referred to hereinafter as the *Gathings Committee Report*.

sexual manners and customs.[3] Those adversaries have frequently found it advantageous, for their respective reasons, to conduct this battle in the courtroom: the censorious, because they see the shock value of bringing before the public selected passages of books that might privately be inoffensive to most literate adults; the defenders of such books, because they see that common sense and most of the law is on their side. The outcome is then in the lap of extremely whimsical deities, and both parties—in defeat— tend to be victimized by the eloquence of their briefs. The literati despairingly conclude that the victories of reason are seldom permanent; the Philistines that so-called decent people are really the most dangerous. "The blackest mud"—the words are Anthony Comstock's—"is to be found behind the trees on which the sun shines brightest. In that shadow the slime lies thick." [4]

In recent years the tide has been running with the literati and against the Philistines. Books are now available at the corner newsstand, like *Lolita* and *Lady Chatterley's Lover,* which would have raised a storm of indignation as recently as five years ago. No audible cries of outrage are heard over such movies as *Some Like It Hot,* with its curious portrayal of a couple of "merry transvestites," as Jay Jacobs called them in *The Reporter,* and their difficulties in convincing anyone that they are in fact males.[5] New York theater audiences have been exposing themselves without riot or other public disturbance to Jean Genêt's *The Balcony,* in which it would be difficult to say whether the language or the subject matter was more flagrantly in defiance of the once-accepted norms.

Nevertheless, though Postmaster General Summerfield may be the only person left in the country who thinks *Lady Chatterley* is obscene, the law under which he sought to suppress it—

[3] Lockhart and McClure, "Literature, the Law of Obscenity, and the Constitution," *Minnesota Law Review* (1954) Vol. 38, p. 343.

[4] Anthony Comstock, *The Evening Mail* (1906), quoted in Ernst and Lindey, *op. cit.,* p. 255.

[5] Jay Jacobs, "A Highly Peculiar Film," *The Reporter,* April 16, 1959.

the Comstock Act, now Section 1461 of the U. S. Code—is still
on the books. District Court Judge Bryan's opinion, in ruling
against him, was the literati's greatest victory to date, but the
most recent and relevant statement from the Supreme Court—
Justice Brennan's opinion in the Roth case, in 1957—still reaf-
firms the legal basis for censorship. How far will the argument
of literary merit carry? Will someone now bring out an American
edition of Henry Miller's *Tropic of Cancer,* or the Marquis de
Sade's *120 Days of Sodom?* Sooner or later there will be a turning, even if it does not amount to the wholehearted revival of
Victorian prudery that has been called for by, among other people, the publisher of *Esquire.*[6]

One of the many ironies of the obscenity issue is the way in
which standards vary, in the eyes of both literati and Philistines,
among the media. What is permissible in one is forbidden in the
next; what would be an unthinkable limitation of freedom on one
hand is tolerated on the other. The older or more established the
medium, generally speaking, the greater the freedom from attack.
When it is new, or exploiting a new audience, it must expect to
be regarded as a potential outlet for the obscene. It was the
nineteenth-century novel, with its exposure of different classes to
one another through serials and lending libraries, which brought
on Victorian censorship; and a similar impetus, in our time,
has been provided by the pocket-size, paperback book. The
burden now rests most heavily of all on the new mass media,
which characteristically—to make matters worse—have a wider
and more penetrating impact on the senses than their predecessors. The movies, radio, and television pose problems in censorship so unfamiliar that the defenders of freedom for the old-
fashioned, hard-cover book hesitate to interfere with them. To
cope with them at all, we have had to evolve and accept im-

---

[6] See Arnold Gingrich, "The Coming Puritan Revolution," address to
Institut Français de Presse of the University of Paris, April 24, 1959, published as "Moral Responsibilities of the Press," in *Esquire,* July, 1959, p. 6.

provised regulations, like the self-policing "codes," which the old media of publishing, press, and stage would regard as unbearably restrictive. No one would dare ask of a newspaper that it observe the same restraints that have continually been demanded of that object of so much solicitude, the comic book.

The nature of any censorship, in other words, is often a function of the anxieties generated by the medium or the milieu which the medium serves. At thirty-five to fifty cents, the pocket-size paperbacks are available not only to many adults who had not thought of themselves as book buyers before, but to adolescents. Concern about them reached its peak in 1952 with a report to the Eighty-second Congress of the Select Committee of the House of Representatives on Current Pornographic Materials, known for short as the Gathings Committee, which tried to show a connection between corruption of the young, pornography, and the seven major paperback publishers then in operation. The Committee seems genuinely not to have desired censorship; it merely desired censorship to be unnecessary. Aware that no definition of obscenity is satisfactory, it tried to evade the word by diffusing it into a cloud of indefiniteness, recommending that the publishing business eliminate on its own initiative not only the conceivably obscene, but "that proportion of its output which may be classified as 'borderline' or 'objectionable' "—in other words, stop haggling about specific books and throw them all out wherever there is the slightest question. The Committee, moreover, wanted to deny to soft-cover books the degree of freedom it knew it must allow to hard-cover ones, on the presumptive grounds that the dissemination of the former constituted a "menace to the moral structure of the nation, particularly in the juvenile segment." [7] The implication was that an adult who could afford to pay $3.50 for obscenity could take care of himself. It was where the paperback book represented a penetration of

[7] *Gathings Committee Report,* p. 3.

"mature" attitudes from the minority bookstore class through to the majority newsstand class that the Committee was alarmed; it wanted this process to be either halted or reversed. It saw its real enemies, as Comstock did, among the respectable, the partisans of the liberal enlightenment who insist upon unloosing evil—in the name of mere principle—on susceptible and unprotected youths.

Censorship and obscenity, as such, were not the real issues here—they were only camouflage for issues so embittered they could not be openly posed. Nor are these, as they have often been said to be, merely religious; one of the least sensible crotchets of the anti-censorship school lies in attributing to Catholicism attitudes which are equally often, and frequently more vigorously, espoused by Protestants. In this respect, the Gathings Committee Report is especially instructive; it is a representative example of the counterattack that was then being made, against various aristocratic views that had been thought to be invulnerable, by the vocal and dissident blocs formed out of the intellectually dispossessed in the aftermath of the Roosevelt era, those forces for revisionist obscurantism that have been called the "discontented classes." [8] The Committee came out against "modern" literature and "liberal" interpretations of the law in virtually the same breath, as though both had equally undermined the Republic. Often, views of this kind were then called anti-intellectual, though they were, in many respects, not so much anti-intellectual as anti-chronological—part of a massive, integrated gripe against the passage of time. Clearly their holders were antagonized less by the work of the mind for its own sake than by the dominant literary and artistic style which had made them feel, for more than two decades, that they were aesthetically out of fashion. Now that the wheel had turned, turned so far that the excesses of "liberalism" and "modernism" were being deplored by those who

[8] David Riesman and Nathan Glazer, "The Intellectuals and the Discontented Classes," *Partisan Review,* Winter, 1955, p. 47.

once committed them, the day had come for revenge. A crusade against pornography, that most helpless of quarries, was made to order.

Thus it is that literature and its advocates have so often found themselves on the defensive, unprotected by the juridical triumphs of one generation from the smut-hunters of the next. The open competition among ideas cannot be relied on, where pornography is concerned. Like Communism or homosexuality, it can be attacked in the secure knowledge that few will dare defend it. It then becomes the focal point for resentments less safe to assert, and everything suspect tends to be lumped together (not surprisingly, numerous citizens, loud in the pursuit of the dirty book, thought it to be somehow connected with the Communists). Often the "liberal" argument, as a way of touching base with respectability, has allowed that "smut for smut's sake" must be rigorously dealt with—forgetting that this is the only concession the would-be censor has ever needed to ask. As long as an exception is made for the indefensible or even the detestable—"Freedom for everybody, except Communists and pornographers"—then there will be people perfectly prepared to state that you or I are Communists and pornographers, or their dupes, until we prove the contrary. It is at such times that one remembers why freedom has been said to be indivisible.

An equally serious objection to the treatment of obscenity as a largely legal issue arises from the distorting effect this has on any discussion of sexual morality. Concentration on what is forbidden, according to arbitrary and variable rules, distracts attention from what is permitted—and from any perspective that might put the two in balance. It would surely seem desirable, where a subject is, by its nature, so delicate, to take into account the extraordinarily wide range of "normal" behavior, the fact that prudes are not the only ones entitled to reticence, and the universal human inability to draw a sharp line between lust and love. An adversary situation over obscenity reduces these factors to their ultimate fragility; it is the native environment of the neurotic, and Comstockery—as Bernard Shaw named the disease—is its natural corollary. One cannot deal fairly with questions of obscenity, at any event, without describing the context out of which they emerge—the muddle of preoccupations and prohibitions which define, at any given time, the standards each individual must reckon with. If the law cannot recognize the effects which would be found in the absence of a given work of putative obscenity, then it cannot very well determine the effect of that work. However haltingly, in a rough-and-ready fashion, it must operate on some kind of theory of the American sex life—of what it is, or ought to be.

American attitudes toward sex illustrate the interrelationship between censorship and provocation in almost clinically pure form; to foreign critics, we offer the most striking example available of a society in which excitation and restraint have the continuous function of intensifying one another. Every censorship breeds evasion; it is in our highly developed techniques for evading our own censorship that the American culture fascinates the visitor—or the few local observers sufficiently interested to notice them. To the European eye, we give the impression of making an unwholesome fetish of the female breast, of overwhelming our adolescents with erotic stimuli, and of hiding behind a "puritan façade" the reality of *"un des pays sexuellement le plus libres du monde."* [9] Confronted with the contrast between our preaching and our practice, we are hard put to refute the thesis propounded a decade and a half ago by Philip Wylie: that the United States is "technically insane in the matter of sex." [10]

To be sure, Americans overemphasize sex partly because they can afford to. If we are the only nation to make love a prob-

<hr>

[9] Claude Roy, *Clefs Pour L'Amérique* (Troi Collines; Paris: 1947), p. 84.

[10] Philip Wylie, *Generation of Vipers* (Rinehart; New York: 1955), p. 57.

lem, we are so in virtue of having emancipated women, reduced
the burden of household routines, and offered both sexes an un-
restricted vista of domestic bliss and self-fulfillment. "Their statesmen are intent on making democracy work," writes a Frenchman
of us. "Everybody is trying to make love work, too." [11] We demand a great deal of it. For modern man, sex has been called
"the last frontier," to which he looks "for reassurance that he is
alive." [12] And while, in a mass-production society, it tends to
become a consumption good like any other, it is a good whose
enjoyment by others remains forever beyond the reach of comparison—an object of limitless potentialities for fantasy and
envy. Our glamor figures, male and female, whose justification is
in most other respects obscure, serve to maintain an illusion that
somewhere, for somebody, sex can be a full-time activity. The
vast majority of us must live on in the knowledge that the indul-
gences of the glamorous are forbidden; and at times, the heavy
puritan hand descends even on a puzzled unfortunate (like Mr.
Jelke, of New York) who was sure that he himself inhabited the
charmed circle.

Expecting much of sex, but feeling as individuals that much
is denied them, Americans create in the substance of suppressed
desire the remarkable symbolic figures that are found here as
in no other culture. The existence of "the great American love
goddess" [13] is more often noted than explained. It is apparent
that she enjoys high status, that she is attended by elaborate cere-
monials, and that the titular embodiment of the divinity (at this
writing, still Marilyn Monroe) is only the reigning head of a
hierarchy of subdivinities, all of whom possess similar attributes.
She is most often a movie star, though her talents as an actress

[11] Raoul de Roussy de Sales, "Love in America," *Atlantic Monthly*,
May, 1938, p. 645.

[12] David Riesman, Reuel Denney, and Nathan Glazer, *The Lonely
Crowd* (Yale; New Haven: 1950), p. 154.

[13] Winthrop Sargent, *Geniuses, Goddesses, and People* (Dutton; New
York: 1949), p. 196.

and the merits of the films in which she appears are plainly immaterial. Her primary function is widely understood but rarely mentioned—that is, to serve as the object of autoerotic reverie. She represents, in brief, the commercial exploitation of the assumption that the American public is composed largely of Peeping Toms.

The assumption would appear to be well founded. It draws sustenance from the approach to sex on similar principles institutionalized by the advertising business. Diverted from literature and the arts, the forces that underlie obscenity and pornography expend themselves in this characteristic American medium. Here sex may be treated as powerful motivation, but only by expressing it in distorted and evasive forms—*e.g.*, the women's underwear that is advertised far out of proportion to the market for it, so that we are daily surrounded with pictures of the feminine bosom, leg, and abdomen tightly constrained by clothing (the difference in effect between these and the "bondage photos" confiscated by the police is one of degree only). To serve the hunger for the unattainable, we have brought into existence an entire class of women whose profession is catering to voyeurs, not even in the flesh, but through photographs—namely, the models. At its top are found the handful who pose for the fashion magazines and set the pace in cosmetics, posture, style, and aura at the outer reaches of unreal sophistication, where their taut, nerveless languor stands unchallenged—for lack of more appealing and imaginable substitutes—as an ideal of the sensual.

Then there is the theme of homosexuality, which runs through American popular culture (as well as literature) like a thread of not-so-innocent deceit. Homosexuality itself, as a phenomenon, has probably been given exaggerated attention. It is the *frisson*, the delectable shiver, of the twentieth century, somewhat as incest was of the nineteenth. Many of the young men who choose it as a way of life undoubtedly do so for a complex of reasons, among which the sexual may not be the most important. For the sensitive young white Southerner or Northern Negro there is scarcely a more rapid avenue of upward social and aesthetic mobility; and many of them, as the late Robert W. Lindner maintained, are not so much homosexual as homoerotic. They keep themselves in physically better trim than most heterosexual males, and they are far better housekeepers than many females. They are pro-sex in a world that is largely anti-sex. With one exception, which I will come to later on, they seem to me to get insufficient credit for their leavening and beneficent effect.[14]

What is deceitful about American homosexuality is not the conspiratorial existence forced on, accepted by, or darkly attributed to homosexuals themselves. It is the connivance of the public in something it wishes to be titillated by, but not mention out loud—in its approval of novelists whose major theme of hatred for women is rarely mentioned; of comedians whose stock in trade is the exhibitionism of spastic, semihysterical effeminacy; of Western and detective-story heroes who rigorously spur their heroines in the search for sadomasochistic purification. All these are not only permitted but profuse. Not a word of complaint about them comes from the self-appointed custodians of morality, who are far too busily occupied protecting teenagers from De Maupassant. Censorship, official and unofficial, lets pass into the social mainstream countless images and innuendos that could only be identified—if they were to be identified—as perverse. Of the normal, the lustful thoughts and desires of one sex for the other, it faithfully removes whatever trace it can.

This paradox has been the subject of a book, the most extraordinary study of Anglo-Saxon censorship yet to appear—

[14] Robert Lindner, Hacker Foundation Lectures, Los Angeles, November 1-5, 1954. ". . . inverts know what the rest of us are just discovering: that we are living in a culture that is not heterosexually oriented but profoundly anti-sexual, mistrustful and rejective of all sex, and bent upon the confinement if not the literal suppression of the sexual instinct." Lecture No. IV, "Changing Attitudes Toward Homosexuality," *Mss.*, pp. 9-10.

Gershon Legman's *Love and Death* (1949). Mr. Legman's subject is the literary sadism which is intensified by the censorship
of sex; his motif is that shameful anomaly of American mores
which has made love, legal in fact, illegal on paper, while murder, though illegal in fact, has been not only legal on paper but
the basis of the greatest publishing successes of all time. To be
sure, affection and hatred are opposite poles of human experience, and art necessarily concerns itself with each—the act in
which life begins and that in which it ends. The highest skill
need not morbidly exaggerate the physical details of either, but
neither will be denied it. Deny one only, and the other takes its
place. Mr. Legman overpoweringly documents his case that in the
modern Anglo-American world this is what has substantially occurred.

Though we often speak of sex and sadism together—as two
equally regrettable qualities in the novels of Mickey Spillane, for
example—in actual practice, we tolerate blood and guts in a
quantity and concreteness denied to sexual love. The time-
tested formula for the "sexed-up" cover of a paperback book
is a near-naked girl with a revolver, and it is curious that critics
should comment so often on the nudity and ignore the invitation
to murder. Within the letter of the law, as in the popular culture,
sex and violence tend to be entangled—we labeled an atomic
bomb with the title of a Rita Hayworth movie and called an ab-
breviated bathing suit a "Bikini"—but in the courts it is exceptional that the two are prosecuted with equal emphasis. The
typical law against obscenity prohibits it in company with other
encouragements to crime as well as lust, but we all take for
granted the state of general acceptance for printed murdering,
whipping, gouging, and wholesale bloodletting which makes half
the law unenforceable.

Mr. Spillane, who must by now be one of the best-selling
novelists of all time, has a standard plot which is simplicity
itself; boy meets girl, boy is seduced by girl, boy kills girl. Here,

on a rough tabulation of his first five books, is what happens to the dozen or so young ladies with whom his hero, Mike Hammer, becomes involved. Two of the novels open with Mr. Hammer's chance meeting with a woman who dies immediately—one by murder, one by suicide. Of the seven with whom he has casual but intimate encounters, six are murdered (three shootings, one strangulation, one drowning, and one slit throat). Of the three in whom he takes a deeper interest he himself shoots two of them in the abdomen, one of them having turned out to be a man, and the third has her head shot off accidentally by a child just as she is about to kill Mr. Hammer.

There are only three other significant female characters. One he beats with his own belt; she is simultaneously shot in the shoulder (though not killed) by someone else. Another is his secretary, for whom he maintains a constant but furiously re-strained affection. In the only book in which he treats her at all tenderly, she is kidnapped by Communists, stripped, hung up by her wrists, and beaten with a knotted rope. Mr. Hammer is suf-ficiently moved by watching this scene to machine-gun an entire roomful of people; three paragraphs describe the physical con-sequences in some detail. That leaves only one woman whose attractiveness to Mr. Hammer does not cause violence to take place. Perhaps the reader is meant to understand that she has already achieved violence in her own fashion, for she is the only genuine nymphomaniac in the lot.

"Whatever its reason," wrote Mr. Legman in *Love and Death*, "through this technique of persistent sexual negation, every detail of ravishing female nudity, lascivious temperament, etc., can be gone into at any desired length . . . as long as the whole is purified by the detective hero's frigid rejection." Love, no; death, yes. In his bitterly polemic book Mr. Legman follows this paradox where it leads him, through comic books to the novels built around the bitch-heroine, and eventually traces it back to the censorship of sex in Anglo-Saxon literature, beginning around 1700, which initiated the literary violence Mr. Spillane has brought to its present mass-producible perfection. Yet Mr. Legman did not suppose that everything would be solved merely by giving incitement to love and incitement to mayhem equal treatment under the law. "The American censorship of sex is internalized," he writes. "The men and women in the street carry it around with them in their heads. *They* are the censor, and to the degree that the law mirrors their wonted censorship, the law can be enforced and will be obeyed." [15]

Now that the lid has been lifted, so to speak, we have had a chance to see how right Mr. Legman was. The freedom of the late fifties came so suddenly and unexpectedly that most of us were unprepared for it. *Lolita,* as Lionel Trilling has remarked, is really the only kind of love story that we are ready to take seriously;[16] while *Lady Chatterley,* now that she is public property, turns out to be almost more embarrassing than stimulating. The writers who were most readily able to profit from the general loosening of moral bonds were those who had already worked out their own patterns of outlet and repression on Mr. Legman's terms. Freedom has proved to be most conspicuously freedom for authors like Tennessee Williams, for castration and cannibalism, and for the endlessly reiterated message of war to the death on women.

Williams' stock formula is the same as Spillane's: females are enthralling, but shared pleasure with them promptly results in the death of one or both partners. I take as an illustration his *Orpheus Descending,* both because it has just appeared as a movie (*The Fugitive Kind*) and because it is a remake of his first play (*Battle of Angels*), and therefore loaded with what were to become his preoccupying themes. This is the Orpheus legend more or less unvarnished. A wandering folk singer

[15] Adapted from Eric Larrabee, "Dames and Death," in "After Hours," *Harper's Magazine,* May, 1952, p. 99. Gershon Legman, *Love and Death: A Study in Censorship* (Breaking Point; New York: 1949), pp. 20, 52, 70.
[16] Lionel Trilling in *Encounter,* October, 1958.

descends upon a representative Hades of the small-town rural South and nearly rescues from it, by his native animality, a full-blooded woman married to a dying man. He gets her with child but also shot by her husband, and himself thrown naked to the county marshal's avenging hounds, which have been mechanically howling offstage for three full acts.

There are various subplots, most of them more interesting than the main one and all revolving around the same conflict—that between instinctive human decency and emotion on the one hand, and the explosive and neurotic puritanism of the dominant Southern community on the other. Williams has a marvelous hatred of the characteristic insanities of the white Protestant American, but whatever he opposes to it comes veiled in layers of symbolism. There is only one Negro in *Orpheus Descending*, and he never speaks an intelligible word. In fact there are essentially no Negroes at all in Williams' synthetic Dixie. They all appear in whiteface. The plays are remarkable for their incredible Italians, onto whom are grafted all the qualities of warmth, spontaneity, and ineffectiveness that Anglo-Saxons conventionally impute to "ethnic" groups. Sensuality, when represented by a character who is not only female but Italian, both fascinates and frightens Mr. Williams. What he seems to be saying is that it gets the wayward white boy into such fatal difficulties that his warped and nay-saying peers will destroy him.

This no doubt is Mr. Williams' considered response to life as he has known it, and he obviously feels entitled to some kind of retribution against the society that has driven him to it. For myself, though I will defend to the death Mr. Williams' right to exalt whatever ideal he chooses, I cannot defend his right to have audiences sit there and drink it all in, as though it were a profound comment on the human situation by a man of no significantly disqualifying bias. The end result of puritan censorship has been this compounded dishonesty of writer and public in which meaningless violence, violence for its own sake, meant merely to shock and terrify the spectator, is never named and identified. Instead, the critics puzzle over the "mystery" of Williams' "dramatic power," and save their choicest laurels for Archibald Mac-Leish's *J.B.*, a tidied-up, Ivy League imitation of Williams' technique for clubbing the audience into emotional insensibility by repeated and insistently pointless acts of mangling, murder, rape, and—the final "poetic" touch—nuclear annihilation. If pornography could cure us of this disease, one would pray for more pornography.[17]

Needless to say, despite these distractions, society survives. The vanity of lawyers in assuming that the law has a significant effect on sexual habits is matched by the vanity of writers in assuming that literature has a comparable effect. Fortunately, there are other forces at work determining conduct, and such enjoyment of life as there is by the vast majority escapes observation and reporting. Young people, determined to explore the mysteries for themselves, continue to grow up without having been successfully convinced that sex is unclean; nor are they always unwilling to scandalize their elders. Throughout this society that resolutely pretends to the contrary, there remains a streak of amiable lewdness and bawdry that has nothing to do with literature and breaks through censorship of any kind at the most unexpected times and places. There is a shudder of outraged horror in each community where a "non-virgin club" is uncovered, but as far as I am aware, these remarkable institutions neither take their inspiration from books nor are in any way discouraged by censorship. They testify to the extent to which sex can be self-induced, self-sustaining, and ultimately self-justified.

The dispute over censorship, no matter how "liberal" the law becomes, is thus likely to continue. The smut-hunters are not the only ones who attack pornography. There are thoroughly intelligent and sophisticated objections to it—on the grounds

[17] Adapted from Eric Larrabee, "Morpheus Ascending," in "After Hours," *Harper's Magazine*, May, 1957.

that it is "calculated to stimulate sex feelings independent of another loved and chosen human being"—which play down any
suggestion that Eros has, in its own right, a civilizing and illuminating potential. This is the view of sex which holds its exclusive
function to be continuation of the race, and is somewhat arbitrary
in its strictures on those whose desires fail to be co-ordinated
with the propagative process. Mrs. Margaret Culkin Banning,
testifying before the Gathings Committee, said that she imagined
the ads in "sexy magazines" to be directed at "frustrated men,
who were too short or too fat or too friendless or too far from
home to have a successful sex relationship";[18] while Margaret
Mead has defined the difference between bawdry and pornography as that between the music hall and the "strip tease,
where lonely men, driven and haunted, go alone. . . ."[19] Such
views impress me as inadequately informed by an appreciation
of sex, not simply as a genetic mechanism, but as one of the
avenues through which reality is exposed to us. This blessing has
been conferred on mankind impartially and is luckily not within
anyone's province to allocate.

But the defense of pornography—and one of the by-products
of censorship's current decline is that an all-out defense has
at last become possible—rests on the assumption that it "reflects a basically healthy and therapeutic attitude toward life."
This is a phrase which the authors of *Pornography and the
Law* (1959) apply only to that subdivision of the literature
which they call "erotic realism," books like Lawrence's, Frank
Harris' autobiography, or Edmund Wilson's *Memoirs of Hecate
County*. Of the rest—the "hard-core" pornography that no judge
has yet been found to condone—Drs. Eberhard and Phyllis
Kronhausen will say only that it cannot be shown to be harm-

---

[18] Margaret Culkin Banning, "Filth on the Newsstands," *Reader's
Digest*, October, 1952, pp. 115, 119, quoted in *Gathings Committee Report*,
pp. 135, 137.

[19] Margaret Mead, "Sex and Censorship in Contemporary Society," in
New American Writing, 3rd Mentor Selection (1953), p. 24.

ful, that its worst qualities result from our "censorial, sex-sup-
pressive attitudes," and that as fantasy it may be preferable to
direct action as an outlet for many antisocial attitudes. But they
do at least rest their entire discussion on the assumption that the
primary purpose of the "hard-core" books is to stimulate the
"lascivious thoughts" and "lustful desires" which the Supreme
Court still frowns upon, and in speaking to any extent favorably
of this "dirt for dirt's sake" they go far beyond the position that
most opponents of censorship have hitherto been willing to
take.[20]

There is a sense in which every nation gets the pornography
it deserves. If we forbid the writing of erotica to all but those
who are willing to break the law, we have no fair complaint
if the results are trivial, mean, and inartistic. We are little entitled to the conclusion that the subject matter of sex cannot be
tastefully—or even beautifully—treated if we have never tried
to treat it so. Least of all can we pride ourselves on our moral
stature as a people until we have further progressed beyond the
outhouse phase, manifested by the Post Office Department's recurrent efforts to agitate public opinion, in which a sniggering
shame is our characteristic approach to sex. The true obscenities
of American life lie in our vicious public consumption of human
suffering, in virtually every form and medium. By comparison,
the literature of sexual love would seem vastly to be preferred.
The only real question is whether pornography is enough,
whether literature alone can do the trick, and whether the ten-
tative liberties now allotted to a handful of authors will undo
the damage of over a century of censorship before another puritan cycle begins. The public now seems to have more literary sex
available than it can assimilate, and there are few signs that
liberation from Comstockery has turned us overnight into profoundly organic and viscerally integrated creatures. Instead, what

[20] Drs. Eberhard and Phyllis Kronhausen, *Pornography and the Law*
(Ballantine; New York: 1959), pp. 23, 266ff.

has come to the fore is that strain of violence in us that D. H. Lawrence saw so clearly, and the sadism that to date has shown no signs of weakening its grip on the American imagination. If the sexual millennium is to arrive, it cannot arrive too soon.

STUDY QUESTIONS

1. Larrabee appears to be defending pornography. Is he actually doing so? What alternatives does he see to pornography? Which does he think is preferable, pornography or its alternatives?
2. According to Larrabee, which is the more important kind of censorship, legal or personal? How does our legal censorship reflect our personal censorship? Is this reflection always accurate? Can you think of specific examples of books or films that were legally permissible but which exceeded your personal grounds for censorship?
3. Larrabee says many Europeans feel that Americans are "sex-mad." What reason have they for this accusation? Is there any defense for Americans' constant attention to sex in advertising and popular arts?
4. What does Larrabee say are the two healthy and creative purposes for censorship? Does our refusal to publish pornography tend to frustrate or aid these purposes? Or does it do both?
5. Larrabee deals at length with perverted expressions of sex that commonly appear in popular literature. Why does he object to these perversions? What forms do they take? What connection has his objection to perversion with his discussion of Gershon Legman's *Love and Death* (1949)?
6. In what respects do the recent novels by Ian Fleming bear clear kinship with Mickey Spillane's stories? Do they seem any healthier than Spillane's stories?
7. Larrabee objects to subjects such as cannibalism and homosexuality on grounds that they represent deviations from normal expressions of sex. Can you think of circumstances in which these sub-

jects might be defensible? What, for example, would Larrabee say about *Lord of the Flies* (1954), or *Catcher in the Rye* (1951)? Is it necessarily the subject or is it the treatment of a subject that renders it unacceptable?

8. Larrabee says that sex has often been a civilizing force, quite aside from its procreative function. What does he mean? Can you think of examples of classical art, literature, or civilization that would tend to support Larrabee's thesis? Does the current treatment of sex in American popular literature in any way seem similar to these classical treatments? How would you explain the similarities and differences?

9. Where there is most disagreement about pornography is in its definition. By this time, you have some idea what you believe constitutes pornography. How would you define it?

GILBERT HIGHET

Gilbert Highet (1906-) is a distinguished classicist
and humanist who has been on the faculty of Columbia
University for many years. His interests are varied; he has
written on the classical tradition (*The Classical Tradition,*
1949), on teacher education (*The Art of Teaching,* 1950),
and on modern literature (*A Clerk of Oxenford,* 1954),
to mention a few of his subjects. He is one of the most
successful informal essayists of the twentieth century. In
his approach to criticism, he seems to reflect the kinds of
neoclassical concerns which we most frequently associate
with eighteenth-century critics: a concern with right reason,
just comparisons, and a sense of proportion which enables
us to take the disparity between the ideal and the actual
with a sense of humor. The following selection reflects all
of these characteristics of Highet's criticism: his sense of
reason and proportion enables him to describe kitsch art
objectively; his sense of justness in literary comparisons
enables him to pinpoint those qualities of kitsch poetry
which are most ludicrous—and most popular; and his sense
of humor enables him to admit cheerfully to his own
affection for kitsch—he can see the disparity between his
own taste and his critical ideals.

Kitsch

If you have ever passed an hour wandering through an antique
shop (not looking for anything exactly, but simply looking),
you must have noticed how your taste gradually grows numb,
and then—if you stay—becomes perverted. You begin to see unsuspected charm in those hideous pictures of plump girls fon-

dling pigeons, you develop a psychopathic desire for spinning wheels and cobblers' benches, you are apt to pay out good money for a bronze statuette of Otto von Bismarck, with a metal hand inside a metal frock coat and metal pouches under his metallic eyes. As soon as you take the things home, you realize that they are revolting. And yet they have a sort of horrible authority; you don't like them; you know how awful they are; but it is a tremendous effort to drop them in the garbage, where they belong.

To walk along a whole street of antique shops—that is an experience which shakes the very soul. Here is a window full of bulbous Chinese deities; here is another littered with Zulu assegais, Indian canoe paddles, and horse pistols which won't fire; the next shopfront is stuffed with gaudy Italian majolica vases, and the next, even worse, with Austrian pottery—tiny ladies and gentlemen sitting on lace cushions and wearing lace ruffles, with every frill, every wrinkle and reticulation translated into porcelain: pink; stiff; but fortunately not unbreakable. The nineteenth century produced an appalling amount of junky art like this, and sometimes I imagine that clandestine underground factories are continuing to pour it out like illicit drugs.

There is a name for such stuff in the trade, a word apparently of Russian origin, kitsch*: it means vulgar showoff, and it is applied to anything that took a lot of trouble to make and is quite hideous.

It is paradoxical stuff, kitsch. It is obviously bad: so bad that you can scarcely understand how any human being would spend days and weeks making it, and how anybody else would buy it and take it home and keep it and dust it and leave it to her heirs. It is terribly ingenious, and terribly ugly, and utterly useless; and yet it has one of the qualities of good art—which is that, once seen, it is not easily forgotten. Of course it is found in all the arts: think of Milan Cathedral, or the statues in Westminster Abbey, or Liszt's settings of Schubert songs. There is a

* The Russian verb *keetcheetsya* means 'to be haughty and puffed up.'

lot of it in the United States—for instance, the architecture of Miami, Florida, and Forest Lawn Cemetery in Los Angeles. Many of Hollywood's most ambitious historical films are superb kitsch. Most Tin Pan Alley love songs are perfect 100 per cent kitsch.

There is kitsch in the world of books also. I collect it. It is horrible, but I enjoy it.

The gem of my collection is the work of the Irish novelist Mrs. Amanda McKittrick Ros, whose masterpiece, *Delina Delaney*, was published about 1900. It is a stirringly romantic tale, telling how Delina, a fisherman's daughter from Erin Cottage, was beloved by Lord Gifford, the heir of Columba Castle, and— after many trials and even imprisonment—married him. The story is dramatic, not to say impossible; but it is almost lost to view under the luxuriant style. Here, for example, is a sentence in which Mrs. Ros explains that her heroine used to earn extra cash by doing needlework.

She tried hard to assist in keeping herself a stranger to her poor old father's slight income by the use of the finest production of steel, whose blunt edge eyed the reely covering with marked greed, and offered its sharp dart to faultless fabrics of flaxen fineness.

Revolting, but distinctive: what Mr. Polly called 'rockockyo' in manner. For the baroque vein, here is Lord Gifford saying goodby to his sweetheart:

My darling virgin! my queen! my Delina! I am just in time to hear the toll of a parting bell strike its heavy weight of appalling softness against the weakest fibers of a heart of love, arousing and tickling its dormant action, thrusting the dart of evident separation deeper into its tubes of tenderness, and fanning the flame, already unextinguishable, into volumes of blaze.

Mrs. Ros had a remarkable command of rhetoric, and could coin an unforgettable phrase. She described her hero's black eyes as 'glittering jet revolvers.' When he became ill, she said he fell 'into a state of lofty fever'—doubtless because commoners have high fever, but lords have lofty fever. And her reflections on the moral degeneracy of society have rarely been equaled, in power and penetration:

Days of humanity, whither hast thou fled? When bows of compulsion, smiles for the deceitful, handshakes for the dogmatic, and welcome for the tool of power live under your objectionable, unambitious beat, not daring to be checked by the tongue of candour because the selfish world refuses to dispense with her rotten policies. The legacy of your forefathers, which involved equity, charity, reason, and godliness, is beyond the reach of their frivolous, mushroom offspring—deceit, injustice, malice, and unkindness—and is not likely to be codiciled with traits of harmony so long as these degrading vices of mock ambition fester the human heart.

Perhaps one reason I enjoy this stuff is because it so closely resembles a typical undergraduate translation of one of Cicero's finest perorations: sound and fury, signifying nothing. I regret only that I have never seen Mrs. Ros's poetry. One volume was called *Poems of Puncture* and another *Bayonets of Bastard Sheen*: alas, jewels now almost unprocurable. But at least I know the opening of her lyric written on first visiting St. Paul's Cathedral:

> Holy Moses, take a look,
> Brain and brawn in every nook!

Such genius is indestructible. Soon, soon now, some earnest researcher will be writing a Ph.D. thesis on Mrs. Amanda McKittrick Ros, and thus (as she herself might put it) conferring upon her dewy brow the laurels of concrete immortality.

Next to Mrs. Ros in my collection of kitsch is the work of the Scottish poet William McGonagall. This genius was born in 1830, but did not find his vocation until 1877. Poor and inadequate poets pullulate in every tongue, but (as the *Times Literary Supplement* observes) McGonagall 'is the only truly memorable bad poet in our language.' In his command of platitude and his disregard of melody, he was the true heir of William Wordsworth as a descriptive poet.

In one way his talents, or at least his aspirations, exceeded those of Wordsworth. He was at his best in describing events he had never witnessed, such as train disasters, shipwrecks, and sanguinary battles, and in picturing magnificent scenery he had never beheld except with the eye of the imagination. Here is his unforgettable Arctic landscape:

> Greenland's icy mountains are fascinating and grand,
> And wondrously created by the Almighty's command;
> And the works of the Almighty there's few can understand:
> Who knows but it might be a part of Fairyland?
>
> Because there are churches of ice, and houses glittering like glass,
> And for scenic grandeur there's nothing can it surpass,
> Besides there's monuments and spires, also ruins,
> Which serve for a safe retreat from the wild bruins.
>
> The icy mountains they're higher than a brig's topmast,
> And the stranger in amazement stands aghast
> As he beholds the water flowing off the melted ice
> Adown the mountain sides, that he cries out, Oh! how nice!

McGonagall also had a strong dramatic sense. He loved to tell of agonizing adventures, more drastic perhaps but not less moving than that related in Wordsworth's 'Vaudracour and Julia.' The happy ending of one of his 'Gothic' ballads is surely unforgettable:

> So thus ends the story of Hanchen, a heroine brave,
> That tried hard her master's gold to save,
> And for her bravery she got married to the miller's eldest son,
> And Hanchen on her marriage night cried Heaven's will be done.

These scanty selections do not do justice to McGonagall's ingenuity as a rhymester. His sound effects show unusual talent. Most poets would be baffled by the problem of producing rhymes for the proper names *General Graham* and *Osman Digna,* but McGonagall gets them into a single stanza, with dazzling effect:

> Ye sons of Great Britain, I think no shame
> To write in praise of brave General Graham!
> Whose name will be handed down to posterity without any stigma,
> Because, at the battle of El-Tab, he defeated Osman Digna.

One of McGonagall's most intense personal experiences was his visit to New York. Financially, it was not a success. In one of his vivid autobiographical sketches, he says, 'I tried occasionally to get an engagement from theatrical proprietors and music-hall proprietors, but alas! 'twas all in vain, for they all told me they didn't encourage rivalry.' However, he was deeply impressed by the architecture of Manhattan. In eloquent verses he expressed what many others have felt, although without adequate words to voice their emotion:

> Oh! Mighty City of New York, you are wonderful to behold,
> Your buildings are magnificent, the truth be it told;
> They were the only thing that seemed to arrest my eye,
> Because many of them are thirteen stories high.
>
> And the tops of the houses are all flat,
> And in the warm weather the people gather to chat;
> Besides on the house-tops they dry their clothes,
> And also many people all night on the house-tops repose.

Yet McGonagall felt himself a stranger in the United States. And here again his close kinship with Wordsworth appears. The Poet Laureate, in a powerful sonnet written at Calais, once reproached the English Channel for delaying his return by one of those too frequent storms in which (reckless tyrant!) it will indulge itself:

> Why cast ye back upon the Gallic shore,
> Ye furious waves! a patriotic Son
> Of England?

In the same vein McGonagall sings with rapture of his return to his 'ain countree':

> And with regard to New York, and the sights I did see,
> One street in Dundee is more worth to me,
> And, believe me, the morning I sailed from New York,
> For bonnie Dundee—my heart it felt as light as a cork.

Indeed, New York is a challenging subject for ambitious poets. Here, from the same shelf, is a delicious poem on the same theme, by Ezra Pound:

> My City, my beloved,
> Thou art a maid with no breasts
> Thou art slender as a silver reed.
> Listen to me, attend me!
> And I will breathe into thee a soul,
> And thou shalt live for ever.*

The essence of this kind of trash is incongruity. The kitsch writer is always sincere. He really means to say something important. He feels he has a lofty spiritual message to bring to an unawakened world, or else he has had a powerful experience which he must communicate to the public. But either his message turns out to be a majestic platitude, or else he chooses the wrong form in which to convey it—or, most delightful of all, there is a fundamental discrepancy between the writer and his subject, as when Ezra Pound, born in Idaho, addresses the largest city in the world as a maid with no breasts, and enjoins it to achieve inspiration and immortality by listening to him. This is like

---

* From *Personae* by Ezra Pound. Copyright 1926, 1954 by Ezra Pound. Reprinted by permission of the publishers, New Directions.—*Ed.*

climbing Mount Everest in order to carve a head of Mickey Mouse in the east face.

Bad love poetry, bad religious poetry, bad mystical prose, bad novels both autobiographical and historical—one can form a superb collection of kitsch simply by reading with a lively and awakened eye. College songs bristle with it. The works of Father Divine are full of it—all the more delightful because in him it is usually incomprehensible. One of the Indian mystics, Sri Rama-krishna, charmed connoisseurs by describing the Indian scrip-tures (in a phrase which almost sets itself to kitsch-music) as

> fried in the butter of knowledge and steeped in the
> honey of love.

Bad funeral poetry is a rich mine of the stuff. Here, for example, is the opening of a jolly little lament, 'The Funeral' by Stephen Spender, apparently written during his pink period:

> Death is another milestone on their way.
> With laughter on their lips and with winds blowing round them
> They record simply
> How this one excelled all others in making driving belts.

Observe the change from humanism to communism. Spender simply took Browning's 'Grammarian's Funeral,' threw away the humor and the marching rhythm, and substituted wind and the Stakhanovist speed-up. Such also is a delicious couplet from Archibald MacLeish's elegy on the late Harry Crosby:

> He walks with Ernest in the streets in Saragossa
> They are drunk their mouths are hard they say *qué cosa*.

From an earlier romantic period, here is a splendid specimen. Coleridge attempted to express the profound truth that men and animals are neighbors in a hard world; but he made the funda-mental mistake of putting it into a monologue address to a don-key.

Poor Ass! Thy master should have learnt to show
Pity—best taught by fellowship of Woe!
Innocent foal; thou poor despised forlorn!
I hail thee brother . . .

Once you get the taste for this kind of thing it is possible to find pleasure in hundreds of experiences which you might otherwise have thought either anesthetic or tedious: bad translations, abstract painting, grand opera . . . Dr. Johnson, with his strong sense of humor, had a fancy for kitsch, and used to repeat a poem in celebration of the marriage of the Duke of Leeds, composed by 'an inferiour domestick . . . in such homely rhimes as he could make':

When the Duke of Leeds shall married be
To a fine young lady of high quality,
How happy will that gentlewoman be
In his Grace of Leed's good company.

She shall have all that's fine and fair,
And the best of silk and sattin shall wear;
And ride in a coach to take the air,
And have a house in St. James's Square.

Folk poetry is full of such jewels. Here is the epitaph on an old gentleman from Vermont who died in a sawmill accident:

How shocking to the human mind
The log did him to powder grind.
God did command his soul away
His summings we must all obey.

Kitsch is well known in drama, although (except for motion pictures) it does not usually last long. One palmary instance was a play extolling the virtues of the Boy Scout movement, called *Young England*. It ran for a matter of years during the 1930's, to audiences almost wholly composed of kitsch-fanciers, who eventually came to know the text quite as well as the unfortunate actors. I can still remember the opening of one magnificent episode. Scene: a woodland glade. Enter the hero, a Scoutmaster, riding a bicycle, and followed by the youthful members of his troop. They pile bicycles in silence. Then the Scoutmaster raises his finger, and says (accompanied fortissimo by most of the members of the audience):

Fresh water must be our first consideration!

In the decorative arts kitsch flourishes, and is particularly widespread in sculpture. One of my favorite pieces of bad art is a statue in Rockefeller Center, New York. It is supposed to represent Atlas, the Titan condemned to carry the sky on his shoulders. That is an ideal of somber, massive tragedy: greatness and suffering combined as in Hercules or Prometheus. But this version displays Atlas as a powerful moron, with a tiny little head, rather like the pan-fried young men who appear in the health magazines. Instead of supporting the heavens, he is lifting a spherical metal balloon: it is transparent, and quite empty; yet he is balancing insecurely on one foot like a furniture mover walking upstairs with a beach ball; and he is scowling like a mad baboon. If he ever gets the thing up, he will drop it; or else heave it onto a Fifth Avenue bus. It is a supremely ridiculous statue, and delights me every time I see it.

Perhaps you think this is a depraved taste. But really it is an extension of experience. At one end, Homer. At the other, Amanda McKittrick Ros. At one end, *Hamlet*. At the other, McGonagall, who is best praised in his own inimitable words:

The poetry is moral and sublime
And in my opinion nothing could be more fine.
True genius there does shine so bright
Like unto the stars of night.

STUDY QUESTIONS

1. How does Highet define "kitsch"? What connection does he see between garish Victorian china and the bad poetry he collects?
2. Why does Highet object to kitsch, yet tolerate it humorously?
3. Compare Ezra Pound's poem, included in the essay, with a section of Hart Crane's poem "Brooklyn Bridge." Then see if you can define what constitutes kitsch in poetry. Why is Edgar A. Guest, who has written more than 11,000 poems, a kitsch poet? Where else is one likely to encounter kitsch poetry? Why?
4. Kitsch is not a quality which belongs exclusively to poetry and ceramics. It also belongs to other arts. Can you find examples of kitsch in contemporary furniture design? (For example, compare the furniture ads in the New York *Times* with the furniture ads in the *Sears and Roebuck Catalogue*.) By comparing some of Frank Lloyd Wright's designs with designs for middle-class housing, suggest some kinds of kitsch which are common in contemporary architecture. What about popular music?
5. Highet explains kitsch almost entirely in terms of poor taste. Are there any economic factors which would encourage the existence of kitsch art? Can you think of any characteristics of mass production which would favor the production of kitsch art?
6. Aline Saarinen—the art critic and widow of the architect Eero Saarinen—believes that some mass-produced art objects actually represent fine examples of functional design. One of her favorite examples is the common square pressed-glass ash trays available in almost every dime store. Can you think of any other mass-produced articles which represent fine design?
7. Highet is ridiculing the taste for kitsch art. How does he avoid giving the impression that he feels superior to his reader? What does his general tone tell about how serious he feels the problem to be?

from *THE TIMES LITERARY SUPPLEMENT*

Occasionally, a foreigner will look at American culture
and, from his perspective outside the culture, discover
qualities which are not apparent to Americans. The following article about the American musical comedy is a
good example of this. It comes from the London *Times
Literary Supplement,* a weekly publication, considered by
many to be one of the best of British literary publications.
In the article, the British critic analyzes the American
musical and points out a number of experimental and
imaginative qualities of the genre which are generally not
immediately apparent to Americans. The British critic is,
in fact, more sympathetic to and appreciative of the musical than Americans are likely to be, since he regards the
musical as an art form and not, as Americans too frequently do, as an escape for tired businessmen.

The Rebirth of the Musical

At unpredictable intervals, and sometimes simultaneously, the
theatres of London, Paris and New York take to what the anxious
doctors in attendance fear may be their death-beds. Hope is
usually at the lowest when one of the perpetual invalids makes
an astonishing rally. The other two capitals then become the
dumping ground for its plays. As soon as this happens there is a
bleat of concern from the scene of the dumping. How can the
native patient possibly survive the shock of the keen alien air?
We are all likely to find ourselves at one time or another among
the bleaters. Experience may tell us that this is the see-saw way
the interchange of plays between the three great play-producing

countries has always worked. It is hard, all the same, as we contemplate the sadly ailing native drama to believe that, so far
from dying of shock, it is more likely in due course to be stung
by the rival invalid's remarkable activity into some competitive
activity of its own. The see-saw way is, after all, the natural way.
The smooth-running mechanism for the swapping of successes
has long ago converted the three theatres into one theatre. Each
section has, of course, its now racially characteristic colour and
manner, but a burst of genuine dramatic energy anywhere is
good for the whole organism. Patriotic Englishmen stand at
present much in need of any consolation this generalization may
afford. They like to think that they invented musical comedy. Its
development into the American musical is something they still
do not understand. Apparently the only practical way open to
them of assisting in the development is to supply the audiences.
This they do with a will; but there is a touch of impotent
jealousy in their appreciation.

'London produces expansive musical shows,' wrote Mr.
Brooks Atkinson, reviewing *Annie Get Your Gun* in the *New York
Times,*

though, if one may be permitted to be smugly isolationist, the London
carousels have less animal gusto than ours. Before the war Paris used
to produce luxuriously bedizened girl shows for the tourists and foot-
loose males, but there was little fun in them. No country except America seems to have the tradition, the organization and the equipment for
these knockabout capers that blow you out of your seat with explosions
of brassy music and whack the funnybone with the slapstick.

This modest survey of how things were a decade ago is
roughly true of how things are to-day. We are bound to add,
however, that the 'knockabout capers' have since grown to a
scarcely believable extent in artistic purposefulness. What disturbs
competitors now is less the animal gusto of the American musical, which is perhaps a racial and inimitable gift, than its enormous confidence, its air of going somewhere, of adventurously

pioneering with happy valiancy into new dimensions of entertainment where mayhap discoveries of some importance to dramatic art are to be made. We are ruefully aware that our own once impressive status in the musical comedy world has dwindled to that of imitators. No sooner do we fall painfully into step than the stride we are trying to match lengthens, changes direction unexpectedly, and we are left once more in the dusty rear.

Many years ago it was the fate of Americans to labour under the same sense of hopeless inferiority. *The Belle of New York* in 1898 was their attempt to muscle in on English musical comedy. George Edwardes certainly learnt from the challenge to handle his Gaiety girls with greater liveliness, and *The Belle* undoubtedly put new pep into the spirit of the genre, but it had no notable successors and the English musical comedy went on its triumphant Edwardian way to reach its apogee in *The Merry Widow*. A flourishing tradition seemingly takes on a bias persistently in favour of those who have created it. That, anyway, is how outsiders have come to feel about the American musical.

This defeatism was comparatively slow to take root in London. *Show Boat* in the last twenties was a spectacle much enjoyed by fanciers of the stupendous, but as a piece of story-telling it was obviously inept. We assumed it would be remembered by a song, 'Old Man River', as the earlier *Rose Marie* was remembered by a dance, the Totem Pole. All through the thirties we grew familiar with fast-moving, lavishly mounted American shows and distinguished between them chiefly by the attractiveness of the music, which might be Jerome Kern's or Sigmund Romberg's or, if we were lucky, George Gershwin's or Cole Porter's. And since these composers often wrote for pieces that were not specifically American the Broadway importations had, on the whole, rather less to say to us than the indigenous musical romance exemplified by such successes as *Cavalcade, Bitter Sweet, Glamorous Nights* and *The Dancing Years*. We got into the habit of telling one another that musical comedy, Daly's and the Gaiety and George Edwardes and all that, was an exhausted form and had better be allowed to fade quietly away. It was *Oklahoma!* that broke it to us that musical comedy had been reborn in a shape that was basically American and, while impossible to resist, seemed to be constructed on principles we had never considered feasible.

All the features of this epoch-opening show conspired to take us slightly aback. Unlike all the musical comedies we had ever ourselves hatched, it told a story of reasonably adult interest and did not suffer the story to be intensified by irrelevant songs, dances, ballets and bursts of comic patter. On the contrary. The authors had aimed at making every song, dance, ballet and joke a means of advancing the story and of holding the mood which they had evoked in the very first words of the opening song—'O, what a beautiful morning . . . everything's going my way'. They achieved their aim with a degree of completeness never before attained in musical comedy and not in fact to be attained again in *Carousel, Guys and Dolls, South Pacific* or any other of its illustrious successors until *West Side Story* came along to refresh a tradition that was beginning after some seventeen years of intense activity to show signs of wear and tear.

Perhaps if you have written a musical as revolutionary in technique as *Oklahoma!* you feel when you come to write another that no sort of technical handicap will prove too onerous. That, at any rate, is how Rouben Mamoulian, Oscar Hammerstein II and Richard Rodgers seem to have approached *Carousel*. They found the new self-imposed difficulty in Molnar's *Liliom,* the fantasy of a disembodied spirit given by a celestial police court a day on earth to undo the harm he has done in his previous existence.

The action of *Carousel* 'shamelessly, consciously and even proudly' followed the rather tortuous symbolical action of *Liliom*. In spite of this staggering handicap the show went home to the publics on both sides of the Atlantic. One half of it was good fresh-air stuff, all nostalgia and period charm yet lively, audacious, taking; the other half rose or declined, according to individual taste, into an exceedingly well managed tear-jerker, with a rather fearsome brand of American sentimentality, as it seemed to some English critics, substituted for Hungarian naïvety. None of the Rodgers songs achieved quite the rushing exhilaration of 'O, what a beautiful morning,' but in 'June is busting out all over' he was as near to it as any composer can hope to get when he tries to say the same thing twice. The importance of the piece seems in retrospect to be that it boldly established the spirit of adventure and of fearlessness in experimentation that has always been the mark of the American musical.

Broadway has asked all sorts of difficult questions about the potentialities of the medium and some of the answers hammered out have been illuminating. Can a musical get by without a hero? Is a song and dance show conceivable without a gay, lovable rascal as its central figure? Rodgers and Lorenz wrote *Pal Joey* about an out-and-out heel. Joey is a terrible fellow with no brains, no morals and no manners. His only human quality is a ferocious ambition to see his name in lights as the kingpin of a night club. Something in him appeals for a short while to the simple heart of the heroine and piques the jaded taste of an adventurous middle-aged lady with a rich husband. The story shows the gigolo exhausting the patience of his protectress ('I have known a dance-band leader with a better mind,' she remarks savagely) and the heel grinding into dust the illusions of the heroine. Yet the show did get by, both in New York and in London, not simply on the strength of the faintly improper 'Bewitched, Bothered and Bewildered' but mainly through the vigour and expressiveness of the dancing.

The expensiveness of the Broadway musical makes it highly desirable that it should keep one alert eye on the London market. *Damn Yankees* asked itself the dangerous question whether it could punch home the excitement and glamour of baseball on audiences with a lifetime's loyalty to cricket. In the event, it turned out that much the most popular scenes in the piece were those dealing directly with the alien game. The team in all the glory of their strange clobber had been provided with some crashing good songs, and that celebrating the importance to players deficient in technical skill of the mysterious quality called 'heart' must be the loudest ever heard in the Coliseum and also one of the most exciting.

But if the musical during its brief career has ever been in danger of taking a wrong turning it is not in the English view through its rash willingness to ask itself daring technical questions at the risk of not finding satisfactory answers. Rather it is the tendency which it shares with the legitimate drama on Broadway to become journalistic. The American playgoer of the last quarter of a century is probably better informed than any other playgoer. His dramatists are inveterate realists and they spend a great deal of themselves in reporting and investigating along the whole range of what may be called newspaper topics. It is possible that, though adding in play after play to his intellectual stock, he remains rather short of the emotional experience that can come only from feeling the stresses of elemental problems treated on the great scale. However this may be, the journalistic style certainly sits somewhat oddly on an entertainment which cannot in the nature of things cope effectively with controversial matter demanding close and patient analysis. This style was most elaborately exercised in *The Pajama Game* where the Grievance Committee of the factory had the heroine at its head, her opposite number was the zealous Works Superintendent, and what interrupted the course of true love between them was a disputed wage increase of 7½ cents.

We might be forgiven for feeling that not only did the dungarees do little to propitiate the light playgoer's pleasure-loving eye, but that we were told at once too much and too little of the rights and wrongs of the dispute and that if this realistic tendency went much farther the musical would soon have bartered its

lyrical heritage for a mess of drab and unsatisfying realistic pottage. But to generalize about the American musical is still to
tread on an upturned rake which flies in your face with a cruel
smack. No sooner had we decided that the form was likely to die
of an excess of niggling realism than we were faced with *My Fair
Lady*, a musical comedy of the first water which we might have
made ourselves if we had come by the idea and had had the sin-
gle-minded organizing power to put the idea into effect.

The only serious word of complaint that can be made against
this extraordinarily happy adaptation of *Pygmalion* is that it does
not conspicuously lead anywhere. It could be called old-fash-
ioned English musical comedy done in the slap-up modern
American way. But to suppose, therefore, that the American
musical is losing its pioneering sense is to be at once contradicted
by the recent appearance of *West Side Story*. This is adventurous
enough to satisfy anybody, for it is the first attempt that the
musical has made on Shakespearian tragedy. Two things are
obviously crucial in the experiment. Every note of music must
say something germane to the action, and this responsibility
Leonard Bernstein discharges with a cleverness which makes a
distinct advance on the notable music that George Gershwin
wrote for *Porgy and Bess*. His success in providing an aria for
Juliet and a love duet for the lovers may not quite meet the needs
of the whistling errand boy, but his efforts to enforce a unity of
sounds on the action and to merge the preparation for the high
dramatic moments with the high moments themselves are a
sinuous succession of small triumphs.

The other vital necessity for the transference of *Romeo and
Juliet* to the musical stage is poetry. This could be found in
words, in melody or in motion. It is natural that Jerome Robbins,
the director, himself trained in the rigour of classical ballet and
in the freedom of American dance styles, should opt for movement. Besides, the choice merely continues a tendency which
has been growing in the American musical for nearly a gen-

eration, for the dancer to take over and run the show. It comes from the instinctive wish that everything should become more fluid, more mobile, faster. Nobody will deny that, in this instance anyway, the choice was the right one. How else could the young street thugs of the rival teen-age gangs of Puerto Ricans and home-bred Americans have been made plausibly to produce even a measure of tragic poetry? Clearly the only way to touch these morons with poetry was by group treatment; and it is remarkable how effectively the transmuting art of the dance draws out the tragic pathos of their social condition and brings them within reach of our sympathy. All the dancing has vibrancy and emotive power, and the total effect of the piece is strongly to confirm our faith in the Broadway musical as an art form in process of evolution. One feels it will never for long be parted from its great maternal images, especially while Miss Ethel Merman, the greatest of them all, who has recently triumphed again as Mama in *Gypsy,* a fine musical made out of the memoirs of Miss Gipsy Rose Lee, has such abundant life and strength. *Candide* was no less ambitious, but less carefully planned.

The American musical is obviously determined to eat up one by one all the world's literary classics. It will some day probably try desperately to resolve into snappy lyrics the highly Latinized, rhythmically complex periods of Sir Thomas Browne's *Urn Burial* and itself perish of a catastrophic indigestion. It would be a noble death. There is no sign meanwhile that its enviable confidence in itself is misplaced.

STUDY QUESTIONS

1. What does the author say are the most important qualities which distinguish the American musical from the English?
2. He says that *Oklahoma!* (1943) first revealed to the English "that

musical comedy had been reborn in a shape that was basically American." What does he mean? What are the principles on which he says *Oklahoma!* was constructed?

3. What does the author feel were the weaknesses of *Carousel* (1945)? Why does he think it was successful despite these weaknesses? Why does he feel it was important?

4. What sorts of questions has Broadway asked "about the potentialities of the medium"? What sorts of answers has it received?

5. Does the author see any danger in the tendency of the musical to become journalistic? Why does he qualify his criticism of this tendency toward realism?

6. He likes *My Fair Lady* (1956). What complaint, then, does he have with it?

7. In what ways does he think *West Side Story* (1958) reveals the "pioneering sense" of American musicals? What are some of its artistic qualities?

8. The author obviously thinks well of American musicals; yet he has a certain ironical tone about them. How does he qualify his praise? What signs of artistic immaturity has he taken into account in making his overall judgment?

9. The author has been discussing Broadway musicals. Do you think he would view the majority of Hollywood film musicals as favorably? Why or why not?

REUEL DENNEY

This essay by Reuel Denney shows another aspect of his criticism of the popular arts (for further information on Denney, see the headnote to his essay "Reactors of the Imagination," p. 112). As a poet, Denney understands that the artist chooses the forms and conventions which best suit artistic purposes; as a social scientist, he understands that artistic forms and conventions also reflect and express the values and beliefs of the audience. In the following essay from his book *The Astonished Muse* (1957), Denney explores the ways in which Al Capp and Walt Kelly have each chosen cartoon conventions peculiarly expressive of their own attitudes and artistic purposes. He also shows what the wide popular acceptance of these conventions reveals about the difference between the popular audience of the 1930's and the popular audience of today.

from
Children of Thoth

The sense of leisure and frivolity that we miss in the humanistic studies is absent also, but in a peculiar way, from adult criticism of comic strips and comic books that, as pointed out at the beginning of this chapter, are read by 90 per cent of American children eight to thirteen years old. An amazing host of men and women twenty to fifty years older than these children habitually regard the comics as a direct, immediate, and profound influence on the behavior of the readers. Thus the seriousness with which the comics are inspected approaches a moral imperative, but, at the same time, the inspectors seem to desire an eventual abundance of "good" comics, that is, light, pleasant, gentle, negligible ones. While searching out evil and waiting for deliverance, these critics fail to see that the comics already in existence are often produced as purposeful leisure and received in kind by adult readers raptly engaged in their popular culture. Moreover, the purposeful leisure of the comics is rooted deeply in literature— the printed literature we have been talking about.

There are a number of good reasons for looking more closely at the "social realism" of the comic strips, comic books, and popular children's books. One reason is that while the content of the strips has been much studied, less attention has been paid to the artistic conventions of various kinds employed by their creators. Thus, while many observers prefer to think of the comic strips and books as being generally fantastic, they fail to observe how much the comics have accepted in recent years the conventions and traditions once associated with the literary and artistic movement known as naturalism.

True, the naturalistic movement and its high period are not easy to define. To use an almost overworked bench mark, let us simply say that some of the tendencies present in the work of Zola have re-emerged in the popular arts. Some people define naturalism in literature as a tendency toward the steno-graphic and documentary, in painting as rivalry with the photograph, and in both literature and graphic art as a willingness to take for granted a materialistic social psychology that expresses itself in terms of a theory of "interests." In this chapter we shall be especially interested in the naturalistic and realistic tendencies that result from the attempt to use pictures in place of words.

In surveying this convention, it is noticeable that naturalistic influences in certain of the popular media and in children's books are the result of a socially downward distribution of fashions. In this sense, much of modern popular culture contains the diffused, reorganized, and to some extent simplified viewpoints of a now aged artistic movement. (It would be unfair, of course, to say that this is all there is to popular culture.) The shift toward social realism in children's books was also, in part, a result of a cheapening of the ideas of John Dewey and in part the result of the Popular Front of the 1930's. Moreover, the shift toward representationalism in the comic strip was largely a result of the motion picture's impact upon artists and their audiences. The 1920's, the period in which the film made its initial impact, happened to be the period during which the older, cruder cartoonist began to lose ground and the new, trained cartoonist began to come into favor. Soon after the early 1920's, we know, the film further increased the social realism of the comic strip by encouraging it to adopt such movie techniques as serialization, continued episodic action, and rapid cutting from scene to scene. Today's comic-viewing eye is an eye trained in part by movie naturalism.

There was no single revolution of comic-strip realism in the years 1900 to 1950 in the United States. There were, on the other hand, a number of changes that can be viewed from one unifying artistic perspective. Some of the major developments are as follows:

1. Skilled draftsmanship was emphasized in the comics following the appearance of the illustrator and advertising artist. Their conquest of the field, which began in the 1920's and was consolidated in the 1930's, put a premium on representational draftsmanship. Some of the cartoonists who started earlier, as, for example, Bud Fisher, the creator of "Mutt and Jeff," might not have been accepted after competence in draftsmanship was firmly established as a prime requisite in cartooning.

2. The continued-story method of narration became the commonest method.

3. Adolescence and babyhood were represented in the comics where previously almost all the children portrayed were drawn from the six-to-ten-year-old group. The shift to adolescent themes was roughly co-ordinate with the great increase in

the number of high-school students in the United States and the resultant rise in normal age at which young people enter the labor market.

4. Current history, as reported on the news pages, was introduced to comic-strip plots. This change was engineered by Milton Caniff, who began "Terry and the Pirates" in 1934, some years after the beginning of illustrative realism. "Terry and the Pirates" did not begin as a China War strip, but it soon became one.

5. Some strips began to provide familial and biographical continuity, as in "Gasoline Alley," with its characters who grew older year by year.

6. Illustrative standards merged with cinematic standards of drawing and narration.

7. Intensive regional and cultural realism appeared, as, for example in the "Li'l Abner" of 1935.

8. The rising status of the women portrayed in the comics brought increased individualization and increased ambivalence of portraiture.

9. Changes in the specifications of social class and class mobility were reflected in the comics.

It appears that draftsmanlike realism in the American comic strip was the result in part of a rationalization of the industry. In the late 1920's one of the syndicates became interested in exploiting the popularity of the Tarzan books in the comic strip. An advertising agent named Harold Foster was engaged to draw the continuity. The very conditions of the public acceptance of "Tarzan" made it necessary to have the strip drawn by someone who could handle the jungle and animal scenery with some cinematic accuracy of representation. Foster and his successor Rex Maxon turned out a strip that soon became the envy of the syndicate world and encouraged other illustrators and advertising artists to consider the possibilities of combining their draftsmanship with someone else's talent for fiction. The success of the "Tarzan" strip appears to have broken a previous myth of the profession—that the successful cartoonist had to be a popular cultural "genius" of some kind.

"Tarzan," with its glamorously realistic portrait of jungle adventure, came out early in 1929. The first more or less realistically drawn feminine heroine appeared in another strip in the fall of that year. This was also the result of a team collaboration (continuity by J. P. McEvoy and drawing by Striebl) in a strip known then as "Show-Girl," based in part on musical-comedy sources, and known now as "Dixie Dugan." In this strip there was far less passion for documentation of special locale than in "Tarzan" or in the later "Terry and the Pirates," but the important thing is that portrayal was dominated by the realism of illustration and advertising. Dixie Dugan, appropriately enough, was one of the first career girls in the American comic strip.

In succeeding years there were numerous attempts to compete with the illustrative realism of these strips. In 1932, "Wash Tubbs and Captain Easy" appeared in a strip in which Buz Sawyer went beyond the "Tarzan" cinematic perspective and actually manipulated the drawing's viewpoint so that it resembled the viewpoint of the camera eye. Such tendencies had been forecast in the "Minute Movies of Ed Whelan" in the late 1920's, but their possibilities had never been fully realized. "Wash Tubbs," like its "Tarzan" predecessor and some of the following draftsmanlike strips, was a continued story with cliffhanger panels, and thus it broke with deep comic traditions on still another score. The attempts to manipulate the same formula have been legion since the 1930's.

In retrospect, the illustrator and the advertising artist affected the comics by introducing three-dimensional shading into an art which previously had been one of conventionalized line and contour. In turn, these commercial artists had been influenced, at a great distance, by illustrators like Winslow Homer and Frederic Remington, who livened the pages of American magazines in the days before photo-mechanical processes. Some of the skills and the manners of the illustrators were developed under the influence of French poster art, and all the illustrators were influenced by the photograph and later by the movie. In part, their realism was a return to the tradition of Charles Dana Gibson, whose drawings purported to be a social history of the American upper-middle class at the turn of the century.

The appearance of such realism in the comics is probably less interesting than its effects. We can say with some assurance that the growth in the draftsman's competence immediately introduced some correlate changes in content. Thus, in the case of "Tarzan," the draftsmanlike competence made possible a near realistic presentation of the jungle and veldt, and this travelogue exoticism was repeated in "Terry and the Pirates" and the later, and much cruder, "Smilin' Jack." This demanded hours and hours of research on the part of the producers in the *realia* and props of the scene to be portrayed. Thus the comic became research-minded as a consequence of its adventure into illustrative realism. This research-mindedness in both "Tarzan" and "Terry and the Pirates," despite its application to science fiction or picaresque fantasy, had its consequences for the psychological and social portraiture of the Americans in the strips. Thrown into semirealistic contrast with primitives or orientals, Americans fictionalized in the strips began to develop certain more specific traits of the American. They acquired regional accents, definite social psychologies, and so on.

At the same time, standards of drawing derived from advertising art meant that the artists depended more than before on the folklore of advertising for their characters. "Dixie Dugan" derives from an illustrator's idea of a standard young American chorus girl of the late 1920's. The comics began to pick up some of the social realism of the advertisements and to betray some of the same concerns as the advertisements. Since the advertisement is almost always a message about social mobility, the treatment of social mobility in the comics began to develop at a similar pace. In place of the old comics that had established a fabulously naïve class position for the characters and then held them to it ("Polly and Her Pals," "Abie the Agent," "Jiggs"), the new comic began to treat mobility dynamically. In modern strips, the best examples are perhaps "The Baers" and "Mary Worth." In these strips the problem of social mobility is handled openly and dynamically and in terms of recognized social variables such as income, ethnicity, and sexual role. Compare this with the primitive handling of the social climber theme in George McManus' "Jiggs."

Doubtless the acceptance of social realism in the new comic strip was hastened by the fact that the 1930's deepened anxiety about the basis of society in the United States. Each class felt itself threatened, and each member of each class felt the whole class structure threatened. The comics began to represent in a much more complete way the different phases in the standard social cycle of the model American, and to some extent the documentary ethos of the strip became for its readers, especially children, a guaranty of its validity as social reporting. Thus, while one effect of the shift was to disclose in a more detailed way the class structure of American society, still another effect was to throw naturalistic draftsmanship into the support of *any* picture of social mobility. Belief in the comic strip as a fictional reporter of the society's demands on the individual became more widespread. The comics stopped being a fantastic escape valve for hurried readers; they became a textbook for oppressed social climbers. They became, in the final analysis, a rhetoric of approved social beliefs. And of course they stopped being comic.

SOUTHERN STYLE

One way to dramatize the contrast between the naturalistic tendency and the fantastic tendency in our comics is to compare two strips possessing some similarity in content and theme but varying widely in the artistic formula employed. Let us take two strips that deal, in different artistic conventions, with rural life in the South. One is Al Capp's "Li'l Abner," a product of early New Deal days, in which a certain amount of naturalism is employed as the basis for caricature, social satire, parody, burlesque. The other is Walt Kelly's "Pogo," a strip in which the highly developed fantasy of an animal community is employed as the basis for social satire expressed largely in terms of the fable or parable. "Li'l Abner" is punitive satire on class relations in the United States; "Pogo" is gentle satire on the social politics of the United States. Both make ultimate reference to the social fact of a community of poor folk in the South. Let us compare their symbolic content and examine the ways in which the similarities in content and differences in artistic convention influence the expectations of the audience and enable this audience to ascribe a determinate meaning to the content.

Who is Pogo, what produces him, who are his readers, and what does he mean to them? The strip is a nationally syndicated comic that dramatizes the lives of a group of talking animals who have deeply distinctive characteristics and concerns. Perhaps the most important characteristic that they share is that they are all a rural group. If it should be objected that most animals in stories are rural because the country is where most animals live, the objections can be met easily. Animals in earlier strips were characterized as urban regardless of their locale. For example, the cat, the mouse, and the bulldog in "Krazy Kat," although they were projected against a southwestern desert locale, were metropolitan characters. The bulldog was a city cop who leaned against city lampposts, and the desert of the locale was surrealistically equipped with fire hydrants. It is important that the characters of "Pogo" are fully rural folk.

The characters of "Pogo" are the inhabitants of the Okefenokee land. They are southern, perhaps because the image of the rural southerner has become the standard American image for the rural man in America in the twentieth century. It is important that these animals live in swampy land and that one of the major characters, Albert the alligator, is a reptile, because this creates a generalized image of a primal world scene—the world of the watery margins from which life came. The swamp locale also serves the purpose of creating a scene of roadless hinterland, backwater seclusion. There is a direct reference from these animals to human beings who are uncitified folk, whose vices and virtues are an aspect of their isolation from the urbanism and urbanity of those who like most to read about them. The rural sociology of "Pogo" is rhythmically dramatized by the appearance and reappearance of a slicker with a different set of values, particularly Mr. Bridgeport, the confidence man and promoter bear.

The economics of Pogoland does not entirely correspond to stereotypes of rural poverty. In "Li'l Abner," for example, we are asked to believe in the existence of a community whose standard of living is so dangerously low that the failure of a turnip crop or the loss of a ham may mean starvation. "Li'l Abner" as a report on rural life was much influenced by the rural disasters of the 1930's. One of its powerful early themes of satire was the relationship between the migrant picker and his labor bosses. By contrast, in Pogoland we see that a little work sustains a standard of living which is generally adequate for all. The appropriateness of this arises, of course, from the character of the animals themselves. They are all able little beasts who evidently spend part of their time collecting stores of food, and they can do it at all times of the year, since they never have to contend with winter. Of course, the struggle for survival in Pogoland is not quite so simple as such a description makes it out to be. The fact is that while Pogo and some of his friends are herbivorous creatures by zoölogical definition, some of the others, including the bear, the tiger, and the alligator, are carnivorous. We shall want to look more closely later at the way in which the economic motivations of these meat-eaters are handled in the story line.

Nevertheless, it is important that these animals are described as living a life in which they possess a certain surplus of goods and leisure time. Otherwise, they would not be able to devote themselves so fully to the activities they engage in: celebrating holidays, having poetry contests, looking for lost children, playing baseball, getting involved in civic controversies over the loyalty of postmen, and running elections for President. Few of the realities that they face are the Aesopian difficulties of getting a living—jumping for grapes, dividing cheese, trapping chickens. The question of economic distribution, it is true, is not absent from their moral struggles with the goldbricking cowbirds, who have a zest for using other people's property, along with an aggressive share-the-wealth philosophy. The cowbirds, however, are no great threat to the economic system of Pogoland, even though they do make away with canned goods now and then. Pogo and his compeers live in a land of decent surplus, which frees their energies for the greater goals of furious involvement with each other in the task of finding the right answers to questions of politics, art, science, medicine, and recreation. The threat of leisure is ever present. One of the sequences, "Slightly Holidazed," begins with Bun Rabbit's assertion that he is going to say to the President: "Put down that piano! An' fix our holiday situation. Every time a man wants to work he got a vacation staring him in the face." One feels that this is not the enforced idleness of a rural community lacking capital and enterprise, like Dogpatch, but the enforced idleness of an economic system that works pretty well.

It is this assumption, we see, that makes it possible for the artist of "Pogo" to achieve his second major reversal of meanings. His first major reversal, the traditional one, is to ask us to believe that animals can act like men; his second one, the one that creates the true Pogo world, is to ask us to believe that these rural animals in these circumstances can act like the people of a small town, a suburb, or a city neighborhood. Given the simplicity of the basic scene, there are few subtleties in social behavior in our urban society that the artist does not exploit. In the book-bound versions of some of the adventures of Pogo the issues range from loyalty checks to political slander, from aesthetic standards to rent-control picketing. In general, the people of Pogoland face these issues with a good deal of naïveté, and it often appears they are going to be exploited by Bridgeport the bear, or Tammany the tiger, or Deacon Mushrat, or by the cowbirds. In the end the "simple people" prevail, and the manipulators and exploiters are discomfited.

Enough has been said here to suggest that the basic political theme of the strips is that the people shall judge and that the people are competent to judge. The threats to liberty and happiness in Pogoland are recognizable in terms of a general American politico-economic mythology. Bridgeport the bear, the Barnumesque figure, is a modern rendition of the confidence man who appeared in America before Herman Melville and Mark Twain wrote books about him. Wearing the garb and using the language of a nineteenth-century swindler, Bridgeport the bear depends heavily on the profile of the late W. C. Fields but displays some knowledge of modern forms of public relations dishonesty. Deacon Mushrat is, of course, the blue-nosed Puritan who was re-introduced to the American public as a symbolic figure when he was employed to symbolize Prohibition in the Rollin Kirby cartoons of the 1920's and 1930's. He is the Paul Pry, the investigator, the self-righteous slander-monger; his pharisaical character is symbolized by the fact that his speech-balloons render themselves in the type face of the old Bible. The cowbirds are Stalinoid birds who make a mock of Marxism by treating larceny as if it were an exemplification of the dictum: "From each according to his capacity, to each according to his needs." It is against such menaces to their political decency that the people of Pogoland are forced to struggle at least half of their waking time.

This suggests strongly that the political ethos which informs the "Pogo" strip is the optimistic ethos of, say, a Lincoln Steffens. We are invited to consider the probability that people are confused by democratic politics and vulnerable to a variety of ills: corruption, authoritarianism, influence-mongering, patronage, and boodling. Forced to organize against these ills, people find it difficult to do so. There is a tendency for every group of men in a democracy to form a splinter party of its own. Crusaders against the same evil, but operating on different principles, trample each other down in the confusion while the pols steal the cupboard bare. Nevertheless, after a crisis of cross-purposes, the steadfast honesty of the people has more staying power than the forces of evil. There is much in "Pogo" to suggest that the ultimate collaboration of these various beasts is imagined somewhat in terms of the collaboration of disparate forces in the American Democratic party. This chaos of strange bedfellows represents in some mythical way the vagaries and subtleties and inner contradictions of the Democratic "caucus" during the later New Deal years.

However, to emphasize the topical political meanings of "Pogo" is to ignore other ranges of meaning that can be found in the strip. One way to evoke those meanings is to remind ourselves that if the political stance of the strip is Democratic and Steffens-like, the literary stance is post-Joycean, and the psychological stance is post-Freudian.

It is no accident that Joyce, in his anthropological and linguistic search for the sources of myth, found Mutt and Jeff quite as interesting as Romulus and Remus or Isis and Osiris. In his later work, he writes as if he believed that the fantasy of the comic strip is another form of the fantasy of the folk tale or the myth. Joyce himself was well steeped in American popular culture and kept written records of the development of American slang, not only in its oral appearances, but also in its recognitions by the media. It is only natural that some sophisticated American cartoonist should exploit in turn some of the artistic devices employed by Joyce to represent the world of myth. The major verbal device in "Pogo" is polyglottism.

The artificial-dialect American speech invented by the artist for general use in "Pogo" is a comic version of rural southern syntax, vocabulary, and pronunciation. ("They sure built that capital awful far up the creek. . . . Figger them folks up there gits outen touch with us ol' mortal critters here at the headwaters?") True, there is no attempt at phonetic accuracy, particularly, for example, in the handling of the vowel values. One guesses that the artist felt that this would be overdoing regionalism. It would certainly make it more difficult for his characters to depart from their basic speech, as they often do, to engage in the creation of new words, to speak in verse, to speak in foreign languages, and to speak in a variety of crypto-languages that can only be called Pogo-Latin, or Okefenokese. The artist's general aim is to introduce every type of semantic and phonetic confusion, but perhaps especially punning and malapropism, into the speech of his characters and to employ the blockages of communication that result from all these private languages as evidences of their neurotically unstable relations with each other. Artistically, the confusion and ambiguity of the language of the animals is offered to the reader somewhat in the same terms that polyglottism is offered to the reader by Joyce: as the representation of a stream of individual and group consciousness—a consciousness the confused fantasy of which cannot be adequately represented by conventionally ordered speech in one language but only by dipping into the muttered dream language.

It is true, to be sure, that the emphasis on problems of verbal communication in "Pogo" bespeaks a semantic slant in the way in which the artist interprets the ills of mankind. One gets the idea that the artist has been influenced by a variety of studies of communication leading up to the claim that a purification of the world of words would lead to an improvement in the world of things. As Albert says to Pogo during the poetry contest: "I made it up. I made it rhyme. Now I gotta make it mean somethin'?" While Albert is almost self-consciously taking a Dadaist artistic position during this interchange, it is also true that his antisemantic tendencies are constantly with him. In the strip, he stands as one of the greatest of sophists, over the straight-faced Socrates of Pogo. This is not to say that the artist is a faddist for semantics. It is to suggest that in a general framework of animal fable the reduction of communication by way of the zoölogical probabilities such as gesture, cries, scent, and so on, along with the corresponding shift of communication to human language, does much to suggest the predicament of American media-minded culture, in which words are expected to do more and more.

To speak of the influence of Joyce on "Pogo" is perhaps to go too far along what some might consider Jungean lines, placing too much emphasis on the problems of some collective unconscious in Pogoland. That, however, is merely the result of looking at "Pogo" in terms of the employment of certain linguistic devices supplied by the artist. If we turn for a moment from dictional texture to plot, character, and motivation, we see post-Freudian psychology at work in a way that invites us to regard human existence as a series of problems posed to individuals in the psychopathology of everyday life. The prime exemplar of this formula is probably Albert the alligator. Consider what he is and what he does. Zoölogically, Albert is a meat-eating predator, situated among a group of animals who, in real swamp life, would be considered his potential prey. It is true that civilization and its discontents bear more heavily on Albert than they do on many of the others because, while Pogo and the Rabbit and many others have only to forswear fighting with and stealing from their neighbors, Albert has to forswear eating them. His suppressed cannibalism, the cap-sheaf of all the cannibalistic themes that run through "Pogo," is one of the reasons that he often seems maladjusted in the society of Pogoland. True, he has the substitute gratification of a cigar, which he chews as vigorously in place of flesh as a smoker chews gum when he is trying to give up cigarettes. However, the suppressed tendency to want to eat everyone emerges in Albert's daily life as a proneness toward the accident of swallowing people. The small creatures of "Pogo" have to be careful what trees they fall out of because, by some mischance as powerful as the fate motif in the novels of Hardy, Albert usually by happenstance is underneath them with his mouth open. Albert, of course, remains quite unconscious of the older tendencies; and when he has actually swallowed something or someone, he resents the event as an invasion of his privacy. This sort of parataxis, or fantastical reversal of his basic unconscious relationship to his friends, even convinces some of his friends and swallowees.

The emphasis on problems of oral aggression, as Freud would call them in his references to zone development and fixation, seems appropriate enough to a society of animals who live largely by their teeth. On first glance, this might suggest that the symbolic world of Pogoland is rather a limited one or that oral aggression is made to substitute for all types of strongly motivated human desire for gratification of physical impulse. However, unless this be too eager a reading of some of the episodes, it seems pretty clear that the artist talks the language of Freudian theories of sexuality in some of the episodes that link Churchy Le Femme the turtle with Mam'selle Hepzibah, the skunk Chloe of the swampland. The turtle is a classic figure of anxiety in myth and fable, and the reader is invited to examine what the artist has made of this possibility in some of his sequences.

This brief inventory of some of the themes suspended and revolved in "Pogo"—themes that the followers of the comic strip have certainly recognized from the beginning—is meant to suggest that the thematic development of "Pogo" is made possible, essentially, by the fabular formula employed by the artist. It is impossible to imagine "Li'l Abner," for example, developing the same low-pressure mode of narration on the same subtleties of social life. The very drawing of "Li'l Abner," in spite of its qualities of caricature, has the naturalistic heaviness of a Sherwood Anderson or a Dreiser, and under its guffaws there is a nervous pressure of social seriousness and solemnity. The characters of "Li'l Abner" live in a world of clear-cut class and power structure, in which the energetic neurotics run everybody else by dint of brass, guile, crime, and paranoia. The strip has never lost its hurt, serious tone of concern with inequality of social opportunity, no matter how much the poor and the sick are made to triumph in the end. Compare the dourness with which Capp pursues and makes fun of radio and the media and the lightness with which Kelly seeks out the same satirical prey.

It seems clear, from the interest taken in a *Life* article through which Capp explained to his readers why he married Li'l Abner to Daisy Mae, that his strip enjoys a massive popularity. Since he specializes in irritable criticisms of both the uppermost and the lowest levels of society, one gets a feeling of class defensiveness in his work, as if he were speaking for a middle class jammed between extremes of delinquency below and irresponsibility above. His punitive satire expresses itself in camp-style boffos about sanitation, food habits, the battle between the sexes, and the constant clashing of class etiquettes. All this suggests that it appeals to those elements in us that are in uneasy flight from lower-middle-class cultural definitions, from ruralism, from any and all connections with the other side of the tracks. Although the actual scene is a hillbilly village, there is reason to guess that one of the actual social scenes he has in mind is the lower-middle-class suburb.

By contrast, "Pogo" is certainly the darling of the intellectuals, their La Fontaine of the comic strip. His readers appear to be the kind of people who take a positive enjoyment in being able to read and interpret an "animal" comic strip that even their own sophisticated children cannot always understand. The mock-pastoral genre of "Pogo" certainly represents, for its readers, a tacit claim that the culturally primitive and the psychologically basic patterns of human affairs are not only very fascinating but also within the scope of reader control. Thus, the strip appears to employ whimsy as a means of releasing the recognition of, and then exercising the power of, the irrational. One might add that while in "Li'l Abner" the individual is threatened generally by social disorganization of some sort (turnip famine, idiotic intervention by urban or bureaucratic forces), in "Pogo" the individual tends to be threatened by the runaway character of his own group's impulses toward organization. The class locus, the content of challenge, and the artistic convention employed in each of the strips appear to interrelate.

There is a residue of cuteness and sententiousness in Kelly's manner, part of it the result of the same topical forces that reduce the universality of the other animal fables and tales such as *The Parlement of Foules, Wind in the Willows, Animal Farm,* and so on. Part of it is just cuteness—an undigested habit closely related, probably, to Kelly's training with Disney. This is sometimes accompanied by a kind of egghead self-consciousness. At the end of a sequence, when one of his small friends asks Pogo if he has been elected President, Pogo says: "Well, I dunno . . . I'll go 'long and vote for EVERYBODY in sight . . . that way we'll get a good one . . . y' know, chile, CRITTERS is nice, but human beans still makes the BEST people." One might be tempted to take this continuity of thought as limp satire on liberal-labor optimism and softheadedness, if one were not sure, on the basis of context, that there is a serious ideological pressure behind the statement and restatement of this hopeful commonplace. Kelly's book publishers, in recent years, have gone far in dressing him up commercially as a "folk-singer" type, a Kin Hubbard of the media-conscious, college-educated set.

Such reservations aside, it remains clear that Kelly's portrait of the social and political gamesmanship of the middle class, as filtered through his swamp scene, is made possible by outright revolt against the habits of illustrator realism in the comic strip. It is the artistic convention—Kelly's symbolism versus the naturalism of, say, "Li'l Abner" that makes the crucial difference. "Pogo" appeals to an audience whose revolt against the sociologese of many of the illustrator strips is in part a matter of class stance.

For more than fifty years now, naturalistic devices have been passed down the social scale to the lower-status sectors of society, while the self-identified elites have turned away from it. Comic-strip changes in style in the period 1920-50 recapitulate, in part, the previous history of literary and artistic style-wars. "Pogo" is a stylistic reaction against the "Li'l Abner" vein in much the same way that Flaubert's whimsical *Bouvard and Pécuchet* provided a counterstatement to his earlier naturalism and in much the same way that the "child's eye" in twentieth-century painting supplanted the "camera eye" of the late nineteenth century. As crucial as the shift in content is the shift in genre.

STUDY QUESTIONS

1. When L'il Abner finally married Daisy Mae, Al Capp wrote the article "It's Hideously True" (*Life,* XXXII [March 31, 1952]). He explained that he had been forced to marry Li'l Abner off because Americans were now so insecure that an unmarried man no longer amused them; furthermore, their insecurity seriously affected their ability to laugh at their own political foibles. Would Reuel Denney's

analysis of "Pogo" tend to support Al Capp's analysis, or does it suggest other explanations for Capp's recent decline in popularity? Does Denney's analysis necessarily negate Capp's analysis?

2. Are the rural characters satirized by Capp the same as those satirized by Walt Kelly? Which seem more relevant to our contemporary world? Why?

3. Denney believes that a cartoonist's drawing conventions reflect the popular culture to which he communicates. To what popular beliefs would Charles Schulz's conventions in "Peanuts" appeal? Can you think of any literary figures who seem temperamentally akin to Schulz? (For example, J. D. Salinger?) How well are Schulz's conventions suited to his subject? To what extent do they actually furnish a comment on the dialogue of his characters?

4. The cartoon conventions of "Terry and the Pirates" and "Steve Canyon" are very different from those of "Pogo" and "Peanuts." Where do Milton Caniff's conventions come from? How well suited to his subject matter are they? How is the reader expected to react to these conventions? Why? Which kind of convention seems to you more perceptive and expressive? Why? Which cartoonist would you say has the greater respect for his audience, Caniff or Kelly?

5. Many cartoonists besides Milton Caniff use drawing conventions which are derived from other popular arts. From what does a strip like "Mary Worth" derive its conventions? What about the strip "Ben Casey"? How do these differences in drawing conventions affect the way the reader looks at the strip and what he expects when he reads it? Do the sources from which the conventions are borrowed tell you anything about what the cartoonist assumes about his audience (age, education, tastes, values)?

6. Chester Gould's characters in "Dick Tracy" are obviously cartoon in conception. Yet many readers take the characters seriously. (For example, when Gravel Gertie gave birth to Sparkle Plenty, Gould received thousands of baby gifts.) How much has Gould's subject matter to do with this kind of public reaction? Why is Gould able to combine his unrealistic drawing conventions with "crime-busting" tales? Does Gould's success help you to understand the nature

of crime fiction and the way in which the audience takes this kind of fiction?

7. Of the cartoonists mentioned in Denney's essay and in these questions, which one seems to you to use his medium with the greatest originality and honesty?

GILBERT HIGHET

"History on the Silver Screen" reveals another aspect of Highet's criticism of popular arts. He leads the reader, through a common-sense approach, from an understanding of the weak uses of history common to most Hollywood productions to a clearer understanding of the nature of meaningful conflict in drama. For Highet, common sense and aesthetics are frequently indistinguishable. (For biographical information on Highet, see the headnote to "Kitsch," p. 185.)

History on the Silver Screen

Suppose we go to the movies.

We might see a new epic about the War of Independence, starring Audrey Hepburn as Martha Washington, Charlton Heston as George Washington, and William Holden as all the other Founding Fathers. (He is a very versatile actor, William Holden.) Among the most stirring scenes are the battles. There is a splendid re-enactment of the Battle of Trenton. On one side, the Hessians, with their red coats and their long muskets and bayonets, on the other side, the small forces of General Washington, in motley uniforms and ill armed; but they have the advantage of surprise, and they are fighting for their own country: they charge gallantly. The Hessians, with the power of long-established discipline, resist; for a moment the issue hangs undecided. Then Charlton Heston jumps forward carrying a heavy machine gun: *trrr, trrrrrrr,* he mows down the Hessians, the first rank, the second, and the third; the American forces move onward in triumph, shouting 'Victory!'; Washington waves his machine gun, and the camera pans from it to the Stars and Stripes.

Or else we might see an epic about the Civil War. The hero is the Southern general, George Edward Pickett (played by William Holden). The big scene is the Battle of Gettysburg. The forces of North and South struggle, locked in deadly conflict, swaying this way and that. The ground is dark with blood, the sky, with the smoke of guns. Pickett's division is held in reserve, until at last, on the fateful July 3rd, the attack on Cemetery Hill is launched, with Pickett and his men in the forefront. Up the deadly slope they charge, with rebel yells almost drowned by the thunder of Federal cannon. Just at the summit, as the lines are about to meet, up spring the defending Federal troops. They are led by a Sioux Indian in full war paint, who is followed by eight hundred whooping Indian tribesmen brandishing stone tomahawks. This decides the battle.

Exciting, isn't it? No? Incredible? Almost disgusting? Yes, it is. But neither of these fantastic scenes is any more incredible, any more disgusting to a man with a sense of history than the distortions of historical fact which are repeatedly perpetrated by the makers of motion pictures. The Civil War is usually quite well represented—because we have photographs of it and reminiscences of it; the very weapons and uniforms used by the combatants still exist; and somehow we understand their manners, their attitude toward life. By the time we go as far back as the War of Independence, a certain vagueness sets in—about manners if not about material objects (I still have in my mind's eye a delicious scene in which Meriwether Lewis, played by Fred MacMurray, said to President Jefferson with a genial grin, like a basketball coach talking to a difficult school principal, 'Oh, congratulations on the Louisiana Purchase!'); and any period beyond that seems to be dim and fabulous. By the time we reach the Greeks and the Romans everything is lost in a world of fantasy.

I must say that I am fascinated, in a horrible way, by motion pictures about ancient Greece and Rome. However silly they may be, they are usually photographed quite beautifully; the costumes are very becoming, particularly to the women; there is a certain thrill in seeing all the famous buildings, like the Acropolis at Athens, looking brand-new and so clean and then the mistakes and the distortions are uproariously funny. They are just as funny as George Washington waving a machine gun, or Meade's troops headed by a detachment of Sioux Indians. And sometimes they are far funnier. The unconscious humor of the movies is one of their strongest assets.

In movies about ancient Greece and Rome, the static parts often look quite real and convincing—no doubt because they have been modeled on pictures and statues. It is the active parts which are usually so funny. Almost every motion picture about ancient Rome I have ever seen showed somebody driving through the streets of the city in a chariot, while the citizens cringed away from his mad career. This is as absurd as showing a cowboy on horseback galloping along the sidewalk of Fifth Avenue, New York. Chariots and such things were absolutely prohibited in the streets of Rome; they were kept for war, or else for hot-pole driving on the highways outside the cities. Everybody walked. The average Roman never rode in a chariot from the day of his birth to the day of his death.

The Greek and Roman armies are usually wrong too. Most Hollywood producers know very little about military tactics, and still less about the more difficult science of strategy. Even in modern movies, they constantly make both the Good Ones and the Bad Ones commit elementary blunders in the art of war.

In *The Robe* we see a group of Roman legionaries rushing into a town and shooting at everyone visible with bows and arrows. In other pictures about Rome we see the legionaries throwing spears with great care and accuracy, as though those were their essential weapons. The reason for these mistakes is quite obvious. The people in Hollywood think that everyone fights by shooting; if not *bang bang*, then *fft fft;* if not smoking guns, then whizzing arrows and hissing spears. But this is nonsense. The Romans conquered the world with swords—short, strong, efficient swords which were used both for cutting and for thrusting. Spears were thrown at the opening of a battle, much as grenades are thrown now, without very careful aim, merely as a device to disrupt the enemy's line; what mattered was the body-to-body conflict. As for bows and arrows, these were left to Arabs and the like, who stayed out in the wings together with slingers. It is as ridiculous to show the Roman soldiers using bows and arrows as it would be to show the U.S. Marines using blowpipes and poisoned darts. The Romans, like the Marines, were realists; they knew that if you want to kill an enemy and defend yourself, the surest way is to face him, eye to eye, and put a sword into him.

In the same way, and probably for the same reason, Hollywood often gets the strategy of Roman warfare quite wrong. (I believe the people out on the Gold Coast think the Romans were stupid, primitive fellows with no power of long-term planning, no maps and no experience in warfare—early medieval minds; whereas in fact they were shrewd statesmen and hard pragmatic thinkers, with a long, long experience of both war and politics reaching over many countries and many centuries.) There was a good motion picture version of Shakespeare's *Julius Caesar,* in which most of the acting and the characterizations struck me as truly splendid; the conspirators might have been the actual men whose faces one sees on the sculptured portraits of the old Roman tombs. But when we came to one of the great crises of the play—a crisis which Shakespeare himself well understood, and did his best to explain within the limits of his small theater— the battle at which the forces of the Republic were beaten by the forces of dictatorship, then we saw that it was misunderstood, or vulgarized, or both. In actual fact, the battle was touch and

go; it was one of those supremely difficult contests in which the
two sides are approximately equal, and each has a chance of win-
ning. One side was victorious on one wing, the other side on the
other wing, the center remaining undecided. It was one of the
Republican commanders, Cassius, who misinterpreted the situation, gave up too soon, committed suicide, and wrecked the
chances of his army. This is a powerful and highly dramatic
situation; Shakespeare grasped it. But as Hollywood presented
it to us, the army of the Republic marched blindly into a long
canyon, without sending out any reconnaissance units to guard
their advance and their flanks. The hills above the canyon were
occupied by the enemy; and, at a given moment, Mark Antony
(played by Marlon Brando) raised his hand in the old gesture so
familiar from Western movies and the stupid Republican forces
were destroyed like walking ducks, mowed down by Sitting Bull.

This kind of oversimplification is supposed to make history
clearer, bolder, more dramatic. In fact, it destroys many of the
best values in history and therefore destroys many of the possibilities of drama which lie in history. For example, take the
screen treatment of the Polish romance about the emperor Nero
and the first persecution of the Christians, *Quo Vadis?* If I remember correctly, the screen play began with a Roman general
(well played by Robert Taylor) leading a triumphal procession
into the city of Rome—and, as he rode at the head of his victorious troops, saluting the indolent and selfish young emperor
Nero. I wrote a piece for *Harper's Magazine* about this absurd
scene, pointing out that, under the Roman empire, no Roman
general except a member of the imperial family could ever lead
a triumphal procession—for a very good reason: namely, that
the triumphant general was, for the time being, supreme in the
state, almost God, and could have seized power in fifteen minutes. I got a letter back from Hollywood saying that this was all
very well for pedants and specialists, but that people who wrote
motion picture scripts had to give the public big spectacular

crowd scenes, and what could be better than a triumphal procession? Well, the answer is that truth is always better than falsehood, and that it nearly always makes better drama. The end of the movie version of *Quo Vadis?* was equally false to history; it had the emperor Nero overthrown by a mutiny of some of his troops mixed with a popular revolt stimulated by horror at the persecution of the Christians. The man who was supposed to lead the mutiny was Robert Taylor. Now, the writers could have made this final piece of nonsense more credible, or 'motivated' it in depth, by sticking to historical truth in the first scene. They could and should have made the Roman general lead his victorious troops up to the very gate of Rome, and then have them taken over by the young emperor, too weak to command but too vain to omit the opportunity of a triumphal procession; wearing a suit of specially made gold armor, Nero would lead the army through cheering crowds, while the war-hardened officers rode grimly in the rear, smouldering with rancor and beginning to plan his final overthrow.

Sometimes, again, entirely imaginary or palpably false scenes are placed on the screen, for no reason whatever that any sane being can conceive, except sheer carelessness or ignorance. Quite early in the film version of *The Robe* we saw the aging emperor Tiberius—looking fairly convincing (although much less sinister than he was in reality), but complaining bitterly about his troubles with his wife, the empress Julia, who appeared for a moment with a magnificent costume and a proud manner. An amusing domestic scene. But at the time when the drama was supposed to take place, Julia had been dead for about twenty years, and Tiberius' inclinations had turned in far different directions. Think of the trouble, the expense, and the needless ingenuity expended on writing in a scene, working out dialogue, providing dress and make-up and hair-do for a character who was not only unnecessary but impossible.

I wonder why they do this sort of thing. Partly it is because they know little or nothing about historical research. They do not believe it is possible to find out the truth about how the Roman army fought, or how a Roman emperor treated his wife. They do not know, apparently, that there are dozens and dozens of reference books filled with details. Often they seem to use cheap and more or less fictional accounts of the life which they are going to put on the screen. Usually, their banquets are as unlike a real Roman banquet as a party given by Al Capone would be unlike a normal American dinner party. This is because the most detailed description which we have of a Roman banquet is a bitterly satirical account of a vulgar millionaire's party in which everything is either exaggerated or in outrageously bad taste— and yet the simple-minded 'researcher' who cannot distinguish satire from truth is apt to accept it as normal. In the same way, I suppose, the Asian nations will accept the portrayal of American life given in such films as *Guys and Dolls* as being truly representative of our culture at its most characteristic.

But partly, also, the people who make such films about history are cynics. They live for the moment. They think that history does not matter; or in the immortal phrase attributed to Henry Ford, 'History is bunk.' And, what is worse, they think that everyone else believes the same. They believe that no one cares about the truth of anything that happened beyond fifty or a hundred years ago. Perhaps that is the worst thing that could be said about them with any pretense to truth: that they despise us, their fellow-citizens and their customers. They imagine that we cannot tell the difference between truth and lies, between sense and stupidity, provided the screen is made extra wide, and covered with beautiful colors, lovely women, expensive costumes, and competent actors (Robert Taylor, Charlton Heston, and William Holden). We are all supposed to be seventeen years old, but almost without the conflicts of seventeen-year-olds. The French had a phrase for this attitude: they said their theater managers sometimes spoke of 'les cochons de payants,' 'those

swine who pay for admission,' or more bluntly, 'the stinking customers.' But that is too bitter for Hollywood. The people who
make these epics do not think we are swine. They merely think
we are children.

STUDY QUESTIONS

1. Does Highet object to the desire of Hollywood for spectacle or
to the way in which Hollywood producers conceive and treat spectacular scenes?
2. Does Highet see any necessary connection between education and
popular appeal? Between historical fact and spectacle? Why or why
not?
3. Highet takes some incidental swipes at the Hollywood star system.
To what extent is the star system responsible for the inaccurate
versions of history frequently found in Hollywood films?
4. Film makers, like other popular artists, frequently feel driven to
imitate success. How much and in what ways do you feel this desire contributes to the production of poor historical films?
5. In "The Twentieth-Century Best-Seller" (p. 297), P. N. Furbank
discusses the ways in which twentieth-century British best-sellers
concentrate on nostalgia and the exotic. How much has the commercial success of these two characteristics influenced the film
producers' use of history? In what ways can you detect this influence?
6. Highet's concern with the historically inaccurate spectacle is in
some ways closely related to Vernon Young's concern with the
consistent use of witness point in a film ("Witness Point," p. 254).
What are the similarities? On what grounds does Highet appeal to
his reader? How does his appeal differ from Young's?

ALBERT HUNT

Albert Hunt (1929-   ) is a well-known British scholar of the mass media. He is Tutor in Adult Education in Shropshire, where he lectures on literature, theatre, and the mass media. He is a member of the British Film Institute and has written numerous essays on film. In this article, Hunt points out the frequent discrepancy between the verbal message of a film and the visual treatment of the subject. He helps the student to understand concretely the meaning of style in a film.

from
The Film

I

A film is, basically, an arrangement of moving pictures and recorded sounds. The man responsible for this arrangement is the director. It is his job to select what the camera is going to record, and to organize it into film shape.

The director has at his disposal a wide range of possibilities, from close-up to long shot, from placing the camera at a low angle to shooting from high above the action, from holding the camera still and allowing the movements inside the frame to speak for themselves, to moving it freely in any direction, coming in close to isolate a particular feature, or drawing back to set it in perspective. The film is, in the end, the sum of the director's choices.

Each of these possibilities contributes to the way a film communicates. When D. W. Griffith composed his close-up of a

233

pair of hands at the climax of the trial in *Intolerance*, he demonstrated a particular way of communicating physical tension. And when Hitchcock, in *Psycho*, shows us a pair of frightened eyes, staring at us through driving rain from behind the hypnotically swinging windscreen-wipers of a car, he presents us with a concrete image of the unease that lies below the surface of the everyday world.

It is through his choices that a director reveals his way of thinking and feeling. In *Paths of Glory*, for example, a film about the First World War, Stanley Kubrick makes the quick cut from one scene to another a part of the fabric of his conception of the war: he sets side by side the misery of the men in the trenches and the luxury of the château behind the front line where the generals plan the next battle. By contrast, the Italian director, De Sica, in *Umberto D*, uses an almost motionless camera to communicate his sense of the importance and mysteriousness of the most habitual actions: he lets his camera rest for several minutes on a servant-girl grinding coffee, so that her every movement becomes interesting and strange.

If the director's response to what he experiences is crude and conventional—or if he thinks of films as junk for the masses —the crudity and lack of conviction will be reflected in the style of his film. But in the hands of a serious artist, the simplest elements of film-making can bear the weight of a complex poetic statement.

For example, in Franju's short film, *Hôtel des Invalides*, there is a shot of the courtyard of victory in the Paris war museum. The picture is geometrical in its composition. A building is all rectangular lines, cannons are arranged in regular patterns, the branches of trees are clipped, straight, and bare. The only movement in the picture comes from a leaf in the foreground which sways gently backwards and forwards in the breeze. On the sound-track, we hear the twittering of birds.

It is difficult to translate the effect of this image into words.

There is the sterility of conquest, the hollowness of military glory, the menacing and destructive rigidity of organized war. But Franju also reminds us of the fragile spontaneity that the war machine has almost, but not quite, crushed; and of the indifference of the leaf and the birds to the grandiose patterns of military honour.

To create this complexity of feeling, Franju has gone right back to the origins of cinema. 'Look, the leaves are moving!' cried somebody in one of the first audiences ever to be confronted with a moving picture. Franju has taken a moving leaf, and has used it as one of the elements in an image that has all the economy and imaginative force of true art.

II

The film, then, is the concrete expression of the director's imagination. It is only by exploring the form of that expression that we can hope to make any valid judgments about film. But if we turn from *Hôtel des Invalides* and examine, in this way, some of the typical products of the film industry, we shall be in a position to understand much more clearly the nature of the links between 'pure entertainment' and the 'values of our civilization'.

These links, together with the effects of the economic pressures inside the film industry, can, perhaps, be most clearly shown by a brief analysis of three fairly recent British productions. The first two, *The Guns of Navarone* and *The Young Ones*, have both been box-office successes in Britain in the last few years, particularly with young people. The third, *The Angry Silence*, was made about five years ago by a new independent company, and was welcomed as an example of a more enlightened attitude in the industry. (In selecting these films, I am aware that I am laying myself open to the charge of rigging the evidence; but most people would, I think, agree that they are typical and are, if anything, better than average productions.)

The Guns of Navarone is about an episode in the last war.

It is one of a series of British films describing war adventures—
they appear less frequently now than they did a few years ago,
but the success of this particular film suggests that the vogue is
far from over. The film is directed by J. Lee Thompson, a technically skilful director, who has made many films of this kind,
and has the benefit of a script by the American, Carl Foreman,
who is well known for his unusually intelligent scripting of a
western, *High Noon*.

The film tells the story of a commando expedition sent to
silence two German guns on the island of Navarone in the Greek
archipelago. The guns command a narrow strip of water through
which men from another island have to be evacuated. There is
plenty of physical excitement, including the destruction of an E-
boat, a storm, and a ship-wreck, a climb up an almost impassable
cliff, a capture and an escape in enemy uniform, the unmasking
of a traitor, and finally in a race against time, the spectacular
destruction of the guns. It is what is sometimes described as a
healthy schoolboy yarn.

But if we stop to examine what the film is communicating,
through its form of expression, a number of important assumptions begin to emerge.

The film opens with a prologue, which is accompanied by a
portentous commentary. Set into the large screen, with its picturesque colour film of the Greek islands, are black and white
newsreels of the Mediterranean campaign. The effect of this is
to establish a link with reality—with a real war about real
issues in which real people were killed. The documentary link is
kept by the device of introducing each part of the story with a
log-book title such as, 'First Day—0.600 hours'.

Moreover, Foreman's dialogue raises several moral problems.
A conversation between two officers approaches the basic dilemma of fighting a modern total war—to win, you have to become as nasty as the thing you're fighting. 'Bearing in mind that
we're on the side of decency and civilization,' says the officer in

command, played by Gregory Peck, 'would you say that was a civilized thing to do?' He has just told another wounded officer a lie, so that under torture he will still be useful in giving false information. And there is a corporal, played by David Niven, who refuses to become an officer because he doesn't want to be responsible for the dirty work of killing; while another man, known as 'the butcher of Barcelona', who has been killing Germans since 1937, says that he now finds the job distasteful. These problems are all clearly and directly related to the 'values of our civilization': and so is the way they are treated.

Consider, for instance, the moment when the corporal discovers that he *is* responsible, that he has to take his share of the moral responsibility. He is laying the fuse to blow up the guns, and he suddenly says, 'I'm up to my neck in it, aren't I?'—and the camera shows him standing in a hole with only his head from the neck upwards visible. It isn't only that a serious moral issue is turned, by the scripting and the placing of the camera, into a joke. The trouble is that the joke is so feeble and trite.

Or consider the scene in which the men discover that one of the Greek girls has betrayed them. The girl claims to have scars on her back that have been inflicted by the Germans. The claim is proved false when her dress is ripped off her shoulders to reveal smooth white flesh. As the officers discuss the morality of shooting her, she is shown lying on the floor and weeping, the front of her dress clutched to her almost visible breasts. What makes the scene so dreary is the sheer glumness of it all; the director goes out of his way to give us a peep at a pretty body— but while peeping we're expected to pretend that all we're interested in is a moral problem.

Again, a man with gangrene in his leg is tortured. A Nazi officer stands over him, moving the splints with the butt of a revolver. He is young, blond, and blue-eyed, with an ice-cold mask of a face (it is worth noting, incidentally, that we are here being invited to adopt the Nazi practice of hating particular racial characteristics). The camera probes in on the leg and then cuts to the victim with a greedy curiosity: but the only response to what is supposed to be unbearable pain is that of a ham actor going through the motions of twisting his face.

One final example: at the top of a cliff the saboteurs have climbed (Gregory Peck crawls agonizingly towards us across a studio floor) is a solitary German guard. He is dressed in a huge, green-grey coat—the sequence is filmed in a mixture of blues and greens and greys. The assailants throw pebbles and make noises to frighten him and he becomes a slightly comic figure as he runs this way and that. Suddenly, we see him in a close-up with hands closing around his mouth: then the camera cuts away to show us a body falling spectacularly over the cliff and hitting the water. In a film which debates the morality of war, killing is *shown* to be fun.

To discover the full crudity of a film like *The Guns of Navarone* it would be necessary to analyse in much greater detail the style of the film—the complete absence of feeling or subtlety in the acting, for example, the deliberate garishness and vulgarity of the colours, the harsh and melodramatic lighting, and the way, for instance, the gun-tunnel is filmed to look like something out of bad science fiction. But it is clear, even from this brief discussion, that this 'pure entertainment' film communicates attitudes which can easily be summed up: war is brutal but fun, the way to win it is to be as uncivilized as your enemies, and the qualities to admire in a person are toughness and insensitivity.

Compared with *The Guns of Navarone*, a musical like *The Young Ones* seems, at first sight, to be scarcely worth discussing. The film tells the story of a group of young people who try to raise the money to keep their Youth Club open. To do this, they put on a show in an old theatre one Sunday night. The show, like the film, is built round the pop singer, Cliff Richard.

The story of a musical rarely matters: what is important, as dancers like Fred Astaire and Gene Kelly, and directors like

Stanley Donen have shown, is the gaiety, wit, and inventiveness
of the singing and the dancing. In *The Young Ones*, the inventiveness is limited, although one sequence, when the Edwardian
theatre is brought back to life in song and dance, has a certain
amount of vitality and is an advance on almost anything before
it in the British musical.

What makes the film worth examining, though, is its treatment of the 'teenager'. A few years ago, the director, Sidney J.
Furie, made a film about the elopement of two young Canadians,
in which he treated their relationship with some understanding.
But in this film, he shows no interest in what young people are
like. Instead, he takes the simplest image offered by the magazines and the pop music industry.

Take his treatment of love: a film about young people in
whom, according to the theme song, 'the flame is strong' might
well be expected to show some interest in the subject. But the
only moment in the film when there is any hint that sexual feeling exists comes when the 'bad girl', a star imported to give the
show publicity, forces Cliff Richard, during a rehearsal of a song,
to caress her while his real girl friend looks on. The emotional
implication is that sex is something nasty. Love, on the other
hand, is linked with a completely different set of images—Cliff
Richard sings the theme song during a visit to a beach in a fast
sports car, and as a background to the song we see blue sea, blue
sky, and water-ski-ing. We are in the world of a Butlin's holiday
camp advertisement, or of 'People Love Players', where love is
just something that goes along with other consumer goods.

Most important of all are the assumptions the film makes
about what *matters* to young people. What matters is Cliff Richard and whether or not he will sing on the Sunday night show.
The tension is built up through a number of sequences in which
his voice is heard over a pirate radio. And when he finally appears, Furie places the camera directly in front of him as he
stands on the stage and at a very low angle, shooting along the

line of his legs and body up to his face. The effect of this is to turn Richard into a heroic, dominating figure—a towering but untouchable sex-symbol.

The image of Cliff Richard in this film is, in fact, exactly the image of the pop singer the magazines and record companies sell. The pop singer is always 'one of us'. He is ordinary working-class, without fancy ideas—only he has been lucky and now has the biggest car and the best collection of Italian suits. In the film, Cliff Richard, too, is 'one of us'. He fights to keep the club open: only he is also the son of the rich speculator who is trying to close it down. So we move in a world that is pictured as 'ordinary', but which has all the glamour of big business deals, long-distance telephone calls, sudden flights to Scotland, and luxury cars. And in the end, the rich speculator also turns out to be 'one of us', when father joins son in a shuffle on the stage. Once again, a 'pure entertainment' film communicates attitudes based on a whole set of social values.

The third film, *The Angry Silence,* is apparently quite different. One of the 'values of our civilization' is, presumably, moral courage, and *The Angry Silence* has as its hero an ordinary little man who refuses to come out on strike because he thinks the strike is wrong. He is an individual conscience standing out against the mob, and he is first sent to Coventry and then beaten up, so that he loses an eye. The film is obviously trying to make an attack on herd-like conformity.

If, however, we examine what the film communicates through its style, we become aware of a completely different level of feeling.

The tone is set by the film's opening sequence. A train steams into the station of an industrial town. A carriage door opens, and out steps a man, ferrety-featured, with horn-rimmed spectacles and a grim earnestness on his sad, 'intellectual' face. He walks out of the station and is picked up by a car, which turns out to be driven by a shop-steward. There is an air of mystery. Over a meal, the stranger says nobody must know they've met before the following morning.

This stranger gets a job with surprising ease, and throughout the film, he stands there in the background, pulling the strings, using the self-important shop-steward as a mouthpiece, receiving orders by telephone from London, talking in sinister tones about rigging meetings ('He must be taught a lesson. No, but a real lesson'), manipulating strikes which have no visible cause. When the strike collapses, he sneaks back to the train, off, presumably, to cause more trouble elsewhere.

Who is this man at the heart of the film? Where has he come from? What are his motives (even Communists, if that's what he is, must have some)? How does he come to have such influence over the shop-steward? The questions are never even put, let alone answered. The truth is that the makers of the film aren't interested in the *real* origins of a wild-cat strike: they have accepted a conventional notion and embodied it in a stock figure.

In the same way, they have accepted the sensational newspaper picture of a strike, all lawlessness and violence and expressed it in a series of isolated, melodramatic shots. The central emotion is fear of the mob, and as the camera cuts dramatically from a stone through a window to a mashed-up bicycle and a burning car, all hackneyed images of violence, the deeper rhythms of a strike—the boredom, men with not much money to spend hanging around pubs, families worried about the latest instalment on the telly—are never investigated.

As a result of this basic lack of concern, there is a feeling of emptiness and unreality hanging over the film. There is, for example, a scene in the factory canteen, after Curtis, the blackleg, has been sent to Coventry. Curtis sits alone at a table. He looks round the room at other people talking and laughing— the camera pans round the tables following his gaze. Gradually, he begins to feel that they are laughing at him: the camera moves round faster, then tilts, in a drunken lurch, with nightmare close-ups of laughing, maniac faces, until Curtis jumps to his feet, bangs the table and yells, 'Shut up!' A strange stillness descends on the room—the verbal cliché I have just used expresses precisely the visual cliché of the film, and everybody remains absolutely still while Curtis screams, 'I don't want you to talk to me!' And then the eyes follow him as he staggers out. There is a blown-up feeling—not a movement anywhere, not a spoon tinkling or the sound of a tea-cup. Everything is frozen in a hack, over-dramatic statement.

Again, when Curtis marches to work alone during the second strike, he walks along streets that are completely empty. The background of houses is authentic—you can see those black rows right across industrial England—but the streets are unnaturally deserted. His footsteps echo hollowly on the pavement as he goes towards the factory gate where a crowd watches his approach.

The film's attitude is most clearly revealed in the climax. Curtis is in hospital. Union leaders are trying to quell a riotous mob, but they fail until Curtis' only friend, Joe who has so far sat on the fence, redeems himself by beating the leading thug to pulp and dragging him in front of the crowd, which becomes —again the literary cliché—strangely calm.

Joe captures the thug—a teddy boy—by pursuing him on a motor-bike. Our indignation is first turned against the teddy boy in a short sequence showing Curtis in bed, his eye bandaged; and then we see Joe, in righteous fury on his motor-bike, bearing down on a running man. We are, in fact, being called on to approve a violent power image. And it is in this that *The Angry Silence* gives itself away.

For the film purports to be an attack on conformity. *But it is entirely conformist itself.* It accepts the conformist image of Communists, shop-stewards, wildcat strikes, and sheep-like work-

ers, and ends by gloating over the violence it sets out to condemn.

Above all, *The Angry Silence* sees people in terms of a mob
to be manipulated—and in this it is a direct reflection of the
way the makers of the film see their audience. For although the
film ostensibly condemns those who manipulate, it is, in itself, a
thorough-going exercise in manipulation. There is no attempt to
work honestly at communicating the truth of human experience.
One eye is always on the shock effect to be produced on the back
stalls. The attitude is summed up completely in one calculated
shot: we are shown a close-up of a drawing-pin being stuck into
the eye of a child, and then the camera pulls back to reveal that
what we are looking at is a newspaper cutting being placed on a
notice-board.

The shot is a gratuitous attempt to manipulate our attention.
It assumes that we can be kept interested only if we are yelled
at. It is the work, not of an artist concerned with the truth of
his communication, but of a salesman who feels he has to put
something across. And this brings us back to the position of the
film as an art that is dependent on industrial processes.

III

For what is striking, when we think again of the three films
I have described, is not the differences between them, but the
ways in which they are alike. One is a war film, one a musical,
and one a film of social comment. Yet they share certain qualities
of tone and feeling.

Firstly, although all these films are, as I have shown, involved with the 'values of our civilization', they all of them
offer an extreme simplification of experience. The strike, for
example, in *The Angry Silence*, is so clearly ridiculous that the
moral complexities surrounding the issue of private conscience
and loyalty to the group can never be approached; while in *The*

Guns of Navarone war, in spite of the apparent ironies, is no more than a boy-scout adventure. Instead of being invited to explore experience, we are asked in these films to respond to a set of empty conventions: heroism is gritting your teeth, jutting out your jaw and looking solemn; death is anonymous creatures in green uniforms being mown down by the score.

Secondly, the simplified versions of experience presented in these films reflect prejudices and assumptions that are shared by large numbers of people. These prejudices are taken and thrown back at us in a particularly crude form. So, if there is to be a strike, it will be violent, because that is the way we usually think of strikes; and the violence will be committed by a teddy boy, because that is the way we think of teddy boys. And if there is a Nazi, he will be a blond, blue-eyed sadist. (Compare the Nazi leaders in a documentary like *Mein Kampf*. They are all the more terrifying for being so obviously human.) There is, as a result, a constant pressure towards the hardening of assumptions that are already generally held.

Thirdly, on examination, these simplified versions turn out to be offered, not only by these three films, but by many of the other forms of mass communication. The importance of a pop singer is not exaggerated in a single, isolated film; the film reinforces an idea that is already there, on the radio, in the record industry, in the gossip columns and the magazines. The image of the unofficial strike in *The Angry Silence* is lifted straight out of the headlines of the tabloid Press. Turn from *The Guns of Navarone* to a *News of the World* story about a Japanese prison camp where there is a 'hate-crazed Jap fanatic' with 'a face like a jaundiced baboon', and you find this account of the torture of a girl: 'This tormentor ripped the girl's coat until she was half-naked, and the exposure caused the girl's eyes to fill with tears.' A fantasy world is being given reality by the repeated insistence with which it is presented.

This tendency to reduce experience to a formula which fits

our most commonplace assumptions can only contribute in the
end to the fixing of sharply defined limits of taste and awareness. Anything which questions the commonplace or challenges
the imagination is likely to be discouraged.

It is this processing of experience that we need to be aware
of in confronting the typical products of the film industry. The
accusations that have been made against the cinema—that it
causes juvenile delinquency and sexual misbehaviour—are not
supported by any reliable evidence. But it is much more difficult
to measure the effects of the constant presentation of a simplified
and mechanical pattern of behaviour, and of a repeated set of
crude assumptions and attitudes. There is no question of measur-
ing off a single film against 'real life'; the attitudes belong to a
wider picture presented by the media in general; and this general
picture becomes itself an important part of the reality that helps
to shape our lives.

The point is, perhaps, most clearly made in a short film
called *Nice Time*, a documentary which gives a very personal
picture of Piccadilly at night. In this film we are shown two
young people holding hands in a cinema queue. They are obviously in love—but behind them is a huge poster of Anita Ek-
berg. And on the sound-track we hear love clichés from the film
they are going to see.

The implication is that a complex and living relationship is
being threatened and dominated by a crude stereotype. The
film the young people are waiting to see is offering them a
picture of love which is mechanical and belongs to a uniform
pattern, and this picture is imposed on their own experience.
The pressure is all the time towards a way of behaviour that is
conventional and lacking in spontaneity.

The image itself is, of course, over-simplified. It isolates the
cinema from all the other areas of experience that contribute to
the young people's knowledge of love. But in doing so it makes
us aware of one of the ways in which that knowledge can be

limited. And above all it calls attention to the inadequacy of the conventional film's response to human experience.

It is on the inadequacy of this response that the films I have described must ultimately be judged. A medium that has shown itself to be capable of extending awareness is being used to reflect the most obvious assumptions shared by the greatest number of people, assumptions which tend, in their turn, to be fixed by their own constant reflexion.

. . . .

IV

I have discussed these films in some detail because they seem to me to be representative of a general attitude in the industry. In each case, the form of the film communication has been dictated by economic pressures. As film costs rise, it becomes increasingly necessary to aim for the widest possible audience. And since only the familiar is safe, any experiment which involves risk becomes more and more difficult. Even the more enterprising British films in recent years, such as *Room at the Top*, *Saturday Night and Sunday Morning*, and *A Taste of Honey*, have been adaptations from best-sellers or stage successes. And although, compared with the films we have been analysing, these productions are fresh and honest in the way they look at contemporary life, they are all, to some extent, limited by the climate in which they have been made. *Room at the Top*, for example, falls back in the closing sequences on cliché violence and self-pity. Joe Lampton, the hero, gets drunk after the woman he has rejected is killed in a car crash, and is beaten up. (In the novel, he deals with his assailants with commando skill.) He comes round to see a child pushing a toy car over the edge of a heap of dirt. The audience, which should be judging Joe, is given an easy bit of sentimentality. In the same way, the relationships which Shelagh Delaney has established with such clear-cut precision in her play are almost bogged down in the literalness of Tony Richard-

son's film, because we have to be given a number of 'cinematic'
set pieces—picturesque shots of boats on the Manchester ship
canal, a trip around Blackpool, a visit to the Derbyshire caves.
Even *Saturday Night and Sunday Morning*, in most ways an
honest and truthful though pedestrian film, scales down Arthur
Seaton's violent rebellion against the society around him by
giving undue emphasis to a comic feud with a gossipy neighbour
whose vast behind he peppers with a shot-gun. The episode is in
the traditional conventions of British comedy. (There are signs
elsewhere that Karel Reisz, the director, is afraid of the *reality*
of violence that makes the driving force of Sillitoe's novel. The
actual beating up of Arthur, by the outraged husband's friends,
is filmed so conventionally as to be meaningless; and in his other
film, *We Are the Lambeth Boys*, about a Youth Club in Lambeth, Reisz carefully avoids any suggestion that young people are
growing up in a violent world.)

The area of experiment in even the best British films is, in
fact, very limited. It is something that working-class characters
are no longer figures of fun. But there has been nothing in our
commercial cinema as experimental as, say, the BBC's *Goon
Show*, which ran for two years to a minority audience before
becoming one of the most popular programmes on the air—and
which proved in doing so that minority taste isn't static. Given
the opportunity, minorities might grow; but the economic structure of the film industry makes it difficult for the opportunity to
be given.

And yet it would be dangerous to dismiss the commercial
cinema, as those concerned with education sometimes tend to
do. Even inside the system, worthwhile films still get made. To
label films in categories—westerns, musicals, war-films, thrillers
—and then write them all off is to cut oneself off from many of
the good things that the cinema has to offer.

To come back to the question of violence, for example. Edu-
cationists tend to assume that people need to be protected from

any experience of violence on the screen. Yet in a film like *Paths of Glory*, the theme of violent death becomes a moral statement. When Kubrick shows us a public execution, he makes us intensely aware of a moral obscenity. In sharp, clear-cut images, he shows us three men on their way to be shot—one of them unconscious on a stretcher, one, who has achieved some sort of control, walking almost blindly along, staring straight in front, and the third, a tall, gangling man, twisting his head from side to side and whimpering like a frightened animal as a priest trots ineffectually alongside reciting words of comfort. The camera picks up, as if in passing, the assembled lines of soldiers, a Press photographer, the face of their Colonel. On the sound-track, drums beat louder and louder as the men are tied up and offered blindfolds. Before the order to fire is given, the drums stop, and in the silence Kubrick places us behind the firing squad. As the bullets strike and the bodies twitch, there is a momentary twitter of birds—and then we are suddenly back with the generals having breakfast.

There is no suggestion in such a sequence of violence for kicks. The light is sharp and clear, there is an austere concentration on essentials, and the effect is one of cold anger. In complete contrast to what happens in *The Guns of Navarone*, death becomes immediate and painful.

Again, compare the raucous, conventional treatment of violent hatred in *The Angry Silence* with the sensitive response to a similar subject—racial hatred—in Buñuel's *The Young One* —a film which the distributors have, incidentally, re-named *Island of Shame* and sent round the circuits as part of a horror programme. The film was shot very quickly on a cheap budget. The acting is, for the most part, poor; the script is often naïve; and the story of a Negro jazz musician who, wrongly accused of raping a white woman, takes refuge on an island occupied only by a racialist game-warden and a young girl, could have been sensational. But in Buñuel's hands it becomes an exploration of how human beings grow in understanding.

The violence is not evaded, as in Reisz's films. It is there all the time below the surface, and it flares out in the conflict between the Negro and Miller, the game-warden. But it is linked with a lack of maturity. As Miller grows in awareness of himself and other people, his racialism begins to crack.

This awareness develops through his relationship with Ewie, the young girl whose father has just died at the beginning of the film. At first Miller sees her only as a desirable object. He can't enter into any feelings she may have about the death of her father: we see him brushing her hair, dressing her in attractive clothes, caressing her on his knee, but casually hitting her when she spoils some food. But after Miller had made love to her— seduced would be too strong a word for the gentle tone in which the sequence is filmed—he gradually becomes aware of her as a person for whom he feels tenderness. Buñuel shows the first break in Miller's racialism when another white man tries to strike Ewie for having helped the Negro to escape. Miller stops him.

And in his treatment of sex, as well as violence, Buñuel shows a sense of complexity. Instead of the cliché image of a deceived young girl, he presents a human being, balanced between innocence and experience. Ewie has the innocence of a child—she can't understand why the Negro should insist on her covering her shoulders after she has taken a shower; and when Miller first kisses her, her response is to rough up her hair which he has so carefully brushed into place. But she is also a maturing woman. One shot at the end of the film places her with precision. We see her walking across the jetty, about to leave the island. She is in her new clothes, but she is a little clumsy in her high heels. Suddenly, she stops walking, and the camera cuts in close to her feet to show her hopping in a swift zig-zag between the cracks. She is joyful at leaving her childhood behind; but the joy is expressed in the gesture of a child.

I have called attention to this film for two reasons. Firstly, it is an indication of what an imaginative director can do, even when he is forced to work with economic limitations. And, secondly, it emphasizes the fact that it is the *treatment* of a subject that we need to examine when we look at a film. By his ability to project, in cinematic language, the contradictions and complexities of relationships between people, Buñuel has dealt with sex and violence in a way that is far removed from the crudities of the newspaper headlines, and has used them to extend our own understanding.

A third point might be made: the distribution companies have tried to bring this particular film back inside the conventions by selling it as a film of—sex and violence. In the same way, they advertised *Rocco and his Brothers* with huge posters crying 'Murder! Rape!' The defence was that in this way they were persuading the public to see a masterpiece.

But if you go to see murder and rape, rape and murder are what you are likely to respond to; a fact which makes it all the more important to bring to the screen an active critical judgement.

V

How are we to develop such judgement? In the absence of any established critical standards, there is no easy answer. In dealing with the culture of the past, we are helped by the fact that only the reasonably worthwhile will have survived. But in the cinema, where we are surrounded by a mass of material, most of it worthless, we have only our experience to guide us. Even those whom one would expect to be most helpful—the film critics of the 'quality' Press—have often assumed a tone of intellectual superiority about the medium, preferring to write slick, amusing columns about bad films, rather than to explain the reasons for their badness.

Yet the first step towards using the film positively must be the creation of standards. By this, I don't mean taking what the distribution catalogues sometimes call 'Film Classics'—adaptations of Shakespeare and Dickens—and seeing how they measure up to the originals; or doing a history of the cinema, with an emphasis on those silent films which are old and remote enough to have acquired an aura of cultural respectability; or studying film technique—it is possible, . . . to be aware of technical achievements without being able to make any judgement about the quality of the experience that is being offered.

The creation of standards involves the building up of a critical response based on an awareness of how film works. And this depends, to begin with, on a willingness to look at films in a much more careful and critical way. The circumstances of cinema-going discourage such attention: in an atmosphere where there are constant distractions, it is much easier to respond to the familiar, to allow oneself to be washed over by the huge, imposing images on the screen, than to remain intellectually alive and questioning. But the cultivation of such attention is important, and it leads at once to a much more active enjoyment of what the cinema has to offer.

There are several ways in which this attention can be focused. Through discussion, for example, it becomes possible to re-create and explore the experience of a film. Such discussion, to be useful, must be based on the concrete details of what has been seen: it is tempting to use a film like *Paths of Glory* as the excuse for a sermon about the futility of war; but this would not help to build up a critical response to the film. What matters is what has appeared on the screen. In *The Guns of Navarone*, for instance, how are we put on the side of the officer in command, as played by Gregory Peck? What are we invited to admire in him? Such questions lead inevitably to a consideration of the *cinematic* qualities, for we know this man only through what we see—through the actions, words, movements, gestures and facial expressions of the actor, and through the way he is photographed; and our feelings are also affected by the music on the soundtrack. It is by exploring these details that we sharpen our critical judgement—a judgement that can be developed further if we set this film alongside others that deal with war in a more serious way.

This kind of attention involves a careful and detailed scrutiny of films. Unfortunately, such a scrutiny is often difficult. The film exists only as a series of fleeting images, and it is normally impossible to go back and examine what one has just seen. This makes it all the more important to bring the film out of the commercial cinema and into the classroom or the youth group or the community centre where a more detailed examination and a directed discussion become possible. But at the same time it is important not to create the idea that film is just one more academic subject: it is better to know what, in the way of good or bad, the local cinema is offering than to show *Henry V* once a year.

It is, in fact, absurd that an art form of such potentiality should still be neglected in liberal education. Nobody asks why we teach music and drama: and nobody should ask why we teach film. But the approach is vital. The aim must be the development of a living response to films of all kinds. This does not mean that the latest musical can be measured against *L'Atalante*. But it does mean that we must be prepared to look at the latest musical critically, searching for freshness and life, and rejecting the mechanical and the dead.

I have emphasized the positive exploration of the film as a means of extending imaginative experience. In any education aimed at developing people critical of the assumptions of their environment, such a study would no doubt be linked with teaching about the other mass media.

But as I said at the beginning, film is not just one more of the media. It is a new and important art, which has already produced works of real stature, the study of which would contribute to the growth of understanding. It is up to those of us who care about our culture to see that this medium is not narrowed down by those whose interests and values are not compatible with our own.

STUDY QUESTIONS

1. What does Hunt say we must explore in order to be able to make valid judgments about film? What does he mean?
2. To what kind of examination does Hunt subject "some of the typical products of the film industry" in order to clarify "the nature of the links between 'pure entertainment' and the 'values of our civilization' "? What are some of those links?
3. Hunt makes a great deal out of the differences between what he calls "the style of a film" and its professed content. Why? Can you think of any other films which were supposed to be against war but actually glorified it? Analyze another film to show what it communicates through its style. Does its style support its surface theme? For example, is there any discrepancy between the style of a number of contemporary bedroom comedies and the morality they profess to communicate?
4. Can you think of any films that "reduce films to a formula which fits our most commonplace assumptions"? Explain.
5. Why does Hunt feel that "it would be dangerous to dismiss the commercial cinema"?
6. Hunt says that "it is the *treatment* of a subject that we need to examine when we look at a film." Does Vernon Young's analysis of "The Witness Point" (p. 254) help us to examine the treatment? Explain.
7. What does Hunt mean when he says that the film can extend one's imaginative experience? Can you explain an analogous way in which a modern novel extends imaginative experience?
8. What kind of standards does Hunt want to establish as a basis for making active critical judgments about film? How does he propose that such standards be developed?

Note: For a more detailed analysis of Buñuel's film see Alan Lovell's *The Anarchist Cinema,* from which some of these comments have been drawn.

VERNON YOUNG

Vernon Young (1912-   ) is both a film critic and a
novelist. His film criticism has most frequently appeared
in the *Hudson Review*. Although he has taught film theory in the United States, he is currently living in Sweden
while he writes a biography of the Swedish film director
Ingmar Bergman. The following article, "The Witness
Point," has been widely recognized as one of the most
significant contributions to film theory and criticism of the
last twenty-five years. In it, Young examines the ways in
which the various techniques available to the film maker
can be made expressive artistic tools rather than gim-
micks for introducing arbitrary variety and excitement into
a film. Young's discussion is particularly valuable to the
beginning student of the popular arts because it furnishes
him not only a way of looking at film but also a valuable
catalogue of film techniques which he recognizes but
which he has probably not heard named or described.

The Witness Point

While the Hollywood motion picture is continually under fire
from a variety of fronts for not being sufficiently radical in its
social interpretation or for being too radical, for appealing to the
twelve-year-old mind or for not appealing to a larger number of
twelve-year-old minds, for not filming the classics or for filming
too many bad classics (or for filming good ones badly), for being
sexually evasive or for being sexually self-conscious, one might
well abandon the area of civic criticism for the amoral and simple question: Just what *is* a movie?

The expense of spirit in a waste of shameful moralizing

over content has ignored the fundamental identity of the motion picture as an art—or shall we say as a synthesis of science and of various art forms?—since it is with some such temporization that we must begin. And before we can conclude with high-minded resolutions as to the motion picture's public obligations, we should come to some agreement on its intrinsic endowments. Means determine, or at least qualify, ends; syntax precedes argument.

The instigator of a form should certainly be listened to and remembered when he coins its definition, even if the form thereafter undergoes mutations which modify the original defining. In the late 1870s an American named Edward Muybridge performed an experiment with twelve still cameras in order to record the motions of a trotting horse for Leland Stanford. This is the first known experiment in the development of what later became "moving pictures." Subsequently, Muybridge defined the movie as "an apparatus for synthetically demonstrating movements analytically photographed from life." No purer definition of the movie as a process has been evolved; all extensions of definition derive from this one, since they have had to derive from the nature of the thing in itself.

Later, when the film as a vehicle of aesthetically organized content was being more widely recognized and more intensively urged, Sergei Eisenstein, one of the most voluble theorists working in the film medium, declared that film form was "a question of creating a series of images in such a way that it provokes an effective movement which in turn awakens a series of ideas. From image to sentiment, from sentiment to thesis." Here is a dialectical description rather than a mechanistic analysis. Between Muybridge and Eisenstein we find the essence and the limits of our definition. All elaborations of statement on this subject must assume the premise that the movie begins with *the art of photographed motion*. The movie is the art of making motion meaningful; it is a dynamic of visual relationships, assisted, generally, by the arts of the scenarist and the actor and by the incorporation of selected sound. Within the framework of the pictorialized problem, the director and editor may augment, distill, or diffuse; increase or decrease tempo by mechanical means, compound images after the event and otherwise arbitrarily complicate, simplify, or intensify the continuity originally devised.

Self-evident, it would seem; yet the commercial movie perennially abdicates its own potential in favor of the lazier chronology of the legitimate theater and the novel of the Fielding tradition, using an unimaginative succession of medium, distance, and close shots, little more dynamic than the magic lantern. The great pioneers of the film art, such as Meliès, D. W. Griffith, Abel Gance, and Pudovkin, empirically established the simple fact that a movie *must be kept moving,* and over the years this principle has been fortified by continuing implementations: moving the camera instead of merely moving the object, and moving it from a variety of positions; employing many brief shots to indicate simultaneity or rapid sequence; balancing "dissolves," "irises," and "fade-outs" with direct cuts; flashing rapidly from detail to larger scene and utilizing music in direct or in counterpoint relation with the photographed images.

Between the experience of watching a play and that of watching a movie the distinction should be elementary, but, from the reactions of the layman and of all but a very few critics, it would appear to be still incompletely understood. Since their modes of presentation materially differ from each other, the stage and the movie, pursuing different formal ends, will arouse qualitatively different perceptions. When the film and the play appear to overlap, they have seceded from their native means. The movie is basically different from the staged play in kind—aside from the patent fact of its being a *recorded* performance—by virtue of its powers of mobility. The stage is three-dimensional, the movie multi-dimensional (even without the amplifications of the new "Cineramic" techniques). The stage play can create epic, for example, only by borrowing movie methods. The movie, likewise, can debate ideas only by imitating the relative stasis of theater and, in pursuit of ideas or not, it unnaturally limits its prowess by containing action within one room or other closely confined area (this constriction is frequently achieved, just to show that it can be done: e.g., *Rope* and *Detective Story*). The imperative of movie motion makes any concession to the working principles of theater a retrograde act, for the form of a play must be violated in order to be converted; if this violation is shirked, the movie's integrity will be sacrificed for that of the play. One cannot possibly imagine a fluid movie adapted from a play by Molière, Chekhov, Sternheim, or Pirandello, unless the original content were disastrously modified. Nor can the social dramas of Ibsen and the discursive comedies of Shaw profit from the movie medium. Their action, in the literal sense, is not going anywhere; their moods and theses can only be dissipated by a compulsively mobile camera.

In this order of playwriting, drama is impelled by people facing each other and exchanging opinions or combatting each other's being in modes dependent upon emotional and intellectual forces irrelevant to or beyond the wiles of the motion-picture apparatus. The inappropriateness of any three-wall play which is screened, retaining its original structure and dialogue, demonstrates functional abuse. Only an ill-educated movie public could have swallowed the uncomfortable versions of Shaw's plays to which we have been exposed, and it is amusing to note that it has been the best educated (in literary ideas only) who have swallowed them whole. But almost any filmed play— *All My Sons, Born Yesterday, Another Part of the Forest, Cyrano de Bergerac*—suffers from the necessity of keeping scenes within limited precincts for long periods, from the superfluous motion resorted to in order to keep not the *idea* but the *scene* moving, and from the tyranny of stage dialogue, highly absolute, rigidly constructed within the otherwise flowing context. (Film dialogue is often less artificial than even the most naturalistic theater talk, seeming to arise more spontaneously from contingencies in the development of action. The privilege of latitude is imposed on it by the interjectional nature of the screen play: sharper than life yet more casual than theater.) That the moral "point" of a play can still be made after its metamorphosis on celluloid need not be disputed, but what we have a right to demand is an almost total translation of aesthetic experience. *A Streetcar Named Desire* was a brilliantly manipulated adaptation. It was still a *screened play*. The producers of *The Importance of Being Earnest* found themselves with a stylized theater product and were forced by honesty to open and close the film with a theater program, pretending whimsically that they had not really made a movie at all! (Shakespeare's multi-ordinal drama, constructed along more serpentine lines of action and form, is the best conceivable exception to this general incompatibility of genre. The Expressionist drama of the first quarter of our century was in many ways a half-cinematic measure, which may largely account for its demise.)

For the modern sensibility, the moviegoing experience is rightly a manifold one. The agents of a play's action move across one's field of vision at an unvarying distance; those of a movie's travel in a stranger sense. With increased ratio to the degree of directorial sophistication, *you* move into the field of vision. You have the illusion of leaving normal dimensions; you are inescapably involved, mute witness and participator as well; not restricted to a set distance from the drama, you may approach it from in front, from above, even from underneath—see it *in toto, in medias res,* or agonizingly from its peripheral inceptions. The helpless filmgoer is a Gulliver, subject to extraordinary and shaking changes of perspective. More unbearably than Gulliver, he inhabits Lilliput and Brobdingnag simultaneously, or at least within shattering accelerations of time, and may find himself transported in the flutter of an eyelid (a change of lens) from a mountaintop to a dark alleyway, from thence to beneath a table, behind a curtain, or within palpitating distance of the heroine's bosom.

In view (and one means just that) of this superior kaleidoscope of momentum, it is surprising how the inveterate filmgoer has taken this wonder for granted, how unaware he is that its artisans have confected an art-science organically expressive of an age that successively finds itself characterized in terms of such process fields as engineering, thermodynamics, psychology, or physics. For the motion picture, so understood, is *the* art of our time analogous with these subjects—mobile, divisive, atomic if you like: a form-breaker, disintegrator, working from specialized and defined mechanical methods toward frequently undetermined ends, incorporating as it goes the ruins of our historical arts of painting, music, and poetry, creating a new whole, plastic, beautiful perhaps, irregularly conditioned by the confused tone of journalism, by the multiple kinesthetic appetites of the driven masses, by our now universal mania for disregarding privacy, for annihilating distance and identity. The movie reflects the inquisitive lust for the panoramic vision indulged by the aviator but present in us all, *malgré nous;* reflects, from each of us, the amateur psychoanalyst, the arrogant sociologist, the latent violator, the cold *voyeur.* (Wouldn't we all rather see Audrey Hepburn than Botticelli's Venus, rising from the foam?) And because it is dedicated to our collateral retinizing, to what Morris Ernst has justly called "the Esperanto of the eye," it is often colossally vulgar. Yet is it more so than Broadway's musical comedies or the average fiction best-seller?

The French, who care pertinently for this subject, have produced, as might be expected, a spokesman with a flair for definition. René Guillère, in an essay primarily concerned with jazz, has provided us with an elegantly exact defense of that world of form in which the cinema finds its justification.

Formerly the science of aesthetics rested content on the principle of fused elements. In music—on the continuous melodic line threaded through harmonic chords; in literature—on the fusion of a sentence's elements through conjunctions and transitions; in art—on a continuity of plastic forms and structures of combinations of these forms. Modern aesthetics is built upon the disunion of elements, heightening the contrast of each other: repetition of identical elements, which serves to strengthen the identity of contrast. . . .

Allowing with a shrug for M. Guillère's cavalier appropriation of the entire scope of modern art, we must concede that he has herein precisely described the qualitative nature of the motion picture. "The disunion of elements, heightening the contrast of each other" is the basis of film assembly: union through disunion, a somewhat more dynamic modification of terms than Eisenstein's Hegelian "from image to sentiment, from sentiment to thesis."

For all these reasons it is significantly the contemporary world that has, by Hollywood, been most fittingly translated into usable movie terms. We live in a fragmented, motile environment, and in the motion picture the seemingly futile activity of daily American urban life acquires, by reason of its decoction into meaningful rhythms and patterns of sound and image, excitement and acceptability. The modern temper, exasperated and energetic, yet passive under bombardment by accessories to nature, receives, in this visual drama of multiplicity, its most authentic revelation. You may beg this question by supporting Yvor Winters' objection to mimetic poetry as "the fallacy of expressive form," or you may defer to the subtler justice in George Williamson's approval of John Donne: "To be contemporary in the right sense means to find the peculiar emotional tension of the time and to mold language to its expression." In what other medium can one find a language so rhythmically molded to express the peculiar emotional tension of *our* time (no irony avoided) as the language of the movie camera? European moviemakers are not so historically restricted; they have an intimate sense of the past. American producers see the past as no less in mindless frenzy than the present; therefore, the strange hollow sound of our Westerns and our costume epics. During the last decade, certainly, the most expertly made American films have been almost all contemporary in subject matter.

(It is noteworthy to observe, in passing, that largely because the writers are permitted more honesty in this direction, the direct subject has been either the underworld of society or the underside of the mind: cf. *The Strange Love of Martha Ivers, The Killers, The Lady in the Lake, Cross Fire, Act of Violence, Champion, Criss Cross, They Live by Night, Caught, The Sniper*.) This phase of the art, if regrettably obsessive, has not been without imaginative value. It has stimulated imagistic reprisal from the greatest among our poets of metamorphosis, Dylan Thomas:

> In this our age the gunman and his moll,
> Two one-dimensioned ghosts, love on a reel,
> Strange to our solid eye,
> And speak their midnight nothings as they swell. . . .
>
> We watch the show of shadows kiss or kill,
> Flavoured of celluloid give love the lie.*

From the literary bias, one could insist that the movie is the art of the novel reduced to absurdity. Like the novel in respect of flexibility, shifts of viewpoint, the ability intimately to dissect or comprehensively to mass, the movie takes the novel one step further, the last, often the disastrous step. It literalizes the novel. (All movie literalism is of course relative; once beyond newsreel immediacy, the artistry is created by a consistent intention and a host of tributary services. And artistry does not necessarily

* From Dylan Thomas, *Collected Poems*. Copyright, 1953, by Dylan Thomas; © 1957 by New Directions. Reprinted by permission of the publisher, New Directions Publishing Corporation; J. M. Dent & Sons Ltd; and the Trustees for the Copyrights of the late Dylan Thomas.—*Ed.*

increase with the degree of expressionism, impressionism, surrealism, or plotless vagary the movie may serve. The important fantasists, from Meliès to Cocteau, have sought to transcend all modes of cinematic realism. Their achievements have often been prodigious. But for purposes of easier reference, I am not attempting, in the ensuing notations, to research the extremist adventure on film.)

On its own naked account, the motion picture cannot take you into the articulated content of thought but it can suggest the content by showing objects so related as to mirror the associations of thought. (Like symbolist poetry it may conceal and delay meaning until its images are completed.) The film version of your literary world banishes ambiguity and alternative renderings. The spectator's private mind is made up for him; the intermediate reaction of the reader is eliminated, his imagination circumscribed, his initiative preëmpted. There is substituted instead this particular image or sequence, dictatorially composed: not any street lined with poplars, vanishing to a distant sky of one's own impalpable painting but this street, these poplars here, this house-front so, this demarcated horizon with no other arrangement than this embodied-in-Technicolor one, no more, no less, and no time to ask or to wonder what is around this exactly measured corner; not any heroine you might individually have imagined from the subtle clues of a prose writer who would allow you, despite his precise order of coloration and anatomy, freedom to wander by yourself with the creature of your own nocturnal imagination, but *this* actress, vivid and irrevocable, her hairline gliding around the tangible curve of an ear you might never have included, hands scorning the poverty of your tactile invention, mouth promising, perhaps, variations you had not yet arrived at. With a recklessness unavailable to the legitimate theater, the movie teases one into an even greater illusion of spontaneity and volition which is the satisfying and sometimes sinister secret of its power. It is a form of literalism which, if insufficiently transformed, will indeed be "strange to our solid eye." It will stupefy, instead of releasing, the imagination of the spectator.

The foregoing character of the motion picture, always leading us into psychological and sociological territory, has been generalized from the sum of its effects as it reaches the observer's subjective and synthetic view. But this sum or "grammar" of cinematography, to risk an academic figure, is evolved from parts of speech usually unidentified by even the more attentive moviegoer who still too often fails to recognize that the foundation of a movie's vital existence is the right relationship of its *details*. Snobbery toward "mere technique" in a movie is untenable. Every inch of a movie *is* technique, under, over, and above all felicities of paraphrasable content and of personality. Just as a poem is, by Mallarmé's sane correction, "written not with ideas but with words," so a movie's totality is made up of concrete syntax, built from experience with the medium, a syntax primarily visual, or today *audio-visual* (tomorrow the 3-D world?). Makers of movies have by now developed a number of refinements instrumental to the greater effectiveness of their art; some of these have been raised into inviolable principles, some are byproducts of a particular context and have not been marshaled into a rationale. A few of the more creative of these refinements may be pointed out, in the hope that moviegoers will recall and then re-look, to the greater glory of their cinema experience:

The device of *moving into a scene from the part to the whole,* rather than the other way around: "From image to sentiment." An easily available example is a fight in *Treasure of the Sierra Madre,* ending with a closeup, floor-level, of the loser's battered face. Scene is "dissolved" into close-up of bloody hands being washed at the plaza fountain. Moving up from the hands to the faces of the victorious combatants discussing their next move, the camera gradually frames a more complete view of the fountain. The older method would have moved us from the bar, probably "fading" instead of dissolving (thereby breaking momentum), out to the entire plaza, then moved us in to the fountain, then out again before picking up the action. By this time, any close-up of the hands would be anti-climactic. The later method obviously saves footage, besides gaining emphasis by concentrating our attention sharply on the transitional detail.

The dissolve through parallel compositional structures: a continuity-design especially gratifying if not overworked. In *Body and Soul,* the shot of a triangulated section of a prize-fight ring is dissolved rapidly into a dressing-room scene where the immediate arrangement of massage table and group of characters repeats the triangle, with a shaded ceiling light as apex. A more poetic illustration can be elicited from *Letter from an Unknown Woman;* an arched railway station in which the woman has just said a strained goodbye to her lover recedes into the similar construction of a hospital corridor among cries from the maternity ward. Here the device was expository, not merely formal. Even without the dissolve in sequence, the *repetition* of a structure at just the right moment, or the introduction of an element which resembles another, can be a compelling reminder or a premonitory announcement. The elevator gates which close on Mary Astor at the end of *The Maltese Falcon* clearly suggest a jail, and in *Madeline* the attorney's feet pacing behind the wicket recall to the woman on trial her poisoned lover, who paced nightly behind the railings of her house.

The transitional caesura, a kind of *delaying* action, is uniquely effective when managed with tact. This process occurs when a fade-out or dissolve leads into an *aftermath* of the next scene logically expected. In *They Won't Believe Me,* Robert Young is shown packing to leave his wife for another woman; she pleads, apparently without success. Dissolve from close-up of Young's suitcase in the bedroom to the same suitcase in a train compartment. As this scene enlarges, we discover that Young is on the train with his wife, having been persuaded by means we discover much later in the film. (This is a shrewd use of anticlimax.) The *symbolic* or *oblique cut* serves a related purpose, as climax to a *suspended* action: an image is abruptly substituted for the deed. In *They Won't Forget*, the cut, from a lynch mob dragging its victim from a train, to a mailbag being jerked from its hook, made a particularly brutal impact. And in the film version of Graham Greene's *The Man Within* (retitled in America *The Smugglers*), the camera boom suddenly left the boy being flogged at the mast to travel swiftly upward and catch a flock of seagulls screaming against a bright sky.

Among the most valuable assets of movie composition, one has to isolate the judicious use of the *closeup* in relation to the larger continuity. A sure knowledge of when to employ closeup so as to emphasize rather than retard action, and to focus instead of dispelling a mood, is one of the cardinal factors. Since Eisenstein's terrifying, and over-prolonged, closeups in the Odessa Steps sequence (*Potemkin*), the management of closeup has come a long and subtle way, even if in the California commodity glamour, not dramatic necessity, seems to be the foremost aim. Anatole Litvak (*The Snake Pit*), Alexander Mackendrick (*Tight Little Island*), and Carol Reed come to mind as having an unfailing sense of the right moment for the appropriate style of closeup. The final cross-examination of the boy, on the stairs of the embassy, in Carol Reed's *The Fallen Idol*, was a superlative example of camera position as the decisive control. It is impossible to imagine the scene being maneuvered, shot for shot, with any better combination of angles. Reed saved his strongest closeup for the moment when the boy's web of prevarication threatened to break.

The use of closeup is governed by another aid to integration, by what I should like to call *the witness point*: this is to say, the camera's coign of vantage not simply within the action of a scene but throughout the entire film. *Whose eye* is the camera, at any moment, intended to represent? Is the strategy to be omnivisual, like Tolstoi's in *War and Peace*, so that the point of view is ricocheted from one participant to another? Is one actor to be concentrated on to the exclusion of others and always seen through another's eyes or is the angle of vision to proceed *from* him? The question of witness point must be initial in the plans of scenarist and director. One remembers Olivier's conspicuous violation of this principle in *Hamlet*, when we saw not only the Ghost but also Hamlet, himself, becoming dim! *Who* is supposed to be looking at Hamlet at this point? Long before the inflated adulation of Olivier's directorial ability, Edward Dmytryk, working with far less elevated material, made no such mistake in *Murder, My Sweet*, where the drugged detective concentrated on clearing his vision; in this case, we saw *him* with *our* eyes open and only blurred *with* him as the stairs, door, and so forth wavered in his focus.

The distinguishing feature of Alfred Hitchcock's early pictures was this working close to a single protagonist, never including more of an incident than could logically be observed by one implicated witness. Since his arrival in Hollywood, he has disowned the method as a controlling style. It found its most extensive assimilation in Robert Montgomery's production, advertised as You *and Robert Montgomery in* THE LADY IN THE LAKE; here the action was seen *exclusively* through the eyes of one narrator. (We never saw *him* except for a brief confrontation by a mirror.) Closeup acting received an extra share of attention and dramatic intimacy was thereby furthered. There are many who find such concentration of means visually monotonous but its possibilities, as Montgomery suggested them, are all in the direction of disciplining the ubiquitous method which, properly handled, does make for greater speed and variety but, if abused, corrupts its privileges by the vice of inordinate maneuvering. (The first-person-singular narration in a novel offers comparative grounds for studying the advantages and the limitations of the restrictive view.)

Deployable view is a startling addition to film narrative: not the mere flashback which is now a Hollywood cliché of storytelling, but a richer extension—the recapitulation of a key action from more than a single viewpoint, a multiple dramatization, as in the Japanese *Rashomon*. Its most intelligent Hollywood employment to date was in Dmytryk's *Cross Fire*, where three G.I.'s told their separate versions of a sadistic and fatal beating, and it was also used to astute psychological advantage in one involved sequence of *The Smugglers*, wherein we first saw a flashback of what had *actually* taken place, followed immediately by another flashback of the same incident deliberately misrepresented by the narrator, under duress of torture.

Musical scoring is a lengthy subject which cannot be more than honored here; its relevance to cinematic success can surely no longer be questioned. If there are any critics remaining who puristically believe that the movie is or should be essentially, or only, visual, and that sound, musical or other, is a gratuitous addition, let them re-view, as test cases, the two worthies, *Treasure of the Sierra Madre* and *The Third Man*, and try subtracting the musical contours from the visual ones. A great deal of the total cinematic thrill will be lost to them, I believe, without Anton Karas's zither and Carlos Chávez' adaptation of the Yaqui Indian theme. A good piece of cinematography will have, of course, a visual logic of its own but a movie, as finished product, is now a *sight and sound* experience. The emotional fruitfulness of thematic music or of orchestrated sounds-in-themselves is indisputable. One needs only to remember the scraping club foot in *Act of Violence*, the harpsichord theme of *Ivy*, the bell in *Day of Wrath*, the Varsovienne of *A Streetcar Named Desire*, the tapping stick and dragging skirts of the Countess' ghost in *Queen of Spades*, the relentless feet stomping and clattering through *Oliver*

Twist, or for that matter the syncopated machine of *The Man in the White Suit* or the unearthly laughter of those girls in the Eiffel Tower elevator sequence of *The Lavender Hill Mob*. *The Thief*, a "silent movie" made in 1952, is the best proof by default we could have. Nobody in it *talked*, sure enough, but sound was carefully retained and the best bit in the film (the *only* one worth remembering) was the covering of a woman's scream by car brakes—an artful, if passé, contrivance!

In the last analysis or, speaking by the card, in the last synthesis, the determining factor of a film's structural purity is *the proportioning of its connective sequences*—no news to the student of the novel or the symphony. In the motion picture, one solid scene following upon another of about equal length, no matter how flexibly directed each of the scenes may be, will be dangerously contrapuntal; whereas a running narrative with brief but punctuating expository shots cut into the more prolonged and fully dramatized sections will "strengthen the identity of contrast" and more fittingly serve that "affective movement" for the recording of which the movie camera was invented. The final responsibility for integrating these elements so that a structure becomes a style falls to the editor (ideally, in collaboration with the director), and it is this vitalizing organization of scene and fragment which is known as *montage*.

It should not be necessary to conclude that a film ought finally to be something better than its most ingenious moments, and something more than the sum of meticulous parts. But the form-and-content dichotomy in the evaluation of movies has been aggravated by the plain fact that American producers rarely know *what* they are doing at the primary creative level: taking pretty pictures, telling a story as eclectically as possible, reproducing the sensations of another form of entertainment, or imitating life.

Carol Reed has claimed that he makes a movie to please him-

self, hoping that it will also please the public, and that so far he
has been lucky. Mr. Reed's honesty is instructive, but obviously
he has been more than lucky. He has been artistic—which is to
say he has kept his eye on his subject. *And* he has been left
alone! Under the Hollywood dispensation, few directors are
given such freedom of authority. The usual result is an irresolution of all but commercial purposes, which has fostered an equal
irresolution of critical approach from the audience. *Portrait of
Jenny* and *Duel in the Sun* included fabulous experiments with
color and photography but their substantial trashiness was unre-
deemable. *Ivy,* produced by William Cameron Menzies in 1947,
remains as perfect a specimen of controlled montage as ever
came out of Hollywood; the critics failed to observe its formal
perfection and one moral snob, without pausing to look and listen for its exceptional charms of texture and pattern, dismissed it
as having a shallow sense of evil. So it had, of course; yet it de-
served a less puritanical concession for its consistent and exciting
elaboration of cinematic means.

No doubt there has never been a film from Hollywood which
has surpassed *Les Enfants du Paradis* or *Panique* in ethical force
and poetic conception, and it must be confessed that neither of
these films is notable for technical brilliance. Faced with such
contradictions, many critics jump to the easy conclusion that the
techniques of film are therefore subordinate to the "story" or the
"acting." The answer is not quite so simple as it may demon-
strably appear by making invidious comparisons. . . . *Day of
Wrath,* the Danish tragedy of witch-burning, had all the necessary ingredients for a great movie: a story of considerable dramatic and moral cogency, responsive actors, and a careful audio-
visual scheme of symbolism and accent. Nonetheless, Carl
Dreyer, who directed the picture, failed in his total operation.
His elements simply did not fuse. It is my opinion that this film
could have been radically improved by correction of certain
faults in the montage (which I will also assert for even *Les En-*

fants and *Panique*). The conceptual values would not have been disturbed; in fact, they would have been enhanced. *Rashomon* is perhaps closer to the perfect union than any film yet produced; it is captivatingly all of a piece, cinema and dialectic.

The subtle uncertainty which belies critical conviction on the subject of what constitutes form is one reason for my having avoided the "final" questions in favor of the less exalted matters of the craft. For I think we are in a safer position to raise the old dilemma of content determining form or form determining content *after* we have acknowledged that movie appreciation should begin with understanding the idiosyncratic contributions of the form, and not by passing judgment, derived from extrinsic standards, on the paraphrasable content. The motion picture in America will not greatly improve in any of the directions demanded of it by the civic intelligentsia until it is at least honored as a potentially independent art, in spite of its derivative composition. The synthesis which we call a *motion picture* is finally something quite different from the media which combine to supply its elements (still photography, the theater, the novel, music). And its peculiar autonomy cannot be respected until the nature of its dependence upon these elements has been clearly defined.

STUDY QUESTIONS

1. Young says that "the commercial movie perennially abdicates its own potential in favor of the lazier chronology of the legitimate theater." Can you think of a movie that does this? In what specific ways does it reveal that it "abdicates its own potential"?
2. From what Young says about the differences between a movie and a play, it would seem that a well-conceived play, with its emphasis on talk, could never be made into a good movie, which must emphasize visual motion. Yet some good critics have said that Lau-

rence Olivier's *Henry V* (1946) was a very good movie. Could this be true? How might you explain the fact that a master playwright like Shakespeare could have written a play that could, without distortion of its intentions, be turned into a good movie? If it is true that the movie *Henry V* is good, does this refute Young's argument?

3. Summarize the various ways in which, according to Young, the movie is a peculiarly modern form of expression. Can you think of any other ways?

4. Young says that "one could insist that the movie is the art of the novel reduced to absurdity." What does he mean? In what ways is the movie more like the novel than like the theater? In what ways does it differ from the novel?

5. Young says that "every inch of a movie *is* technique." What does he mean? He mentions the following creative techniques:
   1. Movement into a scene from the part to the whole,
   2. Dissolve through parallel compositional structures,
   3. The transitional caesura,
   4. The symbolic or oblique cut.

Can you think of some recent films in which these techniques were used creatively? Uncreatively? Explain your reason for each judgment.

6. Young says that the "judicious use of the closeup" is one of "the most valuable assets of movie composition." What does he mean? Can you think of any recent movie in which closeups are used well? Any movie in which they are used improperly? Explain.

7. Are there any similarities between what Young calls "the witness point" and what modern literary critics call "the point of view of a story"? Are there any differences?

8. How valuable do you think Young's concept of the witness point is? Why?

JAMES AGEE

James Agee (1909-1955) was both a film critic and a
film artist, as well as a Pulitzer Prize-winning novelist. For
many years, he wrote film criticism for *Time* magazine.
Later he went to Hollywood and wrote a number of distinguished film scripts, probably the best known being
the one for *The African Queen* (1952). He also wrote
and produced a short television film on Abraham Lincoln's
early years. In his later years, he was also film critic for
The Nation. His novel, *A Death in the Family*, was published posthumously in 1957 after his untimely death in
1955; it won the Pulitzer Prize in 1958. The following
article originally appeared in *Life* magazine in 1949. It is
a loving description of silent film comedy. One sees silent
film here through the eyes of a perceptive critic who is
possessed of both a nostalgic delight in his own past
experience and a novelist's gift of description.

Comedy's Greatest Era

In the language of screen comedians four of the main grades of
laugh are the titter, the yowl, the bellylaugh and the boffo. The
titter is just a titter. The yowl is a runaway titter. Anyone who
has ever had the pleasure knows all about a bellylaugh. The
boffo is the laugh that kills. An ideally good gag, perfectly constructed and played, would bring the victim up this ladder of
laughs by cruelly controlled degrees to the top rung, and would
then proceed to wobble, shake, wave and brandish the ladder until he groaned for mercy. Then, after the shortest possible time
out for recuperation, he would feel the first wicked tickling of
the comedian's whip once more and start up a new ladder.

The reader can get a fair enough idea of the current state of screen comedy by asking himself how long it has been since he has had that treatment. The best of comedies these days hand out plenty of titters and once in a while it is possible to achieve a yowl without overstraining. Even those who have never seen anything better must occasionally have the feeling, as they watch the current run or, rather, trickle of screen comedy, that they are having to make a little cause for laughter go an awfully long way. And anyone who has watched screen comedy over the past ten or fifteen years is bound to realize that it has quietly but steadily deteriorated. As for those happy atavists who remember silent comedy in its heyday and the bellylaughs and boffos that went with it, they have something close to an absolute standard by which to measure the deterioration.

When a modern comedian gets hit on the head, for example, the most he is apt to do is look sleepy. When a silent comedian got hit on the head he seldom let it go so flatly. He realized a broad license, and a ruthless discipline within that license. It was his business to be as funny as possible physically, without the help or hindrance of words. So he gave us a figure of speech, or rather of vision, for loss of consciousness. In other words he gave us a poem, a kind of poem, moreover, that everybody understands. The least he might do was to straighten up stiff as a plank and fall over backward with such skill that his whole length seemed to slap the floor at the same instant. Or he might make a cadenza of it—look vague, smile like an angel, roll up his eyes, lace his fingers, thrust his hands palms downward as far as they would go, hunch his shoulders, rise on tiptoe, prance ecstatically in narrowing circles until, with tallow knees, he sank down the vortex of his dizziness to the floor, and there signified nirvana by kicking his heels twice, like a swimming frog.

Startled by a cop, this same comedian might grab his hatbrim with both hands and yank it down over his ears, jump high in the air, come to earth in a split violent enough to telescope his spine, spring thence into a coattail-flattening sprint and dwindle at rocket speed to the size of a gnat along the grand, forlorn perspective of some lazy back boulevard.

Those are fine clichés from the language of silent comedy in its infancy. The man who could handle them properly combined several of the more difficult accomplishments of the acrobat, the dancer, the clown and the mime. Some very gifted comedians, unforgettably Ben Turpin, had an immense vocabulary of these clichés and were in part so lovable because they were deep conservative classicists and never tried to break away from them. The still more gifted men, of course, simplified and invented, finding out new and much deeper uses for the idiom. They learned to show emotion through it, and comic psychology, more eloquently than most language has ever managed to, and they discovered beauties of comic motion which are hopelessly beyond reach of words.

It is hard to find a theater these days where a comedy is playing; in the days of the silents it was equally hard to find a theater which was not showing one. The laughs today are pitifully few, far between, shallow, quiet and short. They almost never build, as they used to, into something combining the jabbering frequency of a machine gun with the delirious momentum of a roller coaster. Saddest of all, there are few comedians now below middle age and there are none who seem to learn much from picture to picture, or to try anything new.

To put it unkindly, the only thing wrong with screen comedy today is that it takes place on a screen which talks. Because it talks, the only comedians who ever mastered the screen cannot work, for they cannot combine their comic style with talk. Because there is a screen, talking comedians are trapped into a continual exhibition of their inadequacy as screen comedians on a surface as big as the side of a barn.

At the moment, as for many years past, the chances to see silent comedy are rare. There is a smattering of it on television—

too often treated as something quaintly archaic, to be laughed at, not with. Some two hundred comedies—long and short—can be rented for home projection. And a lucky minority has access to the comedies in the collection of New York's Museum of Modern Art, which is still incomplete but which is probably the best in the world. In the near future, however, something of this lost art will return to regular theaters. A thick straw in the wind is the big business now being done by a series of revivals of W. C. Fields's memorable movies, a kind of comedy more akin to the old silent variety than anything which is being made today. Mack Sennett now is preparing a sort of pot-pourri variety show called *Down Memory Lane* made up out of his old movies, featuring people like Fields and Bing Crosby when they were movie beginners, but including also interludes from silents. Harold Lloyd has re-released *Movie Crazy*, a talkie, and plans to revive four of his best silent comedies (*Grandma's Boy, Safety Last, Speedy* and *The Freshman*). Buster Keaton hopes to remake at feature length, with a minimum of dialogue, two of the funniest short comedies ever made, one about a porous homemade boat and one about a prefabricated house.

Awaiting these happy events we will discuss here what has gone wrong with screen comedy and what, if anything, can be done about it. But mainly we will try to suggest what it was like in its glory in the years from 1912 to 1930, as practiced by the employees of Mack Sennett, the father of American screen comedy, and by the four most eminent masters: Charlie Chaplin, Harold Lloyd, the late Harry Langdon and Buster Keaton.

Mack Sennett made two kinds of comedy: parody laced with slapstick, and plain slapstick. The parodies were the unceremonious burial of a century of hamming, including the new hamming in serious movies, and nobody who has missed Ben Turpin in *A Small Town Idol,* or kidding Erich von Stroheim in *Three Foolish Weeks* or as *The Shriek of Araby*, can imagine how rough parody can get and still remain subtle and roaringly funny. The plain slapstick, at its best, was even better: a profusion of hearty young women in disconcerting bathing suits, frisking around with a gaggle of insanely incompetent policemen and of equally certifiable male civilians sporting museum-piece mustaches. All these people zipped and caromed about the pristine world of the screen as jazzily as a convention of water bugs. Words can hardly suggest how energetically they collided and bounced apart, meeting in full gallop around the corner of a house; how hard and how often they fell on their backsides; or with what fantastically adroit clumsiness they got themselves fouled up in folding ladders, garden hoses, tethered animals and each other's headlong cross-purposes. The gestures were ferociously emphatic; not a line or motion of the body was wasted or inarticulate. The reader may remember how splendidly upright wandlike old Ben Turpin could stand for a Renunciation Scene, with his lampshade mustache twittering and his sparrowy chest stuck out and his head flung back like Paderewski assaulting a climax and the long babyish back hair trying to look lionlike, while his Adam's apple, an orange in a Christmas stocking, pumped with noble emotion. Or huge Mack Swain, who looked like a hairy mushroom, rolling his eyes in a manner patented by French Romantics and gasping in some dubious ecstasy. Or Louise Fazenda, the perennial farmer's daughter and the perfect low-comedy housemaid, primping her spit curl; and how her hair tightened a good-looking face into the incarnation of rampant gullibility. Or snouty James Finlayson, gleefully foreclosing a mortgage, with his look of eternally tasting a spoiled pickle. Or Chester Conklin, a myopic and inebriated little walrus stumbling around in outside pants. Or Fatty Arbuckle, with his cold eye and his loose, serene smile, his silky manipulation of his bulk and his satanic marksmanship with pies (he was ambidextrous and could simultaneously blind two people in opposite directions).

The intimate tastes and secret hopes of these poor ineligible dunces were ruthlessly exposed whenever a hot stove, an electric fan or a bulldog took a dislike to their outer garments: agonizingly elaborate drawers, worked up on some lonely evening out of some Godforsaken lace curtain; or men's underpants with big round black spots on them. The Sennett sets—delirious wallpaper, megalomaniacally scrolled iron beds, Grand Rapids *in extremis*—outdid even the underwear. It was their business, after all, to kid the squalid braggadocio which infested the domestic interiors of the period, and that was almost beyond parody. These comedies told their stories to the unaided eye, and by every means possible they screamed to it. That is one reason for the India-ink silhouettes of the cops, and for convicts and prison bars and their shadows in hard sunlight, and for barefooted husbands, in tigerish pajamas, reacting like dervishes to stepped-on tacks.

The early silent comedians never strove for or consciously thought of anything which could be called artistic "form," but they achieved it. For Sennett's rival, Hal Roach, Leo McCarey once devoted almost the whole of a Laurel and Hardy two-reeler to pie-throwing. The first pies were thrown thoughtfully, almost philosophically. Then innocent bystanders began to get caught into the vortex. At full pitch it was Armageddon. But everything was calculated so nicely that until late in the picture, when havoc took over, every pie made its special kind of point and piled on its special kind of laugh.

Sennett's comedies were just a shade faster and fizzier than life. According to legend (and according to Sennett) he discovered the sped tempo proper to screen comedy when a green cameraman, trying to save money, cranked too slow.* Realizing the tremendous drumlike power of mere motion to exhilarate, he gave inanimate objects a mischievous life of their own, broke

* Silent comedy was shot at 12 to 16 frames per second and was speeded up by being shown at 16 frames per second, the usual rate of theater projectors at that time. Theater projectors today run at 24, which makes modern film taken at the same speed seem smooth and natural. But it makes silent movies fast and jerky.

every law of nature the tricked camera would serve him for and made the screen dance like a witches' Sabbath. The thing one is surest of all to remember is how toward the end of nearly every Sennett comedy, a chase (usually called the "rally") built up such a majestic trajectory of pure anarchic motion that bathing girls, cops, comics, dogs, cats, babies, automobiles, locomotives, innocent bystanders, sometimes what seemed like a whole city, an entire civilization, were hauled along head over heels in the wake of that energy like dry leaves following an express train.

"Nice" people, who shunned all movies in the early days, condemned the Sennett comedies as vulgar and naive. But millions of less pretentious people loved their sincerity and sweetness, their wild-animal innocence and glorious vitality. They could not put these feelings into words, but they flocked to the silents. The reader who gets back deep enough into that world will probably even remember the theater: the barefaced honky-tonk and the waltzes by Waldteufel, slammed out on a mechanical piano; the searing redolence of peanuts and demirep perfumery, tobacco and feet and sweat; the laughter of unrespectable people having a hell of a fine time, laughter as violent and steady and deafening as standing under a waterfall.

Sennett wheedled his first financing out of a couple of ex-bookies to whom he was already in debt. He took his comics out of music halls, burlesque, vaudeville, circuses and limbo, and through them he tapped in on that great pipeline of horsing and miming which runs back unbroken through the fairs of the Middle Ages at least to ancient Greece. He added all that he himself had learned about the large and spurious gesture, the late decadence of the Grand Manner, as a stage-struck boy in East Berlin, Connecticut and as a frustrated opera singer and actor. The only thing he claims to have invented is the pie in the face, and he insists, "Anyone who tells you he has discovered something new is a fool or a liar or both."

The silent-comedy studio was about the best training school

the movies had ever known, and the Sennett studio was about as free and easy and as fecund of talent as they came. All the major comedians we will mention worked there, at least briefly. So did some of the major stars of the twenties and since—notably Gloria Swanson, Phyllis Haver, Wallace Beery, Marie Dressler and Carole Lombard. Directors Frank Capra, Leo McCarey and George Stevens also got their start in silent comedy; much that remains most flexible, spontaneous and visually alive in sound movies can be traced, through them and others, to this silent apprenticeship. Everybody did pretty much as he pleased on the Sennett lot, and everybody's ideas were welcome. Sennett posted no rules, and the only thing he strictly forbade was liquor. A Sennett story conference was a most informal affair. During the early years, at least, only the most important scenario might be jotted on the back of an envelope. Mainly Sennett's men thrashed out a few primary ideas and carried them in their heads, sure the better stuff would turn up while they were shooting, in the heat of physical action. This put quite a load on the prop man; he had to have the most improbable apparatus on hand—bombs, trick telephones, what not—to implement whatever idea might suddenly turn up. All kinds of things did—and were recklessly used. Once a low-comedy auto got out of control and killed the cameraman, but he was not visible in the shot, which was thrilling and undamaged; the audience never knew the difference.

Sennett used to hire a "wild man" to sit in on his gag conferences, whose whole job was to think up "wildies." Usually he was an all but brainless, speechless man, scarcely able to communicate his idea; but he had a totally uninhibited imagination. He might say nothing for an hour; then he'd mutter "You take . . ." and all the relatively rational others would shut up and wait. "You take this cloud . . ." he would get out, sketching vague shapes in the air. Often he could get no further; but thanks to some kind of thought-transference, saner men would take this cloud and make something of it. The wild man seems in fact to have functioned as the group's subconscious mind, the source of all creative energy. His ideas were so weird and amorphous that Sennett can no longer remember a one of them, or even how it turned out after rational processing. But a fair equivalent might be one of the best comic sequences in a Laurel and Hardy picture. It is simple enough—simple and real, in fact, as a nightmare. Laurel and Hardy are trying to move a piano across a narrow suspension bridge. The bridge is slung over a sickening chasm, between a couple of Alps. Midway they meet a gorilla.

Had he done nothing else, Sennett would be remembered for giving a start to three of the four comedians who now began to apply their sharp individual talents to this newborn language. The one whom he did not train (he was on the lot briefly but Sennett barely remembers seeing him around) wore glasses, smiled a great deal and looked like the sort of eager young man who might have quit divinity school to hustle brushes. That was Harold Lloyd. The others were grotesque and poetic in their screen characters in degrees which appear to be impossible when the magic of silence is broken. One, who never smiled, carried a face as still and sad as a daguerreotype through some of the most preposterously ingenious and visually satisfying physical comedy ever invented. That was Buster Keaton. One looked like an elderly baby and, at times, a baby dope fiend; he could do more with less than any other comedian. That was Harry Langdon. One looked like Charlie Chaplin, and he was the first man to give the silent language a soul.

When Charlie Chaplin started to work for Sennett he had chiefly to reckon with Ford Sterling, the reigning comedian. Their first picture together amounted to a duel before the assembled professionals. Sterling, by no means untalented, was a big man with a florid Teutonic style which, under this special pressure, he turned on full blast. Chaplin defeated him within a few minutes with a wink of the mustache, a hitch of the trousers, a quirk of the little finger.

With *Tillie's Punctured Romance*, in 1914, he became a major star. Soon after, he left Sennett when Sennett refused to start a landslide among the other comedians by meeting the raise Chaplin demanded. Sennett is understandably wry about it in retrospect, but he still says, "I was right at the time." Of Chaplin he says simply, "Oh well, he's just the greatest artist that ever lived." None of Chaplin's former rivals rate him much lower than that; they speak of him no more jealously than they might of God. We will try here only to suggest the essence of his supremacy. Of all comedians he worked most deeply and most shrewdly within a realization of what a human being is, and is up against. The Tramp is as centrally representative of humanity, as many-sided and as mysterious, as Hamlet, and it seems unlikely that any dancer or actor can ever have excelled him in eloquence, variety or poignancy of motion. As for pure motion, even if he had never gone on to make his magnificent feature-length comedies, Chaplin would have made his period in movies a great one single-handed even if he had made nothing except *The Cure*, or *One A.M.* In the latter, barring one immobile taxi driver, Chaplin plays alone, as a drunk trying to get upstairs and into bed. It is a sort of inspired elaboration on a soft-shoe dance, involving an angry stuffed wildcat, small rugs on slippery floors, a Lazy Susan table, exquisite footwork on a flight of stairs, a contretemps with a huge, ferocious pendulum and the funniest and most perverse Murphy bed in movie history—and, always made physically lucid, the delicately weird mental processes of a man ethereally sozzled.

Before Chaplin came to pictures people were content with a couple of gags per comedy; he got some kind of laugh every second. The minute he began to work he set standards—and continually forced them higher. Anyone who saw Chaplin eating a boiled shoe like brook trout in *The Gold Rush*, or embarrassed by a swallowed whistle in *City Lights*, has seen perfection. Most of the time, however, Chaplin got his laughter less from the gags, or from milking them in any ordinary sense, than through his genius for what may be called *inflection*—the perfect, changeful shading of his physical and emotional attitudes toward the gag. Funny as his bout with the Murphy bed is, the glances of awe, expostulation and helpless, almost whimpering desire for vengeance which he darts at this infernal machine are even better.

A painful and frequent error among tyros is breaking the comic line with a too-big laugh, then a letdown; or with a laugh which is out of key or irrelevant. The masters could ornament the main line beautifully; they never addled it. In *A Night Out* Chaplin, passed out, is hauled along the sidewalk by the scruff of his coat by staggering Ben Turpin. His toes trail; he is as supine as a sled. Turpin himself is so drunk he can hardly drag him. Chaplin comes quietly to, realizes how well he is being served by his struggling pal, and with a royally delicate gesture plucks and savors a flower.

The finest pantomime, the deepest emotion, the richest and most poignant poetry were in Chaplin's work. He could probably pantomime Bryce's *The American Commonwealth* without ever blurring a syllable and make it paralyzingly funny into the bargain. At the end of *City Lights* the blind girl who has regained her sight, thanks to the Tramp, sees him for the first time. She has imagined and anticipated him as princely, to say the least; and it has never seriously occurred to him that he is inadequate. She recognizes who he must be by his shy, confident, shining joy as he comes silently toward her. And he recognizes himself, for the first time, through the terrible changes in her face. The camera just exchanges a few quiet close-ups of the emotions which shift and intensify in each face. It is enough to shrivel the heart to see, and it is the greatest piece of acting and the highest moment in movies.

Harold Lloyd worked only a little while with Sennett. During most of his career he acted for another major comedy producer, Hal Roach. He tried at first to offset Chaplin's influence and establish his own individuality by playing Chaplin's exact opposite, a character named Lonesome Luke who wore clothes much too small for him and whose gestures were likewise as un-Chaplinesque as possible. But he soon realized that an opposite in itself was a kind of slavishness. He discovered his own comic identity when he saw a movie about a fighting parson: a hero who wore glasses. He began to think about those glasses day and night. He decided on horn rims because they were youthful, ultravisible on the screen and on the verge of becoming fashionable (he was to make them so). Around these large lensless horn rims he began to develop a new character, nothing grotesque or eccentric, but a fresh, believable young man who could fit into a wide variety of stories.

Lloyd depended more on story and situation than any of the other major comedians (he kept the best stable of gagmen in Hollywood, at one time hiring six); but unlike most "story" comedians he was also a very funny man from inside. He had, as he has written, "an unusually large comic vocabulary." More particularly he had an expertly expressive body and even more expressive teeth, and out of his thesaurus of smiles he could at a moment's notice blend prissiness, breeziness and asininity, and still remain tremendously likable. His movies were more extroverted and closer to ordinary life than any others of the best comedies: the vicissitudes of a New York taxi driver; the unaccepted college boy who, by desperate courage and inspired ineptitude, wins the Big Game. He was especially good at putting a very timid, spoiled or brassy young fellow through devastating embarrassments. He went through one of his most uproarious Gethsemanes as a shy country youth courting the nicest girl in town in *Grandma's Boy*. He arrived dressed "strictly up to date for the Spring of 1862," as a subtitle observed, and found that the ancient colored butler wore a similar flowered waistcoat and moldering cutaway. He got one wandering, nervous forefinger dreadfully stuck in a fancy little vase. The girl began cheerfully to try to identify that queer smell which dilated from him; Grandpa's best suit was rife with mothballs. A tenacious litter of kittens feasted off the goose grease on his home-shined shoes.

Lloyd was even better at the comedy of thrills. In *Safety Last,* as a rank amateur, he is forced to substitute for a human fly and to climb a medium-sized skyscraper. Dozens of awful things happen to him. He gets fouled up in a tennis set. Popcorn falls on him from a window above, and the local pigeons treat him like a cross between a lunch wagon and St. Francis of Assisi. A mouse runs up his britches-leg, and the crowd below salutes his desperate dance on the window ledge with wild applause of the daredevil. A good deal of this full-length picture hangs thus by its eyelashes along the face of a building. Each new floor is like a new stanza in a poem; and the higher and more horrifying it gets, the funnier it gets.

In this movie Lloyd demonstrates beautifully his ability to do more than merely milk a gag, but to top it. (In an old, simple example of topping, an incredible number of tall men get, one by one, out of a small closed auto. After as many have clambered out as the joke will bear, one more steps out: a midget. That tops the gag. Then the auto collapses. That tops the topper.) In *Safety Last* Lloyd is driven out to the dirty end of a flagpole by a furious dog; the pole breaks and he falls, just managing to grab the minute hand of a huge clock. His weight promptly pulls the hand down from IX to VI. That would be more than enough for any ordinary comedian, but there is further logic in the situation. Now, hideously, the whole clockface pulls loose and slants from its trembling springs above the street. Getting out of difficulty with the clock, he makes still further use of the instrument by getting one foot caught in one of these obstinate springs.

A proper delaying of the ultrapredictable can of course be just as funny as a properly timed explosion of the unexpected. As Lloyd approaches the end of his horrible hegira up the side of the building in *Safety Last*, it becomes clear to the audience, but not to him, that if he raises his head another couple of inches he is going to get murderously conked by one of the four arms of a revolving wind gauge. He delays the evil moment almost interminably, with one distraction and another, and every delay is a suspense-tightening laugh; he also gets his foot nicely entangled in a rope, so that when he does get hit, the payoff of one gag sends him careening head downward through the abyss into another. Lloyd was outstanding even among the master craftsmen at setting up a gag clearly, culminating and getting out of it deftly, and linking it smoothly to the next. Harsh experience also taught him a deep and fundamental rule: never try to get "above" the audience.

Lloyd tried it in *The Freshman*. He was to wear an unfinished, basted-together tuxedo to a college party, and it would gradually fall apart as he danced. Lloyd decided to skip the pants, a low-comedy cliché, and lose just the coat. His gagmen warned him. A preview proved how right they were. Lloyd had to reshoot the whole expensive sequence, build it around defective pants and climax it with the inevitable. It was one of the funniest things he ever did.

When Lloyd was still a very young man he lost about half his right hand (and nearly lost his sight) when a comedy bomb exploded prematurely. But in spite of his artificially built-out hand he continued to do his own dirty work, like all of the best comedians. The side of the building he climbed in *Safety Last* did not overhang the street, as it appears to. But the nearest landing place was a roof three floors below him, as he approached the top, and he did everything, of course, the hard way, that is, the comic way, keeping his bottom stuck well out, his shoulders hunched, his hands and feet skidding over perdition.

If great comedy must involve something beyond laughter, Lloyd was not a great comedian. If plain laughter is any criterion

—and it is a healthy counterbalance to the other—few people have equaled him, and nobody has ever beaten him.

Chaplin and Keaton and Lloyd were all more like each other, in one important way, than Harry Langdon was like any of them. Whatever else the others might be doing, they all used more or less elaborate physical comedy; Langdon showed how little of that one might use and still be a great silent-screen comedian. In his screen character he symbolized something as deeply and centrally human, though by no means as rangily so, as the Tramp. There was, of course, an immense difference in inventiveness and range of virtuosity. It seemed as if Chaplin could do literally anything, on any instrument in the orchestra. Langdon had one queerly toned, unique little reed. But out of it he could get incredible melodies.

Like Chaplin, Langdon wore a coat which buttoned on his wishbone and swung out wide below, but the effect was very different: he seemed like an outsized baby who had begun to outgrow his clothes. The crown of his hat was rounded and the brim was turned up all around, like a little boy's hat, and he looked as if he wore diapers under his pants. His walk was that of a child which has just gotten sure on its feet, and his body and hands fitted that age. His face was kept pale to show off, with the simplicity of a nursery-school drawing, the bright, ignorant, gentle eyes and the little twirling mouth. He had big moon cheeks, with dimples, and a Napoleonic forelock of mousy hair; the round, docile head seemed large in ratio to the cream-puff body. Twitchings of his face were signals of tiny discomforts too slowly registered by a tinier brain; quick, squirty little smiles showed his almost prehuman pleasures, his incurably premature truthfulness. He was a virtuoso of hesitations and of delicately indecisive motions, and he was particularly fine in a high wind, rounding a corner with a kind of skittering toddle, both hands nursing his hatbrim.

He was as remarkable a master as Chaplin of subtle emotional and mental process and operated much more at leisure. He once got a good three hundred feet of continuously bigger laughs out of rubbing his chest, in a crowded vehicle, with Limburger cheese, under the misapprehension that it was a cold salve. In another long scene, watching a brazen showgirl change her clothes, he sat motionless, back to the camera, and registered the whole lexicon of lost innocence, shock, disapproval and disgust, with the back of his neck. His scenes with women were nearly always something special. Once a lady spy did everything in her power (under the Hays Office) to seduce him. Harry was polite, willing, even flirtatious in his little way. The only trouble was that he couldn't imagine what in the world she was leering and pawing at him for, and that he was terribly ticklish. The Mata Hari wound up foaming at the mouth.

There was also a sinister flicker of depravity about the Langdon character, all the more disturbing because babies are premoral. He had an instinct for bringing his actual adulthood and figurative babyishness into frictions as crawley as a fingernail on a slate blackboard, and he wandered into areas of strangeness which were beyond the other comedians. In a nightmare in one movie he was forced to fight a large, muscular young man; the girl Harry loved was the prize. The young man was a good boxer; Harry could scarcely lift his gloves. The contest took place in a fiercely lighted prize ring, in a prodigious pitch-dark arena. The only spectator was the girl, and she was rooting against Harry. As the fight went on, her eyes glittered ever more brightly with blood lust and, with glittering teeth, she tore her big straw hat to shreds.

Langdon came to Sennett from a vaudeville act in which he had fought a losing battle with a recalcitrant automobile. The minute Frank Capra saw him he begged Sennett to let him work with him. Langdon was almost as childlike as the character he played. He had only a vague idea of his story or even of each scene as he played it; each time he went before the camera Capra would brief him on the general situation and then, as this finest of intuitive improvisers once tried to explain his work, "I'd go into my routine." The whole tragedy of the coming of dialogue, as far as these comedians were concerned—and one reason for the increasing rigidity of comedy ever since—can be epitomized in the mere thought of Harry Langdon confronted with a script.

Langdon's magic was in his innocence, and Capra took beautiful care not to meddle with it. The key to the proper use of Langdon, Capra always knew, was "the principle of the brick." "If there was a rule for writing Langdon material," he explains, "it was this: his only ally was God. Langdon might be saved by the brick falling on the cop, but it was *verboten* that he in any way motivate the brick's fall." Langdon became quickly and fantastically popular with three pictures, *Tramp, Tramp, Tramp, The Strong Man* and *Long Pants;* from then on he went downhill even faster. "The trouble was," Capra says, "that high-brow critics came around to explain his art to him. Also he developed an interest in dames. It was a pretty high life for such a little fellow." Langdon made two more pictures with high-brow writers, one of which (*Three's A Crowd*) had some wonderful passages in it, including the prize-ring nightmare; then First National canceled his contract. He was reduced to mediocre roles and two-reelers which were more rehashes of his old gags; this time around they no longer seemed funny. "He never did really understand what hit him," says Capra. "He died broke [in 1944]. And he died of a broken heart. He was the most tragic figure I ever came across in show business."

Buster Keaton started work at the age of three and one-half with his parents in one of the roughest acts in vaudeville ("The Three Keatons"); Harry Houdini gave the child the name Buster in admiration for a fall he took down a flight of stairs. In his first movies Keaton teamed with Fatty Arbuckle under Sennett. He went on to become one of Metro's biggest stars and earners; a Keaton feature cost about $200,000 to make and reliably grossed $2,000,000. Very early in his movie career friends asked him why he never smiled on the screen. He didn't realize he didn't. He had got the dead-pan habit in variety; on the screen he had merely been so hard at work it had never occurred to him there was anything to smile about. Now he tried it just once and never again. He was by his whole style and nature so much the most deeply "silent" of the silent comedians that even a smile was as deafeningly out of key as a yell. In a way his pictures are like a transcendent juggling act in which it seems that the whole universe is in exquisite flying motion and the one point of repose is the juggler's effortless, uninterested face.

Keaton's face ranked almost with Lincoln's as an early American archetype; it was haunting, handsome, almost beautiful, yet it was irreducibly funny; he improved matters by topping it off with a deadly horizontal hat, as flat and thin as a phonograph record. One can never forget Keaton wearing it, standing erect at the prow as his little boat is being launched. The boat goes grandly down the skids and, just as grandly, straight on to the bottom. Keaton never budges. The last you see of him, the water lifts the hat off the stoic head and it floats away.

No other comedian could do as much with the dead pan. He used this great, sad, motionless face to suggest various related things: a one-track mind near the track's end of pure insanity; mulish imperturbability under the wildest of circumstances; how dead a human being can get and still be alive; an awe-inspiring sort of patience and power to endure, proper to granite but uncanny in flesh and blood. Everything that he was and did bore out this rigid face and played laughs against it. When he moved his eyes, it was like seeing them move in a statue. His short-legged body was all sudden, machinelike angles, governed by a daft aplomb. When he swept a semaphorelike arm to point, you could almost hear the electrical impulse in the signal block. When he ran from a cop, his transitions from accelerating walk to easy jogtrot to brisk canter to headlong gallop to flogged-piston sprint—always floating, above this frenzy, the untroubled, untouchable face—were as distinct and as soberly in order as an automatic gearshift.

Keaton was a wonderfully resourceful inventor of mechanistic gags (he still spends much of his time fooling with Erector sets); as he ran afoul of locomotives, steamships, prefabricated and over-electrified houses, he put himself through some of the hardest and cleverest punishment ever designed for laughs. In *Sherlock Jr.,* boiling along on the handlebars of a motorcycle quite unaware that he has lost his driver, Keaton whips through city traffic, breaks up a tug-of-war, gets a shovelful of dirt in the face from each of a long line of Rockette-timed ditch-diggers, approaches a log at high speed which is hinged open by dynamite precisely soon enough to let him through and, hitting an obstruction, leaves the handlebars like an arrow leaving a bow, whams through the window of a shack in which the heroine is about to be violated, and hits the heavy feet-first, knocking him through the opposite wall. The whole sequence is as clean in motion as the trajectory of a bullet.

Much of the charm and edge of Keaton's comedy, however, lay in the subtle leverages of expression he could work against his nominal dead pan. Trapped in the side-wheel of a ferryboat, saving himself from drowning only by walking, then desperately running, inside the accelerating wheel like a squirrel in a cage, his only real concern was, obviously, to keep his hat on. Confronted by Love, he was not as dead-pan as he was cracked up to be, either; there was an odd, abrupt motion of his head which suggested a horse nipping after a sugar lump.

Keaton worked strictly for laughs, but his work came from so far inside a curious and original spirit that he achieved a great deal besides, especially in his feature-length comedies. (For plain hard laughter his nineteen short comedies—the negatives of which have been lost—were even better.) He was the only major comedian who kept sentiment almost entirely out of his work, and he brought pure physical comedy to its greatest heights. Beneath his lack of emotion he was also uninsistently sardonic; deep below that, giving a disturbing tension and grandeur to the foolishness, for those who sensed it, there was in his comedy a freezing whisper not of pathos but of melancholia. With the humor, the craftsmanship and the action there was often, besides, a fine, still and sometimes dreamlike beauty. Much of his Civil War picture *The General* is within hailing distance of Mathew Brady. And there is a ghostly, unforgettable moment in *The Navigator* when, on a deserted, softly rolling ship, all the pale doors along a deck swing open as one behind Keaton and, as one, slam shut, in a hair-raising illusion of noise.

Perhaps because "dry" comedy is so much more rare and odd than "dry" wit, there are people who never much cared for Keaton. Those who do cannot care mildly.

As soon as the screen began to talk, silent comedy was pretty well finished. The hardy and prolific Mack Sennett made the transfer; he was the first man to put Bing Crosby and W. C. Fields on the screen. But he was essentially a silent-picture man, and by the time the Academy awarded him a special Oscar for his "lasting contribution to the comedy technique of the screen" (in 1938), he was no longer active. As for the comedians we have spoken of in particular, they were as badly off as fine dancers suddenly required to appear in plays.

Harold Lloyd, whose work was most nearly realistic, naturally coped least unhappily with the added realism of speech; he made several talking comedies. But good as the best were, they were not so good as his silent work, and by the late thirties he quit acting. A few years ago he returned to play the lead (and play it beautifully) in Preston Sturges's *The Sin of Harold Diddlebock*, but this exceptional picture—which opened, brilliantly, with the closing reel of Lloyd's *The Freshman*—has not yet been generally released.

Like Chaplin, Lloyd was careful of his money; he is still

rich and active. Last June, in the presence of President Truman, he became Imperial Potentate of the A.A.O.N.M.S. (Shriners). Harry Langdon, as we have said, was a broken man when sound came in.

Up to the middle thirties Buster Keaton made several feature-length pictures (with such players as Jimmy Durante, Wallace Beery and Robert Montgomery); he also made a couple of dozen talking shorts. Now and again he managed to get loose into motion, without having to talk, and for a moment or so the screen would start singing again. But his dark, dead voice, though it was in keeping with the visual character, tore his intensely silent style to bits and destroyed the illusion within which he worked. He gallantly and correctly refuses to regard himself as "retired." Besides occasional bits, spots and minor roles in Hollywood pictures, he has worked on summer stages, made talking comedies in France and Mexico and clowned in a French circus. This summer he has played the straw hats in *Three Men on a Horse.* He is planning a television program. He also has a working agreement with Metro. One of his jobs there is to construct comedy sequences for Red Skelton.

The only man who really survived the flood was Chaplin, the only one who was rich, proud and popular enough to afford to stay silent. He brought out two of his greatest nontalking comedies, *City Lights* and *Modern Times,* in the middle of an avalanche of talk, spoke gibberish and, in the closing moments, plain English in *The Great Dictator,* and at last made an all-talking picture, *Monsieur Verdoux,* creating for that purpose an entirely new character who might properly talk a blue streak. *Verdoux* is the greatest of talking comedies though so cold and savage that it had to find its public in grimly experienced Europe.

Good comedy, and some that was better than good, outlived silence, but there has been less and less of it. The talkies brought one great comedian, the late, majestically lethargic W. C. Fields, who could not possibly have worked as well in silence; he was

the toughest and the most warmly human of all screen comedians, and *It's A Gift* and *The Bank Dick*, fiendishly funny and in-
cisive white-collar comedies, rank high among the best comedies
(and best movies) ever made. Laurel and Hardy, the only comedians who managed to preserve much of the large, low style
of silence and who began to explore the comedy of sound, have
made nothing since 1945. Walt Disney, at his best an inspired
comic inventor and teller of fairy stories, lost his stride during
the war and has since regained it only at moments. Preston
Sturges has made brilliant, satirical comedies, but his pictures
are smart, nervous comedy-dramas merely italicized with slapstick. The Marx Brothers were side-splitters but they made their
best comedies years ago. Jimmy Durante is mainly a nightclub
genius; Abbot and Costello are semiskilled laborers, at best; Bob
Hope is a good radio comedian with a pleasing presence, but
not much more, on the screen.

There is no hope that screen comedy will get much better
than it is without new, gifted young comedians who really belong in movies, and without freedom for their experiments. For
everyone who may appear we have one last, invidious comparison to offer as a guidepost.

One of the most popular recent comedies is Bob Hope's *The
Paleface*. We take no pleasure in blackening *The Paleface;* we
single it out, rather, because it is as good as we've got. Anything
that is said of it here could be said, with interest, of other comedies of our time. Most of the laughs in *The Paleface* are verbal.
Bob Hope is very adroit with his lines and now and then, when
the words don't get in the way, he makes a good beginning as
a visual comedian. But only the beginning, never the middle or
the end. He is funny, for instance, reacting to a shot of violent
whisky. But he does not know how to get still funnier (*i.e.,* how
to build and milk) or how to be funniest last (*i.e.,* how to top or
cap his gag). The camera has to fade out on the same old face
he started with.

One sequence is promisingly set up for visual comedy. In it, Hope and a lethal local boy stalk each other all over a cow town through streets which have been emptied in fear of their duel. The gag here is that through accident and stupidity they keep just failing to find each other. Some of it is quite funny. But the fun slackens between laughs like a weak clothesline, and by all the logic of humor (which is ruthlessly logical) the biggest laugh should come at the moment, and through the way, they finally spot each other. The sequence is so weakly thought out that at that crucial moment the camera can't afford to watch them; it switches to Jane Russell.

Now we turn to a masterpiece. In *The Navigator* Buster Keaton works with practically the same gag as Hope's duel. Adrift on a ship which he believes is otherwise empty, he drops a lighted cigarette. A girl finds it. She calls out and he hears her; each then tries to find the other. First each walks purposefully down the long, vacant starboard deck, the girl, then Keaton, turning the corner just in time not to see each other. Next time around each of them is trotting briskly, very much in earnest; going at the same pace, they miss each other just the same. Next time around each of them is going like a bat out of hell. Again they miss. Then the camera withdraws to a point of vantage at the stern, leans its chin in its hand and just watches the whole intricate superstructure of the ship as the protagonists stroll, steal and scuttle from level to level, up, down and sidewise, always managing to miss each other by hair's-breadths, in an enchantingly neat and elaborate piece of timing. There are no subsidiary gags to get laughs in this sequence and there is little loud laughter; merely a quiet and steadily increasing kind of delight. When Keaton has got all he can out of this fine modification of the movie chase he invents a fine device to bring the two together: the girl, thoroughly winded, sits down for a breather, indoors, on a plank which workmen have left across sawhorses. Keaton pauses on an upper deck, equally winded and puzzled.

What follows happens in a couple of seconds at most: air suction whips his silk topper backward down a ventilator; grabbing frantically for it, he backs against the lip of the ventilator, jacknifes and falls in backward. Instantly the camera cuts back to the girl. A topper falls through the ceiling and lands tidily, right side up, on the plank beside her. Before she can look more than startled, its owner follows, head between his knees, crushes the topper, breaks the plank with the point of his spine and proceeds to the floor. The breaking of the plank smacks Boy and Girl together.

It is only fair to remember that the silent comedians would have as hard a time playing a talking scene as Hope has playing his visual ones, and that writing and directing are as accountable for the failure as Hope himself. But not even the humblest journeymen of the silent years would have let themselves off so easily. Like the masters, they knew, and sweated to obey, the laws of their craft.

STUDY QUESTIONS

1. Agee is discussing comedy that is essentially visual in its appeal. How would you compare this kind of comedy with the large group of recent American comedies which center around extramarital affairs? In what respects are these recent comedies more verbal than visual? Do they have marks of visual comedy? Can you cite specific examples?
2. Most modern film comedies differ not only in technique but also in subject matter from the silent comedies. What seem to be the dominant subjects for comedy in our time? How do these subjects seem to require different treatment from that which Charlie Chaplin, Harold Lloyd, and other silent masters employed?
3. Probably the two most successful practitioners of film comedy today are Sir Alec Guinness and Peter Sellers. To what extent are their films more intellectual than some of the silent comic films? To

what extent do both men imitate the tradition of comedy begun by Chaplin? Both men employ the technique of comic understatement to good advantage. Are the situations in which they find themselves equally understated? How does this relationship between situation and acting technique compare with the silent comedies?

4. Agee says that modern films have few belly laughs. Does the absence of belly laughs necessarily make modern film comedy inferior to silent comedy? Why?

5. The tradition of silent film comedy has most obviously been carried on in television—particularly by Lucille Ball and Red Skelton. Skelton's comedy is the more obviously visual of the two, especially in the silent spot on his programs. Why is he so much more successful as a visual comedian than as a verbal comedian? Does he actually treat the two kinds of comedy as if they were different from each other? In what sense is Lucille Ball a silent comedian? What is the function of the dialogue on her shows?

6. In this essay, Agee wishes to share with his readers the enjoyment of an experience which is now mostly inaccessible to them. He uses essentially a novelist's approach. What is this approach? Why is it particularly appropriate to the general subject of silent film? Agee's article might properly be called an "appreciation." Compare it with Gilbert Highet's "History on the Silver Screen" (p. 185). What is the difference between Agee's general purpose and Highet's? Why is Highet's approach generally classified as criticism? Do the two approaches necessarily conflict with each other?

P. N. FURBANK

P. N. Furbank (1920-   ) was born in Surrey, England,
and educated at Emmanuel College, Cambridge, where he
was a fellow and director of studies in English from 1947
to 1953. He now works with Macmillan and Company,
London. Besides regular reviews for *The Listener* and
many various articles, he has published *Samuel Butler:
1835-1902* (1948) and *Italo Svevo: The Man and the
Writer* (1966). Although this analysis of best-sellers deals
primarily with British fiction, the thoughtful observer of
American popular fiction will readily see that the qualities
Furbank finds most popular with the British public are
equally popular with the American public. The books' titles
may be different, but the books' characteristics are completely familiar. Furbank's analysis applies to more than the
best-sellers; it also applies to many of the daily programs on
television, and is reflected, to some extent, in the human-
interest stories prevalent in the popular press.

The Twentieth-Century
Best-Seller

The best-seller (and here we shall only be dealing with best-
selling fiction) forms a large but very recognizable category
somewhere between literature proper, in the sense in which the
word has been used elsewhere in these volumes, and more pulp
fiction. *Uncle Tom's Cabin* is a best-seller in our sense, perhaps
the most celebrated there has been. It is also a 'steady-seller'. The
best-seller, according to S. H. Steinberg, is

a book which, immediately on, or shortly after, its first publication, far
outruns the demand of what at the time are considered good or even

large sales; which thereafter sometimes lapses into obscurity, making people wonder why it ever came to the front; but which sometimes graduates into the rank of 'steady-sellers'.

(*Five Hundred Years of Printing*, 1955)

The strongest objection to the 'mass' organization and dissemination of culture is that it may foist off on the public something that it would never have positively wanted. Its menace is the menace of the trivial, the thing which is too dead and empty to have intrinsic interest, but yet is thrust down people's throats until they become accustomed to triviality and expect it. This cannot fairly be said of the best-seller, and even less of the steady-seller, for they have a life of their own and express strong needs and deeply felt beliefs.

What, then, makes a best-seller? There is first of all its intrinsic appeal; and later in this chapter I try to analyse one or two favourite themes and patterns in best-selling writing in the hope of throwing light on this. Otherwise, a number of more or less accessory factors come in: the effect of advertisement, of reviewing, of the novel's being made into a film or television play or becoming a paper-back, of its success with the circulating libraries or its adoption by a book-club, of some exceptionally deliberate and successful calculation on the author's part, or finally of pure luck—the novel having some unexpected topical appeal or becoming notorious for some accidental reason.

Publishers' advertising departments can obviously do a great deal towards creating a best-seller, both by buying space in newspapers and journals and persuading booksellers to exhibit publicity material (a book is sure of success if certain important booksellers agree to devote a whole show-window to it), and by less direct means, such as placing articles in gossip columns or the trade press, or arranging television interviews, literary luncheons, and cocktail parties.

It is less easy to generalize about the effect of reviewing. The lowbrow best-selling author is frequently not reviewed at all. And

the famous and record-breaking best-sellers have not often owed
their popularity to reviewers (though the success of Margaret
Kennedy's *The Constant Nymph,* which sold slowly for the first
six weeks, seems to have been precipitated by a review by Au-
gustine Birrell). On the other hand, reviewers certainly help to
perpetuate the reputation of best-selling novelists. It is an important fact of publishing economics that a novelist tends to get
fixed at a certain level of sales, so that if he happens to leap up
into a higher category, he is likely to stay there. There are obvious reasons for this. Fiction-readers and the libraries that cater
for them like to know what they are buying; and if they have
bought once, they will buy again; the sales of fiction are not
much affected by competition. And once a middlebrow novelist
has achieved very high sales, editors and reviewers naturally tend
to give his work proportionate attention. Thus, unless novel-
reviewers are scrupulous or frank enough to say, when necessary,
that an author's reputation is inflated, they are tacitly helping to
bolster the reputation up. And of course they rarely do say so,
because of the special conventions within which novel-reviewing
is done.

Chief of these, perhaps, is the tradition that novels should
be reviewed by well-known novelists. This goes back as far as the
best-selling industry itself. The public like it, because they feel
that these writers are in sympathy with what they are reviewing,
and ought therefore to be good judges of it. And in fact they do
tell the public what it wants to know; but they tell it with such
relaxed standards that for their own self-respect they have tacitly
to imply that they are writing in a kind of code. 'Do not think',
they hint, 'that when I use the word "great" I mean it in any
sense outside this context.' They deal out their 'real *tour de
force*' and 'a redeeming vein of poetry' with great liberality, and
though they usually know that such things have not much to do
with real writing, a thousand generous motives and some pruden-
tial ones argue against their saying so. One must remember, too,

that literary and artistic society in England, from the late nineteenth century on, went through a marked anti-highbrow phase (probably accentuated and prolonged by the Wilde débâcle), and this has no doubt helped to establish the convention that the best sort of critic is not only not the expert, but actually the man who has never bothered consciously to think out the bases of the art he is criticizing, but relies on his common human sympathies to take him to the truth.

Reviewers do not influence opinion merely by their reviews, for reviewers are also likely to be publishers' readers, or performers on television or radio discussion panels, or members of official organs of patronage or the selection committees of book societies and literary awards. This close interlocking of literary society has its dangers, for the mere fact that a given work receives attention from all quarters also takes it two-thirds of the way to success; and whereas a good writer will, no doubt, seldom be deliberately and concertedly ignored, a second-rate writer (second-rate, that is, by whatever standards happen to apply) may, because everyone knows him personally, get the kind of attention he doesn't really deserve.

The book-club is an important factor in the growth of a bestseller. The first general club of this kind in England was formed in 1937, though the idea had already been put into practice in Germany in the 1920s. There are four notable ones at the time of writing, aiming at somewhat different groups of readers, the largest having a membership in the region of 200,000. They reprint books in a different format some time after the first year of publication. (There is also the 'Book Society', which does not publish books, but whose monthly recommendations ensure sales of between 10,000 and 20,000 copies.) These societies are a very natural application of modern business methods, and publishers generally favour them, though booksellers now mostly refuse to cooperate with them. There is little evidence that they seriously influence writers' choice of what they shall write, or publishers' of what they shall publish (as they do to some extent in America). They are, in fact, a useful amenity for a wide class of middlebrow readers, and the fear that they stifle individual curiosity and choice is probably not very real, for this class of readers is not adventurous at the best of times.

The paper-back has similarly opened an enormous new market to the best-seller. The competition for paper-back rights is now very fierce, and they are often sold even before a book has been completely written, let alone published. The major paper-back publishers usually issue a popular novel reprint in a first edition of about 30,000 to 50,000. The real formula for success, however, is publication as a paper-back immediately after a successful film version—as may be seen from the case of John Braine's *Room at the Top*, which sold half a million paper-back copies in seven months.

Finally, it may be asked, to what extent does the best-selling novelist ever deliberately manipulate his public, in the sense of foisting off on it what he knows to be inferior? It is usually said that to have true best-seller appeal a writer must believe passionately and absolutely in what he writes. But of course there may very well be absolute conviction at one level and calculation at another. In her indispensable *Fiction and the Reading Public*, Q. D. Leavis quotes a number of popular authors who discuss their own artistic intentions. I shall content myself here with a passage from Denis Wheatley's Cantor Lecture to the Royal Society of Arts (1953), which nicely catches the mixture of innocence and cunning with which much best-selling writing is done:

The novelist . . . must settle on the type of people he wishes to interest with his book.

Is it to be the more intellectual public that appreciates fine prose and takes pleasure in following the involved ramifications of the human mind; or is it to be some section of the vast public which gets its weekly supply of light literature mainly from what used to be known as the twopenny libraries? If the former, he must concern himself with some unusual personality, the eternal triangle, or a family, and with these people's psychological reactions to certain more or less normal events . . .

Of course there is a limited number of authors who have succeeded in having the best of both worlds. John Buchan, Graham Greene, Dorothy Sayers, Nevil Shute, Agatha Christie, and Francis Iles spring to mind. . . . I, too, have been most fortunate in that respect, but only owing to a most laborious technique which consists of writing two separate books and dovetailing them into one another.

* * *

The rise of the best-seller in England may conveniently be dated from the mid nineties, when the convention of the three-volume novel was at last abandoned. The implications of this event were twofold: it made possible the commercialization of fiction on a scale hitherto impossible, but plainly called for by the new reading public brought into being by the Education Act of 1870; and at the same time it opened the way for the sort of aesthetically or socially 'advanced' novel which would not have found a publisher previously. A novel which would only appeal to the few could be published, and might sell sufficiently, at the price of six shillings without the aid of the circulating libraries; and the short novel, which many serious novelists of the period wanted to attempt (in imitation of the French) need not now be padded out to three-volume length. This event, therefore, both expresses the separating paths of popular and highbrow fiction and assisted this separation, and thus inaugurated the modern fictional scene, with its double or multiple standards and its divided audience.

The best-seller, and especially the middlebrow best-seller, is in many ways a special genre, and not merely a special version of an accepted genre of literature. It explores a special tract of country, and has particular techniques and a peculiar potency of its own. Its apologists usually say, in various tones of voice, that at least it has powerful emotional force, and unlike highbrow fiction it does tell a story. There is more to it than that, though; the best-seller has laws of its own, and much ingenuity and novelty in obeying them. There is, first, a feature that has always belonged to sentimental fiction, but has been developed and elaborated in many ways in our period. Mary Berry (Horace Walpole's Miss Berry) once very sensibly pointed it out.

The false pictures given of human life in most novels, and which alone (in my opinion) makes them dangerous reading for young people, is, not that the sentiments and conduct of the hero and heroine are exalted above the common level of humanity, for there is no well-conceived novel which is not read by many an ingenuous and noble mind, who can reflect with pleasure that they have acted on some occasion with all the high sense of honour, the exalted generosity, the noble disinterestedness described in their author. But what they must not look for in real life, what they would expect in vain, what it is necessary to guard them against, is supposing that such conduct will make a similar impression on those around them, that the sacrifices they make will be considered, and the principles on which they act understood and valued, as the novel writer, at his good pleasure, makes them.

(*Extracts of the Journals and Correspondence of Miss Berry from the year 1783 to 1852*, ed. Lady Theresa Lewis, 1865)

Popular sentimental novels, that is to say, tend to take the form of a 'congratulation-system'. For instance, in *A Town Like Alice* (1950), Nevil Shute tells the story of his heroine through the lips of a staid old family lawyer who himself falls gradually in love with her. And further, when she courageously rides forty miles through the Australian bush to get help for an injured farmer (though she had scarcely ever ridden before), the story of her heroism is at once made known to everyone concerned by being broadcast from the local radio station. In Warwick Deeping's *Sorrell and Son* (1925), the ex-officer hotel-porter, persecuted by a bullying sometime-N.C.O. who is placed over his head, thinks his wrongs are ignored and misunderstood; but all the time the

God-like owner of the hotel has been aware of all that is happening, has recognized the sacrifices he is making for his son's career, secretly acknowledges him as a gentleman and an equal, and finally gives him a hotel to run for himself.

If characters, by accident or design, have their actions misinterpreted, then the whole dynamic of the book will be to make the reader wait anxiously for the moment of explanation. An ingenious device of this kind is used in Florence Barclay's *The Rosary* (1909). It is a splendidly preposterous novel, of course; yet at first sight you can't say that the course of the plot is itself illogical. A very plain, masculine-looking woman, with, however, a fine singing-voice, discovers that the beautiful and successful young painter Garth Dalmain, adored of many women, has fallen in love with her (he has been swept off his feet by the beauty of character revealed by her singing). She fears that if he marries her, his love of physical beauty would soon make him regret it, and so she tells him that she cannot take his love seriously. They part. He accidentally blinds himself on a shooting expedition. She meanwhile has repented of having refused him. But how shall she now persuade him that she is returning out of anything more than pity? A friend suggests that she go to him under the assumed identity of the petite, fluffy Nurse Gray, and whilst nursing him back to health and restoring his will to live, hope that the truth can eventually be brought home to him. Marvellously farfetched though this is, at first sight there seems nothing wrong with it logically. But why, one then asks, does the masquerade part of the novel go on so long? Not, it transpires, because of the necessities of the plot, but from the requirements of a 'best-friend' or 'built-in-audience' device. For the longer Jane Garth can masquerade as Nurse Gray, and encourage Garth to talk about his old love, the more tributes she can elicit to herself.

A second feature of the best-seller is what we may call 'romantic disproportion', the use of incongruity to introduce the emotion of the wonderful or the pathetic. The hero of W. J.

Locke's *The Beloved Vagabond* (1906), for instance—the un-shaven, Bohemian, absinthe-drinking 'wandering scholar' Paragot —has been to Rugby, and thirteen years ago won the Prix de Rome for architecture. Raffles, again, is a gentleman and a cracks-man. The same quality appears in the love of disproportionate human relationships: Paragot makes a companion of a small boy; the heroine of *The Constant Nymph* (1924) is a child with adult problems; in *Sorrell and Son* father and son share a passionate, quasi-marital, relationship. (Of course much of the pathos in Dickens springs from just such anomalous relationships—the adult as child or the child as adult.) This vein of sentimental dis-proportion is a very powerful and precarious one, and easily turns into a positive delight in disproportion—so that Deeping is led on to propose (what would be rather monstrous if you took it seriously) that not only should the father sacrifice health and social position to his son's career, but that he should constantly remind the son that he is doing so, and that the son should make it the great sacrificial task of his life to repay the debt.

A third feature of best-selling writing is dependence on nostalgia, the feeling that past things are moving and significant simply because they are past. Here we are in strictly best-seller country. The popular novelist can depend on this distancing of events, by itself, to create pathos. Arnold Bennett sometimes used it in this way. Bennett was not a best-selling novelist proper; but he delighted to play the part of the business man of letters, and his whole career is very important for our subject. When he writes deliberately in a best-selling vein, as in *Sacred and Profane Love*, his cynicism is too obvious for the thing to have the power of the natural article. On the other hand, when he is writing with complete integrity, certain weaknesses of a best-selling kind hamper him. In *The Old Wives' Tale* (1911) he means to show, in accordance with naturalist doctrine, that every detail of these commonplace lives is interesting and moving when you see the pattern it contributes to. But in fact he gives significance to the lives of his heroines, less by the logic of events, than by a constant appeal to 'Life', a facetiously ecstatic tone in describing their commonplace emotions, which sometimes sounds like genuine imaginative sympathy and sometimes like contempt; and, again, by an appeal to nostalgia, a dwelling on the pastness of what is past for them. There is a passage in Maupassant's *Une Vie* (Bennett's model for *The Old Wives' Tale*) in which Jeanne, old and half-crazy, finds a bundle of calendars belonging to her youth, and, pinning them to the wall, spends whole days asking herself 'Now, what was I doing then? and then?' In the later pages of *The Old Wives' Tale* Bennett sometimes seems to have no more to say than poor Jeanne in her morbid nostalgia.

❋   ❋   ❋

Various elements in English culture and contemporary history have their best-selling exponents. The imperial idea is important in the earlier part of our period, especially for that group of novelists (Buchan, Sapper, Dornford Yates, Edgar Wallace in *The Four Just Men*, 1905) who present a self-elected élite of friends, of high position or connexions, leaving their clubs or their Scottish castles to defend the country or the Empire's interests—or perhaps merely to right private wrongs. There is an echo of the Boer War in this, the group forming a kind of 'Commando', skilled in self-defence, masters of disguise and cover, using Europe as their 'veldt'. As Richard Usborne points out, the keynote is success; everyone is 'highly thought of in the White House' or 'the second most dangerous man in Europe'. For Buchan himself, the idea must have been partly inspired by Milner's 'kindergarten', of which he was a member; it must, indeed, have seemed natural to these young men, picked from the universities to do the business of the Empire, to think of themselves as a chosen, privileged, inside group called on to arrange the world at their own pleasure.

If one looks for the father of the modern thriller of this kind, that is to say the adventure story in a contemporary social setting, it is probably Conan Doyle, with some hints from Stevenson's *New Arabian Nights*. From Doyle comes the concept of the master criminal with his extreme technical inventiveness—this combines with a late Romantic conception of the criminal as artist. As the thriller has developed, the hero has increasingly employed the same technical ingenuity as the villain. And at the same time the moral status of the hero has sunk. Novels of the Peter Cheyney, Ian Fleming school work on the assumption that violent and treacherous enemies can only be combated by violence and treachery; thus the reader can enjoy in fantasy the full criminal life, save that he remains theoretically on the side of law, virtue, and patriotism. Sapper's Bulldog Drummond remains a gentleman, with Edwardian standards of honour, entering into competition with his enemies with only his courage and various sporting skills to defend him (though in an emergency discovering unsuspected mental resources—a mixture of Watson and Holmes, in fact). The issues remain ostensibly moral, for Drummond's motives are decency and patriotism as against vicious and alien codes and designs. He uses his fists to defend himself, since they are the weapons proper to his code and class—though (an interesting ethical distinction) he cheerfully uses tortures and beatings to *punish* his quarry when he has captured them, should they belong to the categories—such as foreign fiends, Bolshevik Jews, or trade-union leaders—for whom they are suited. In the newer thriller the moral issue becomes perfunctory, or, as in James Hadley Chase, non-existent; 'topping girls' are replaced by casual or tough sex; and the hero is no longer a gentleman, but, as in Ian Fleming's recent James Bond series, an efficient and savage animal, with gleaming teeth, lean body, and narrow hips; an anonymous engine for detection, murder, and fornication, the driving of fast automobiles and the consumption of branded goods.

Some other favourite themes of the first period of the best-seller were scandal-in-high-life (Marie Corelli), highly coloured soul-drama (Hall Caine), Ruritanian romance, and erotico-Ruritanian as refurbished with tiger-skins and mad passion by Elinor Glyn in *Three Weeks* (1907). Ruritania was invented by 'Anthony Hope' in *The Prisoner of Zenda* (1894), which itself looks back to the romance-writing school of the eighties. Stevenson was in some sense its father, as he was of other elements in the best-seller. It is interesting how many of the themes which he started in his oblique, playful, mandarin manner were taken up more seriously, or at least more literally, by later popular writers.

The First World War inspired one or two from-school-to-war novels, such as Ernest Raymond's *Tell England* (1922), of a high, romantic-religious, class-conscious, idealized-homosexual ethos, an ethos still Edwardian, and close, for example, to that of Horace A. Vachell's famous school story *The Hill* (1905). A reversal of these values in the name of romanticized post-war disillusion and sexual emancipation produced a complementary best-seller, Michael Arlen's *The Green Hat* (1924), in which the idealized young upper-class hero who 'dies for purity' is really a sham, who kills himself on his wedding-night because he has syphilis. Two important best-sellers, *Sorrell and Son* (already mentioned) and A. S. M. Hutchinson's *If Winter Comes* (1921), concern the returned officer in a post-war world, out of a job and up against the 'mob', who resent his pretensions to gentlemanliness. By the end of the novel these heroes assume almost Christlike dimensions as representatives of the 'new poor'.

The First World War seems to have remained English society's true inoculation to death, and the shock of it can still be felt; its bitter division of soldier and civilian and angry aftermath of class-antagonism are reflected in the hysteria and romanticism of its popular novels. The country was psychologically better prepared for the Second World War and less profoundly stirred by it. Best-sellers on the subject, like Nigel Balchin's *The Small Back Room* (1943) and Nicholas Monsarrat's *The Cruel Sea* (1951), are full of technical information and matter-of-fact in tone. Nevil Shute, perhaps the most characteristic post-war best-seller, carries on this tradition. He takes his reader through some enterprise detail by detail, step by step. His heroes are the people who get things done, ordinary people obsessed by some vision; the last section of *A Town Like Alice*, in which the heroine introduces shoe-manufacture into a remote Australian farming settlement, is a sort of parable of private enterprise, with strong political overtones. Against this element of new-style Defoe, which is his most original feature, he sets up a more commonplace 'congratulation-system' of heroism and sentiment.

The country novel had its heyday in the twenties, when the builders were also dotting the Home Counties with their fake Tudor farmhouses, called 'Duffers End' or 'Old Hatcheries'. We can distinguish the country novelists who write what in essence might have taken place equally well in a town or garden suburb, but who obtain certain qualities of largeness and simplicity from a country setting—for example Sheila Kaye-Smith—and those, like Mary Webb, who create a country poetry and country phantasmagoria of their own. Mary Webb's novels of the Welsh border, with their shy, earthy, wildwood heroines amid scenes of rustic violence and oddity, their pungent speech and erotic nature-poetry, are clearly the offspring of *Tess of the D'Urbervilles*, though shorn of any wider meaning. They are the most odd, and perhaps the most interesting, of these novels, and had a great though rather brief vogue after Stanley Baldwin's public tributes to *Precious Bane* (1924)—their reputation suffered a good deal of damage from Stella Gibbons's parody *Cold Comfort Farm* (1932).

Of comic novelists the best known and most lasting has been P. G. Wodehouse. His material is the completely shadowy one of stage farce and musical comedy, with its comic butlers, silly-ass young men, slangy girls, and impecunious peers engaged in plots to steal cow-creamers or to out-manoeuvre rich aunts. The speed, the highly machined and elaborate plotting, the sudden exits and entrances and innumerable peripeteia all spring from the same stage conception; and Wodehouse has been a technical source-book for writers like Evelyn Waugh and Kingsley Amis. What gives his work character, however, is its linguistic side. Over all his work hangs a comic pretence of verbal precision, an exhibition of lexicology. His sentences run the gamut between pomposity, literary quotation, parodied cliché, and some exactly placed slang word; the whole style is a joke about literacy, an affectation of precision in defining the mental processes of imbeciles and dilation into tautologies to express the most elementary of facts.

When we come to the historical romance and the detective story, it is less individual novels than a certain formula which raises the author into the best-selling class. The writers of historical romances often tell us quite frankly what they are doing. 'My story will take you into times and spaces alike rude and incivil,' says Maurice Hewlett, in his best brocaded style, on the first page of *The Forest Lovers* (1898). 'Blood will be spilt, virgins suffer distresses; the horn will sound through woodland glades; dogs, wolves, deer and men, Beauty and the Beasts, will tumble each other, seeking life or death with their proper tools . . .' Most authors of this kind write with some such formula or recipe of ingredients in their mind. The charm of the genre lies in its being, to some extent, a charade, the modern bodies and feelings remaining recognizable under the period disguise. And, characteristically, the authors often make their plots turn on dressing-up. Thus, in an early Georgette Heyer, *Powder and Patch* (1923), the hero, a rugged country-bred youth (a hearty modern boy, as we really feel), though despising the effeminacy of wigs and patches and paint, is compelled to make himself into a model fine gentleman. Again, Jeffrey Farnol's *The Amateur Gentleman* (1913) tells of an innkeeper's son who studies to impose himself on high society. And, in rather a similar way, the young republican hero of Rafael Sabatini's *Scaramouche* (1921) makes himself the best swordsman in France, so that he can turn the hated symbol of the *ancien régime*, the duel, against its devotees. This kind of 'dressing-up' plot is the most natural way of bringing period stage-properties into the foreground of the novel.

The more recent favourites in this genre, like C. S. Forester, have a touch of self-consciousness not present in the full-blooded narratives of Sabatini and the Baroness Orczy, and hint faintly that they are playing at this sort of thing. Georgette Heyer achieves quite a skilful pastiche of a Jane Austen plot and style in *Bath Tangle* (1955), the values and the drift of the dialogue, however, remaining essentially modern, and contrasting intentionally with the well-caught Regency phraseology. C. S. Forester sophisticates his material (and gets the best of both worlds) by making his hero a bluff, hearts-of-oak seadog straight out of Marryat, who is at the same time a sensitive and self-doubting modern soul consciously impersonating this simple period role. The staple of Forester's Hornblower novels, however, is a loving and extremely technical analysis of nautical operations. It is this that gives a degree of conviction to the odd amalgam, and it links him, of course, with the 'technological' school of Nevil Shute (so that, indeed, he really gets the best of three worlds).

Finally there is the detective story, 'use-literature' in its extremest form. Unlike the novels of Wilkie Collins, the modern detective novel is deliberately designed to raise and solve its problems without emotionally involving the reader. It seems to offer the normal constituents of fiction without actually doing so. It makes little difference if the background and characters are taken from life or simply from other fiction, for what happens is not meant to illuminate them, but only to make bewildering use of them. If the motive for a murder turns out to be concealed paranoia on the part of a *Cranford*-esque spinster, then the important lesson is that the reader could never unaided have guessed this; it takes the superior intellect of the detective to reveal such things. It is a middle-class art and taste. The problem is set against a background of absolute security; and though this security is momentarily interrupted by violence, order is soon efficiently though miraculously restored. The detective puzzle, moreover, enables the reader to remain detached from, and superior to, the human issues involved. The conventions of the genre are now set and will obviously be fruitful for many years ahead.

The transcendent and eccentric detective; the admiring slightly stupid foil; the well-intentioned blundering and unimaginativeness of the official guardians of the law; the locked-room convention; the pointing finger of unjust suspicion; the solution by surprise, deduction by putting one's self in another's position (now called psychology); concealment by means of the ultra-obvious; the staged ruse to force the culprit's hand; . . . the expansive and condescending explanation when the chase is done . . .

(H. Haycraft, *Murder for Pleasure*, N.Y., 1941)

One should add that the detective novel has the distinction of being the first best-selling genre to celebrate not deeds but the human reason. It has handed over its heroic elements (battle of wits with the master-mind of crime) and its atmospheric elements (pursuit and chase in the urban labyrinth) to the thriller, and what it has left to offer is a game or pastime. Its value to its readers (who are traditionally schoolmasters, clergymen, lawyers, dons, etc.) is purely therapeutic; and since they form the modern 'clerisy', it is fitting that their pastime literature should be a celebration of the intellect.

STUDY QUESTIONS

1. Furbank lists a number of qualities which are characteristic of British best-sellers. Do these seem to you qualities which are also

noticeable in American best-sellers? Can you cite particular best-selling novels which exhibit these characteristics?

2. William Faulkner might well be accused of trading on our fascination with nostalgia and the exotic. What is the difference between the way Faulkner handles the past and the exotic and the way a typical novelist of best-sellers handles the same material?

3. Are the best-sellers' characteristics that Furbank lists typical only of popular fiction, or can these characteristics also be found in other popular arts? For example, to what extent can they be found in such television programs as *Peyton Place* (1964) on the one hand and Jackie Gleason's productions on the other?

4. In *The American Experience* (1947), H. B. Parkes says that a sense of loneliness and of being overwhelmed by machines was typical of American best-sellers in the 1930's. His analysis seems to indicate that in some respects the American sensibility differs from the British. Can you think of any historical reasons for this difference? Does Parkes' thesis invalidate Furbank's thesis? Or can the two exist side by side? Can you think of examples which would support both theses? Is there any sense in which the American fear of machines might be classified as a kind of nostalgia?

5. Has either the United States or Britain ever escaped from the rather materialistic desire to see virtue concretely rewarded? How is this desire reflected in our contemporary popular arts?

6. In "The Gangster as Tragic Hero" (p. 155), does Robert Warshow's analysis of the gangster hero help to explain our desire for material reward on grounds other than sentimentality? Does John Williams' analysis of the western hero in "The 'Western': Definition of the Myth" (p. 98) help to explain this desire?

7. Do the visual natures of film and television encourage the use of materialistic schemes of values? Why?

ABRAHAM KAPLAN

Abraham Kaplan is professor of philosophy at the University of Michigan. He was born in Russia, came to the United States as a child, and was educated at the College of St. Thomas in Minnesota, the University of Chicago, and the University of California at Los Angeles. He has taught at New York, Harvard, and Columbia Universities, and at U.C.L.A. He is co-author of *Power and Society* (1950), and author of *The New World of Philosophy* (1961) and *The Conduct of Inquiry: Methodology for Behaviorial Science* (1964). In the following article, Professor Kaplan does something unusual. He deals with what he calls the "disvalues" in art, with the problems, that is, of understanding and evaluating the less than ideal embodiments of art we call the "popular arts." By following his argument carefully and distinguishing with him between such terms as pop art, bad art, minor art, folk art, and popular art, we can better understand the kinds of taste these arts satisfy, the forms they use, the emotions they express and the ways in which they express them, and, finally, the social functions they serve. Unless we seriously consider such matters, we cannot possibly understand the value of studying the popular arts, or, for that matter, why we should study them at all.

The Aesthetics
of the Popular Arts*

Aesthetics is so largely occupied with the good in art that it has little to say about what is merely better or worse, and especially about what is worse. Unremitting talk about the good, however, is not only boring but usually inconsequential as well. Aesthetic theory that is preoccupied with artistic virtue is largely irrelevant both to artistic experience and to critical practice, confronted as they are with so much vice. The study of *dis*-values may have much to offer both aesthetics and criticism for the same reasons that the physiologist looks to disease and the priest becomes learned in sin. Artistic taste and understanding might better be served by a museum of horribilia, presented as such, than by the unvarying display of perfection, whose natural habitat comes to be confined to the museum. It is from this standpoint that I invite attention to the aesthetics of the popular arts.

Most aestheticians, I think, are Platonists at least in this respect: they analyze the realm of value by looking chiefly to its ideal embodiments. Disvalues are left to implicit negation: if artistic excellence is *this*, what is not this specifies the inferior product. The vulgar and tasteless, the derivative and academic, brummagem, borax, and kitsch—such as these are left to purely tacit and inferential analysis. Are there, after all, Ideas of hair, mud, and dirt? The time will come, says Parmenides, when philosophy will not despise even the meanest things, even those of which the mention may provoke a smile.

* Based on a paper read for the American Philosophical Association, Milwaukee, May, 1964.

I

By the popular arts I do not mean what has recently come to be known as pop art. This, like junk art and some of the theater of the absurd, is the present generation's version of dada. In some measure, no doubt, it serves as a device for enlarging the range of artistic possibilities, exploring the beauty in what is conventionally dismissed as meaningless and ugly, as well as the ugliness in what is conventionally extolled as beautiful. Basically, it is a revolt against the artistic establishment, a reaction against the oppressiveness of the academic and familiar. As such, it is derivative, as though to say, "You call *this* junk?" If it is lacking in artistic virtue, its vice is like that of watching a voyeur—the sins of another are presupposed. It is what pop art presupposes that I am calling *popular art*.

Second, I do not mean simply *bad art,* neither the downright failures nor those that fall just short of some set of critical requirements. It is a question of *how* they fail and, even more, to what sort of success they aspire. Maxwell Anderson's verse dramas and Dali's *Last Supper* are not very good, but they are not popular art in the sense I intend it. Popular art may be bad art, but the converse is not necessarily true. It is a particular species of the unaesthetic that I want to isolate.

Similarly, I set aside what may be deprecated as merely minor art. Its products are likely to be more popular, in the straightforward sense, than those which have greatness. The *Rubaiyat* may be more widely read than *De rerum natura,* and *The Hound of the Baskervilles* more than *Crime and Punishment,* but each is excellent after its own kind. A work of minor art is not necessarily a minor work. Greatness, that is to say, is a distinctive aesthetic attribute—a matter of scope or depth and so forth; the word is not just a designation for the highest degree of artistic value. The lack of greatness may be a necessary condition for popular art, but most surely it is not a sufficient condition.

Neither is popular art to be confused with folk art, though it is by no means always easy to differentiate them in specific cases. Folk art is popular in the special sense of being produced by "the people"—that is to say, anonymously, without self-consciousness, and not in an explicitly aesthetic context. Yet this is, strictly speaking, a matter of accident rather than essence. What is involved is again a distinctive aesthetic attribute, which need not be produced only in that way. Some folk art has been created deliberately to be just that, and by identifiable and even contemporary artists—Carl Sandburg, Stephen Vincent Benét, and many others in other media. *The Song of Songs*, Byzantine icons, and perhaps Gothic cathedrals are products of folk art, but none of them is in the least representative of what I intend by the popular arts.

We come closer with the category of mass art, what is mass-produced or reproduced, and is responded to by vast numbers of people. Yet here, too, qualifications must be made. The specification of origin and destination does not of itself determine just what it is that is being produced and responded to. There is no fixed a priori relation between quantity and quality, and especially not between quantity and certain specific qualities as distinguished from worth in general. Vulgarity after all, in spite of its etymology, is not *constituted* by being popular. Spinoza's dictum that all things excellent are as difficult as they are rare has much merit, but it is the difficulty that I want to track down; rarity may be the mark of what is difficult, but it is not, surely, the substance of the difficulty.

The *kind* of taste that the popular arts satisfy, and not how widespread that taste is, is what distinguishes them. On this basis, I provisionally identify my subject as *midbrow art*, to be contrasted with what appeals to either highbrow or lowbrow tastes. Popular art is what is found neither in the literary reviews nor in the pulp magazines, but in the slicks; neither in gallery paintings nor on calendars, but on Christmas cards and billboards; neither in serious music nor in jazz, but in Tin Pan Alley. The popular arts may very well appeal to a mass audience, but they have characteristics that distinguish them from other varieties of mass art, and distinctive contexts and patterns of presentation. A work of popular art may be a best seller, but it is not assigned in freshman English nor reprinted as a comic. It may win an Academy Award, but it will be shown neither at the local Art Cinema nor on the late, late show.

Many social scientists think that these symptoms—for they are no more than that—provide an etiology of the disease. Midbrow art, they say, is more properly designated *middle-class art.* It is a product of the characteristic features of modern society: capitalism, democracy, and technology. Capitalism has made art a commodity, and provided the means to satisfy the ever widening demands for the refinements of life that earlier periods reserved to a small elite. Democracy, with its apotheosis of majorities and of public opinion, has inevitably reduced the level of taste to that of the lowest common denominator. The technology of the mass media precludes the care and craftsmanship that alone can create works of art. For a time it was fashionable to lay these charges particularly at American doors, to view the popular arts as the distinctive feature of American culture; but by now, I think, most of those who take this line see popular art more generally, if not more generously, as only "the sickness of the age."

I have no doubt that a good case can be made for this point of view. The trouble with such an explanation, however, is that it explains too much, and none of it with the illumination hoped for. Sidney Morgenbesser once pointedly suggested as an examination question for a course in the history of civilization, "Name two important events since 1600 *not* connected with the rise of the middle class." To be sure, this rise is one of the most significant determinants of modern culture, its effects as far-reaching as they are profound. But what are we saying about the culture when we characterize it as middle-class? The social forms and institutions to which reference is being made provide the possibility of satisfying popular taste, and perhaps also explain why society tries to satisfy it. But they do not explain what that taste is, what interests its satisfaction serves, nor how these interests relate to those satisfied in genuinely aesthetic experience.

My thesis is this: that popular art is not the degradation of taste but its immaturity, not the product of external social forces but produced by a dynamic intrinsic to the aesthetic experience itself. Modern society, like all others, has its own style, and leaves its imprint on all it embraces. But this is only to say that our popular art is *ours*, not that it is our sole possession. Popular art is usually said to stem from about the beginning of the eighteenth century, but in its essence it is not, I think, a particularity of our time and place. It is as universal as art itself.

II

We might characterize popular art first, as is most often done, with respect to its *form*. Popular art is said to be simple and unsophisticated, aesthetically deficient because of its artlessness. It lacks quality because it makes no qualifications to its flat statement. Everything is straightforward, with no place for complications. And it is standardized as well as simplified: one product is much like another. It is lifeless, Bergson would say, because it is only a succession of mechanical repetitions, while what is vital in art is endlessly variable. But it is just the deadly routine that is so popular. Confronted with that, we know just where we are, know what we are being offered, and what is expected of us in return. It is less unsettling to deal with machines than with people, who have lives of their own to lead. For we can then respond with mechanical routines ourselves, and what could be simpler and more reliably satisfying?

Yet this account of the matter is itself too simple to be satisfactory. For why should simplicity be unaesthetic? Art always strips away what is unessential, and purity has always been recognized as a virtue. Put the adjective *classic* before it and simplicity becomes a term of high regard. What is simple is not therefore simple-minded. Art always concentrates, indeed it owes its force to the power of interests that have been secured against distraction and dissipation. Art, we may say, does away with unnecessary complications. We can condemn popular art for treating as expendable the *necessary* complications, but nothing has been added to our aesthetic understanding till we have been given some specification of what complexity is necessary and what is not.

There is a similar lack in the condemnation of popular art as being standardized. If the term is to have more than a persuasive definition, its meaning must be distinguished from the *stylizations* that unite the works of a particular culture, period, school, or individual artist. One Egyptian statue is much like another, after all, just as there are marked resemblances among Elizabethan tragedies or among Italian operas. Such works are not for that reason assigned the status of popular art. The standardization of popular art does not mean that forms are stylized but that they are *stereotyped*. The failing does not lie in the recurrence of the forms but in deficiencies even in the first occurrence. The characters and situations of the usual movie, words and music of popular songs, the scenes and sentiments of magazine illustrations are all very much of a piece, each after its own kind. (There was a time in my youth when every great man of history talked and looked like either George Arliss or Paul Muni.) It would be more accurate to say that the fault of these stereotypes—what makes them stereotypes—is not that each instance of the type so closely resembles all the others, but that the type as a whole so little resembles anything outside it.

The stereotype presents us with the blueprint of a form, rather than the form itself. Where the simplifications of great art show us human nature in its nakedness, the stereotypes of popular art strip away even the flesh, and the still, sad music of humanity is reduced to the rattle of dry bones. It is not simplification but schematization that is achieved; what is put before us is not the substance of the text but a reader's digest. All art selects what is significant and suppresses the trivial. But for popular art the criteria of significance are fixed by the needs of the standardization, by the editor of the digest and not by the Author of the reality to be grasped. Popular art is never a discovery, only a reaffirmation. Both producer and consumer of popular art confine themselves to what fits into their own schemes, rather than omitting only what is unnecessary to the grasp of the scheme of things. The world of popular art is bounded by the limited horizons of what we think we know already; it is two-dimensional because we are determined to view it without budging a step from where we stand.

The simplification characteristic of popular art amounts to this, that we restrict ourselves to what *already* comes within our grasp. Every stereotype is the crystallization of a prejudice— that is, a prejudgment, a reduction of the empirical to the a priori. This is reflected in the ease with which popular art lends itself to the categorization of genres; even the inanimate materials of its medium have been type-cast.

Popular art is dominated throughout by the star system, not only in its actors but in all its elements, whatever the medium. Every work of art, to be sure, has its dominant elements, to which the rest are subordinate. But in popular art it is the dominant ones alone that are the objects of interest, the ground of its satisfaction. Everything else is an unnecessary complication, only blunting the point to be made. By contrast, great art is in this sense pointless; everything in it is significant, everything makes its own contribution to the aesthetic substance. The domain of popular art is, paradoxically, an aristocracy, as it were: some few elements are singled out as the carriers of whatever meaning the work has while the rest are merged into an anonymous mass.

The life of the country is reduced to the mannered gestures of its king. It is this that gives the effect of simplification and standardization. The elements of the schema, of course, need not be characters in the strict sense; action, color, texture, melody, or rhythm may all be simplified and standardized in just this way.

What popular art schematizes it also abstracts from a fully aesthetic context. Such an abstraction is what we call a *formula;* in formula art the schema is called upon to do the work of the full-bodied original, as though a newspaper consisted entirely of headlines. The abstraction can always be made, as is implied in the very concept of style, and of specific stylistic traits. We can always apply formulas to art; the point is that popular art gives us the formula but nothing to apply it to. Popular art uses formulas, not for analysis but for the experience itself. Such substance as it has is only the disordered residue of other more or less aesthetic experiences, themselves well on the way towards schematization. Popular art is thus doubly derivative: art first becomes academic and then it becomes popular; as art achieves style it provides the seeds of its own destruction.

This whole line of analysis might be summarized in the statement that popular art simply lacks form—not that it is in the literal sense formless, that is, chaotic, but that form in the aesthetic sense has no useful application to it, is irrelevant to its status and function as popular art. The order exhibited by any organized whole I call *shape;* it is an attribute of the objects of popular art as of any other objects. But *form* attaches to the work of art rather than the art product, to use Dewey's terms. Form is a displacement onto the object of the structure of our experience of the object; it is this experience that is the primary locus of aesthetic quality. What we say about form refers at bottom to the pull of the perceptual and psychodynamic forces at work when the art object is experienced in an ideal context.

In denying form to popular art, I am saying that no such work of structuring is involved in it. In the usual idiom, popular

a reaction, in the sense I intend it, is almost wholly determined by the initial stimulus, antecedently and externally fixed, while a response follows a course that is not laid out beforehand but is significantly shaped by a process of self-stimulation occurring then and there. Spontaneity and imagination come into play; in the aesthetic experience we do not simply react to signals but engage in a creative interpretation of symbols. The response to an art object shares in the work of its creation, and only thereby is a work of art produced. But in popular art everything has already been done. As Dwight Macdonald put it, the spectator's reactions are included in what is presented to him; there is nothing that calls upon him to make his own responses. Thus the background music for the popular movie signalizes the birth of love with melodious strings and the approach of death by chords on the organ; contrast these signals with the demanding substance of, say, Prokofieff's music for Eisenstein's *Alexander Nevsky*. To vary the metaphor, popular art is a dictatorship forever organizing spontaneous demonstrations and forever congratulating itself on its freedoms.

In the taste for popular art there is a marked intolerance of ambiguity. It is not just that we shrink from doing that much work—the work, that is, of creative interpretation. At bottom, aesthetic ambiguity is frightening. That is why the newest art is always either funny or infuriating: we laugh at what we cannot understand so as to discharge the tension of the fear it arouses, and what is perceived as a threat may also provoke anger. But art is always a challenge; the artist assumes responsibility only for marking out the scope of our own responsible effort. Art is a confrontation with our freedom to create, plunging us into an inchoate world with the awesome words "Let there be . . . !" forming on our own lips. Popular art is a device for remaining in the same old world and assuring ourselves that we like it, because we are afraid to change it. The paradigmatic expression of popular taste is J. Alfred Prufrock's, "Do I dare disturb the universe?" But the artist dares, and dares his audience to share his daring, and the art depends upon the disturbance.

At best, popular art replaces ambiguity by some degree of complexity. This is most clearly demonstrated by the so-called *adult Western*, which has moved beyond the infantilism of "good guys" and "bad guys," by assigning virtues and vices to both heroes and villains. But the moral qualities themselves remain unambiguous in both sign and substance. The genre, for the most part, is still far from the insight into the nature of good and evil invited, say, by Melville's Captain Ahab or, even more, by his Billy Budd. Yet, *High Noon* is undeniably a far cry from *The Lone Ranger*.

In short, popular art is simple basically in the sense of easy. It contrasts with art in the markedly lesser demands that it makes for creative endeavor on the part of its audience. An artistic form, like a life form, is a creation, and like the living thing again, one which demands a coöptive effort, in this case between artist and audience. We cannot look to popular art for a fresh vision, turn to it for new directions out of the constraints of convention. Unexplored meanings call for their own language, which must be fashioned by a community with the courage and energy of pioneers. But for a new language there must be something new to say; what the pioneer can never do without is—a frontier.

III

Quite another approach to the analysis of popular art is by way of feeling rather than form. Popular art may be characterized by the kinds of emotions involved in it, or by its means of evoking or expressing them.

Thus there is a common view that popular art is merely *entertainment,* in a pejorative sense. It does not instruct, does not answer to any interests other than those aroused then and there; it is just interesting in itself. Popular art offers us something with which to fill our empty lives; we turn to it always in quiet desperation. It is a specific against boredom, and is thus an inevitable concomitant of the industrial civilization that simultaneously gives us leisure and alienates us from anything that might make our leisure meaningful.

Whatever merits this view may have as sociology, as aesthetics I do not find it very helpful. That the interests satisfied by popular art are self-contained is hardly distinctive of the type. All art has inherent value, independent of its direct contributions to extra-aesthetic concerns. And all art has a certain intrinsic value, affording delight in the form and color of the aesthetic surface, independent of depth meaning. That something is entertaining, that it gives joy to the beholder without regard to more serious interests, so-called, is scarcely a reason, therefore, for refusing it artistic status. It is surely no more than snobbery or a perverted puritanism to disparage entertainment value, or to deny it to art. That art must be boring is a prejudice of popular taste; the aesthetician may have been subtly influenced by the same prejudice when he identifies popular art as entertainment. His logic might be compared to that pseudo-Kantianism which infers that we are moral only when we help those we hate, for only then can we be sure that we are actuated by duty and not by mere inclination.

In any case, the question still remains, What makes popular art entertaining? To invoke a contrast with boredom is not of much help, for that is a descriptive category, not an explanatory one; as well say that work is an antidote to laziness. Indeed, I think the claim might be more defensible that popular art, far from countering boredom, perpetuates and intensifies it.

We are entertained, in the primary sense, when we are housed and fed, and not merely amused; popular art only makes us guests in our own home. This is to say that popular art is not, as is often supposed, a *diversion*, redirecting our interests, diverting them to other and more satisfying objects of interest. It does not arouse new interests but reinforces old ones. Such satisfaction as it affords stems from the evocation in memory of past satisfactions, or even from remembered fantasies of fulfillment. What we enjoy is not the work of popular art but what it brings to mind. There is a nostalgia characteristic of the experience of popular art, not because the work as a form is familiar but because its very substance is familiarity.

The skill of the artist is not in providing an experience but in providing occasions for reliving one. The emotions that come into being are not *expressed* by his materials but are *associated* with them. They are not embodied in the object but are conveyed by it, transmitted. The object is only an intermediary between past and present; emotional investment and even attention are withdrawn from it as soon as it has delivered its message. In the experience of popular art we lose ourselves, not in a work of art but in the pools of memory stirred up. Poetry becomes a congeries of poetic symbols which now only signalize feeling, as in the lyrics of popular songs; drama presents dramatic materials but does not dramatize them—brain surgery, or landing the crippled airliner; painting becomes illustration or didactic narrative from Jean Greuze to Norman Rockwell.

Conventions are, to be sure, at work; the associations aroused are not wholly adventitious and idiosyncratic. But *convention* is one thing and *style* is another. One is extrinsic to the materials, giving them shape; the other is the very substance of their form. The difference is like that between a railroad track and a satellite's orbit: convention is laid down beforehand, guiding reactions along a fixed path, while style has no existence antecedent to and independent of the ongoing response itself. For this reason popular art so easily becomes dated, as society changes its conventional associations; seen today, A *Father's Curse* surely evokes laughter rather than pity or fear. On the other hand, a work of art may become popular as its expressive substance is replaced by associations—Whistler's *"Mother"* is a case in point.

Rather than saying, then, that popular art provides us with *substitute* gratifications, I think it would be less misleading to credit it with giving us the *same* gratifications, such as they are, all over again. It is not even quite right to say that at least a symbolic object replaces the real one—the feelings evoked by the painting are after all directed towards the viewer's mother, not Whistler's. If there is in some sense a substitution, there can be no question, at any rate, of a sublimation. There is little empirical evidence supporting the view that popular art provides catharsis, in the operational sense that exposure, say, to stories of violence makes us less violent in behavior, or that if we can look lustfully we are content with committing adultery only in our hearts. For that matter, there is even less evidence that popular art, on the contrary, *produces* corresponding behavior, as alarmist guardians of public morals so loudly proclaim. The point is that popular art leaves our feelings essentially unchanged, and therefore also leaves unchanged their relation to action. It neither transforms nor fulfills our desires but only reminds us of them. Its gratifications are those of touching an aching tooth.

Popular art wallows in emotion while art transcends it, giving us understanding and thereby mastery of our feelings. For popular art, feelings themselves are the ultimate subject matter; they are not present as a quality of the experience of something objectified, but are only stimulated by the object. The addiction to such stimuli is like the frenzied and forever frustrated pursuit of happiness by those lost souls who have never learned that happiness accrues only when the object of pursuit has its own substance. Popular art ministers to this misery, panders to it, we may say. What popular art has in common with prostitution is not that it is commercialized; art also claims its price, and the price is often a high one. The point is that here we are being offered consummations without fulfillment, invited to perform the gestures of love on condition that they remain without meaning. We are not drawn out of ourselves but are driven deeper into loneliness. The vestments of our passions are very much in evidence in popular art; what could throb more with human feeling than our soap operas and bedroom sonatas? Yet it is all "but a paltry thing, a tattered coat upon a stick"—there is no life within. Emotion is not a monopoly of popular art, as Dickens, Tschaikovsky, or Turner might testify; but these artists do not traffic in emotion. Popular art, on the contrary, deals in nothing else. That is why it is so commonly judged by its impact. To say truly that it is sensational would be high praise; what we usually get is an anaesthetic.

IV

There is yet another reason for questioning whether popular art provides relief from boredom, bringing color into grey lives. The popular audience may be chronically bored, but this is not to say that it is without feeling. On the contrary, it is feeling above all that the audience contributes to the aesthetic situation and that the popular artist then exploits. Popular art does not supply a missing ingredient in our lives, but cooks up a savory mess from the ingredients at hand. For that matter, art is never engaged in the importation of feeling. The stuff of aesthetic experience, so far as emotions are involved in it, is universal. There is no man—this side of downright pathology, at any rate —for whom affect is a rare and strange delight, and for which he must turn to art. What *is* true is that feelings are commonly undergone without awareness, experienced without perspective, blurred both in their own detail and in the interconnections that give them significance. In a word, they are usually lacking in *depth*, whatever their intensity. Popular art is correspondingly shallow.

In a fully aesthetic experience, feeling is deepened, given new content and meaning. Till then, we did not know what it was we felt; one could say that the feeling was not truly ours.

It is in this sense that art provides us with feeling: it makes us aware of something that comes to be only in the intense and structured experience of the awareness. We become selves as we come to self-consciousness, no longer unthinking creatures of feeling but men whose emotions are meaningful to us. But popular art provides no such mirror of the mind, or if we do find our feelings dimly reflected in it, we cannot pass through the looking glass to confront our hidden selves. We are caught up on the surface, and our feelings remain superficial and deficient, as unreal as their reflections. The shades with which the world of popular art is peopled seem to us substantial when we ourselves are still only fictitious characters.

Superficial, affected, spurious—this is the dictionary meaning of *sentimental*. So far as feeling goes, it is sentimentality that is most distinctive of popular art. There is a sense, I suppose, in which we could say that all feeling starts as sentiment: however deep down you go you must begin at the surface. The point is that popular art leaves our feelings as it finds them, formless and immature. The objects of sentiment are of genuine worth—cynicism has its own immaturity. But the feelings called forth spring up too quickly and easily to acquire substance and depth. They are so lightly triggered that there is no chance to build up a significant emotional discharge.

Dewey has criticized sentimentality as being disjoined from action, but it is only action within the experience itself that is relevant here. Maintaining a certain psychic distance is essential to the aesthetic attitude. In another connection William James tells of the Russian aristocrat who weeps at the tragedy on the stage while her waiting coachman is freezing to death outside the theater. What makes her tears sentimental is not that she does not hurry to his relief, but that she is incapable of more than the very beginnings of pity even at the play: her eyes are dry within. She is not experiencing a catharsis, for there is scarcely anything there to be purged. She does not participate in the action of the drama but only reacts to it, that is, reenacts feelings she has not made truly her own. The tears are real enough, but they have no reason—only a cause.

In the eighteenth century a "sentiment" meant a moralistic apothegm (as in *The School for Scandal*). The words are full of feeling, but the speaker is not. The object of the sentiment so well defines the feelings called for that the definition itself is mistaken for the feeling. The true man of sentiment is far from being a hypocrite; his feeling is sincere enough as far as it goes, but it goes nowhere. Sentimentality is a mark always of a certain deficiency of feeling; it is always just words, a promise that scarcely begins to move toward fulfillment.

Yet, paradoxically, there is also something excessive about sentimentality. Stephen Pepper has characterized it as a violation of "emotional decorum," an abandonment of proper restraint. But it is easy for us to beg the question of how much is excessive. There are no a priori limits to the intensity of feeling that art can encompass. There is boundless depth in David's cry, "O my son Absalom, my son, my son Absalom! Would I had died instead of you, O Absalom, my son, my son!" No doubt there are those who would find it excessive; undeniably it does not express an Anglo-Saxon attitude, but it is also undeniably free from sentimentality. Cultures may differ in their tolerance for sentimentality, or even proclivity towards it, but the quality itself is not wholly a cultural variable.

It is only an excess of a special kind that is in question here. We must distinguish sentimentality from sensibility, that is, a ready responsiveness to demands on our feelings. Art has no purchase at all on insensibility. Unless a man is capable of being moved, and moved deeply, in circumstances where his antecedent interests are not engaged, art has nothing for him. Of such a man we may well ask, "What's Hecuba to him or he to Hecuba, that he should weep for her?" Sensibility becomes sentimental when there is some disproportion between the response and its object, when the response is indiscriminate and uncontrolled. Emotion, Beethoven once said, is for women, and I think we all understand him; but we are to keep in mind the difference between such women as Elizabeth Bennet and her mother.

It is this difference that we want to get at. Dewey comes very near the mark, I believe, in characterizing sentimentality as "excess of receptivity without perception of meaning." It is this lack of meaning, and not intensity of feeling, that makes the receptivity excessive. Popular art is not sentimental because it evokes so much feeling, but because it calls for so much more feeling than either its artist or audience can handle. The trouble is not too much feeling but too little understanding; there is too little to be understood. The tear-jerker provides an occasion for the tears it invites, but *why* we weep lies outside the occasion and beyond our perception. In art, apprehensions are enlarged; we feel in more detail and in broader perspective. It is in this sense that there is a catharsis: emotions are transcended as we move along the dimension of their meaning from a subjective state to the objective forms in which feeling has become patterned.

The sentimentalist makes himself the standard of proportionality of feeling; the only meaning that matters to him is what he has stored up within. As R. H. Blythe has beautifully said (in his treatise on *haiku*, I think), sentimentality is loving something more than God does. It is viewing things in their significance only for the viewer; his emotions are decisive, and they are their own justification.

There is a systematic rationalization of this "subjectivist madness"—romanticism. The metaphysics of romanticism first reads the ego into the cosmos, then triumphantly produces an ontological basis for its self-centeredness. To be is to be felt— by me; and my own being is defined by the depth of my feeling. Reality is perceived by the romantic only as the locus and ground of his emotional response; his sentimentality is rationalized by the defense-mechanism of projection. It is noteworthy that the style of popular art—in so far as it achieves style—tends always toward the romantic: that is the best that it can do with its sentimentality.

Here at last we may have come upon an underlying connection between popular art and the organization of modern society. The connection is not by way of democratization and the technology of mass production. It is, rather, by way of the ideological import of the bourgeois revolution, from which Huizinga, Hauser, and many others date the rise of popular art. For in this ideology, social reality is defined for each individual by himself. It is a world of his own choosing, not a feudal order externally fixed; it is constituted by free contract rather than imposed status. The sober bourgeois becomes a hero of romance, as in Shaw's *Arms and the Man*. The rationalizations of the entrepreneur are refined into the metaphysics of romanticism and vulgarized into popular art. Midbrow art may be really middle-class after all.

Sentimentality, then, moves in a closed circle around the self. The emotions released by a stimulus to sentiment satisfy a proprietary interest, and one which is directed inward. The important thing is that they are *my* feelings, and what is more, feelings about *me*. The prototype of sentimentality is self-pity. Popular art provides subjects and situations that make it easy to see ourselves in its materials. We await only a signal to rush into identification. All art invites the self, but it does so in a way that draws us out of ourselves. Art enlarges and transforms the self that has been brought to the aesthetic encounter. The aesthetic experience begins with empathy: we must give ourselves to it. But in the consummation art repays our willing identification by giving us an identity. We do not see ourselves in art but truly *find* ourselves there, become what before was only a bare potentiality. Popular art accepts and discharges the obligation on our own recognizance. It takes us at face value, but leaves us to contemplate our own empty features. Narcissus, W. H. Auden conjectured, was probably a hydrocephalic idiot, who stared into the pool and concluded, "On me it looks good!" The self-centeredness of popular art is the measure of our own diminishing.

V

Perhaps the most common characterization of popular art is that it is *escapist*. There is no doubt that it can produce a kind of narcosis, a state of insensibility arresting thought and feeling as well as action—in a word, a trance. We do not look at popular art, we stare into it, as we would into flames or moving waters. I think it not accidental that the most popular media, movies and television, are viewed in the dark; as the nightingale trills her commercial we may well ask with Keats, Do I wake or sleep? The medium itself is such stuff as dreams are made on.

If there is any responsiveness, it is focused largely on sensory values. What we are fed is not only predigested but also attractively packaged. Technicolor and vistavision, all that Aristotle called "spectacle," make up for shortcomings in character and action. A source of delight itself is sweetness of sound, shape, and color. Indeed, this is what is popularly known as beauty, and what art recurrently has revolted against. (It is not only modern art that has cultivated the ugly, though the academy makes of the cultivation a cult.) For such beauty is indeed only skin-deep. A truly aesthetic surface does not preclude depth meanings but shows them forth, embodying them in the materials presented to sense. A face with character is not necessarily much to look at.

Popular art seeks to escape ugliness, not to transform it. There is nothing like a pretty face to help you forget your troubles, and popular art can prettify everything, even—and perhaps especially—the face of death. It provides an escape first, therefore, by shutting out the reality, glossing over it.

But popular art is said to do more; it seems to provide an escape not only *from* something but also *to* something else, shuts out the real world by opening the door to another. We do not just forget our troubles but are reminded of them to enjoy the fantasy of overcoming them. I once met a man whose occupation was driving truckloads of explosives; his recreation was reading adventure stories—*they* all end happily. Popular art is as likely to relieve anxiety as boredom.

The world of popular art is unreal not just in the sense that it consists of symbols rather than realities—"it's only a movie." Science, too, replaces things by abstract representations of them, but it is not for that reason derogated as an escape from reality. It may serve as such for some scientists: they may turn to symbols because they cannot relate happily to people and things. But what makes it science, after all, is that it is capable of bringing us back to the realities, however far from them it de-tours in its abstractions. Whether symbols are essentially an escape depends at bottom on what they symbolize. Popular art is unreal, not as being sign rather than substance, but because what it signifies is unreal. All art is illusion, inducing us as we experience it to take art for life. But some of it is true to life, illusory without being deceptive. Popular art is a tissue of false-hoods.

Popular art depicts the world, not as it is, nor even as it might be, but as we would have it. In that world we are neither strangers nor afraid, for it is of our own making. Everything in it is selected and placed in our interest. It is a world exhausted in a single perspective—our own—and it is peopled by card-board figures that disappear when viewed edgewise. Art opens to us a landscape over which we may roam freely, unfolds events that can be seen through the eyes of even the least of their participants. Popular art limits our identifications, and restricts our movements. We are not to ask whether the rescued maiden can cook, nor do we see the gallant knight through the eyes of

scientific imagination. We do not escape from the reality but from the constrictions of our unimaginative experience of it. Art may be produced for children—Lewis Carroll and Robert Louis Stevenson—or with a childlike quality—Paul Klee and Joan Miro —but it is not therefore childish. It is this childishness, however, that characterizes popular art: the fairy tale is retold for adult consumption, but stripped of just those qualities of creative imagination in which lies the artistry of the original.

In mature fantasy both the reality principle and the pleasure principle are at work. Popular art is concerned only with the pleasure, and for just this reason it can provide only immature satisfactions. Where art makes manifest such significance in the reality as gives pleasure in its apprehension, popular art gives pleasure only in encouraging the pretence that we have been pleased. The circle is closed within: we ourselves have the desires and we ourselves satisfy them. The difference is that between masturbation and a mature love that reaches outside the self. In responding to popular art we do not escape from reality —we have not yet attained to the reality. Beneath the pleasure in popular art is the pathos of the note lying outside the orphanage wall: "Whoever finds this, I love you!"

What popular art does, Ernest Vandenhaag points out, is to blur the line between fantasy and reality. It is not a question of escaping, for we do not even know where we are. Plato's attack on all art has unmistakable force when applied to popular art— *that* is a dream within a dream. The aesthetic experience calls for—and contributes to—a certain maturity, a capacity for enough distance to give perspective, and enough wisdom to see oneself in perspective. It is only in such objectification that both self and world attain reality. The magic of art may have its genesis in infantile delusions of omnipotence, but these delusions persist just in so far as self and world, fantasy and reality, remain undifferentiated. Art does not feed the delusion that we can do anything, but on the contrary shows forth the limits of our powers. The magic is that we transcend those limits in our aesthetically structured awareness of them. Popular art is escapist only in so far as it turns its back on a world it has never known.

VI

Now, what are the social functions of popular art? What, after all, makes popular art so popular? The usual reply follows the account that conceives of popular art in terms of distinctive features of modern society. The major premise is the alienation and deracination of modern man; the minor premise is that popular art serves to counter these forces, providing a basis for at least an ersatz community. Popular art reaches out to the lowest common denominator of society; it provides the touch of nature that makes all men kin, or, at least, all men who share the conventions of a common culture.

Unfortunately, empirical data to support this conclusion are lacking; on the contrary, such evidence as we have tends to refute it. Popular art does *not*, as is so commonly supposed, leave out whatever might offend anyone. Its mass appeal seems to derive from "a distinctive 'majority taste' rather than widespread satisfaction of a polyglot of tastes." Popular art does not answer to the mean of our tastes but to the mode, in the sense both of statistics and of fashion. It is art that might better be said to appeal to a common denominator; this is what we call the universality of art. If the appeal is not universally responded to, it is because the art is not understood, and because we do not understand ourselves well enough to know what is in us.

In so far as the function of popular art today is to be explained in terms of social conditions rather than psychic processes, the situation seems to me to be the reverse of what the previous account relies on. It is not man who is alienated and uprooted, but art. In our time art has become increasingly dissociated from the cultural concerns with which it has been so intimately involved throughout most of its history—religion, love, war, politics, and the struggle for subsistence. Art today is, in Dewey's brilliant phrase, "the beauty-parlor of civilization." Popular art at least pretends to a social relevance, and is not only willing but eager to find a place for itself outside the museum.

But I hope that nothing I have said is heard as a cry of despair over the decadence of the times. On the contrary, I believe that popular art today is neither worse nor more common than it always has been. There is a wider audience today for art of every kind: the mass of the Athenian population were slaves, and not much more than that in Renaissance Italy or Elizabethan England. There may be more poor stuff produced today because there are more people to consume it, but this is even more true, proportionately, for the superior product. Nor do I sympathize with the view that ours is an age of barbarism to be defined, according to Ortega y Gasset, as "the absence of standards to which appeal can be made." What is absent, to my mind, is only a cultural elite that sets forth and enforces the standards; and I say, so much the better! It is ironic that popular art is taken as a sign of barbarism; every real development in the history of art, and not only the modern movement, was first greeted as a repudiation of aesthetic standards. My objection to popular art is just the contrary, that it is too rigidly bound to the standards of the academy. Kitsch is the homage paid by popular art to those standards: Oscar and Emmy are avatars of the muse.

Art is too often talked about with a breathless solemnity, and viewed with a kind of religious awe; if high art needs its high priests, I hope that aesthetics will leave that office to the critics. To put it plainly, there is much snobbery in the aesthetic domain, and especially in the contempt for popular art on no other basis than its popularity. We speak of popular art in terms of its media (paperbacks, movies, television) as though to say, "Can any good come out of Nazareth?"; or else by the popular genres (western, mystery, love story, science fiction) as though they can be condemned wholesale. For audiences, art is more of a status symbol than ever; its appearance in the mass media is marked by a flourish of trumpets, as befits its status; the sponsor may even go so far as to omit his commercials. I am saying that even where popular art vulgarizes yesterday's art, it might anticipate tomorrow's—baroque once meant something like kitsch. I am willing to prophesy that even television has art in its future.

But if not, what then? Aesthetic judgment is one thing and personal taste another. The values of art, like all else aesthetic, can only be analyzed contextually. There is a time and a place even for popular art. Champagne and Napoleon brandy are admittedly the best of beverages; but on a Sunday afternoon in the ballpark we want a coke, or maybe a glass of beer. "Even if we have all the virtues," Zarathustra reminds us, "there is still one thing needful: to send the virtues themselves to sleep at the right time." If popular art gives us pleasant dreams, we can only be grateful—when we have wakened.

STUDY QUESTIONS

1. What value can the study of less-than-perfect art have?
2. Why does Kaplan distinguish between "popular art" and other terms like "pop art," "bad art," "minor art," "folk art," and "mass art"? How does he distinguish between them?
3. Why does he identify popular art with "midbrow art" rather than "middle-class art"?
4. He says that part of his thesis is "that popular art is not the degradation of taste but its immaturity." What is the difference? Why is this an important distinction?
5. According to Kaplan, what is formless about the popular arts?
6. Why does Kaplan feel that we cannot look to the popular arts today "for a fresh vision"?

7. What makes the popular arts entertaining?
8. In what ways are the popular arts given to sentimentality?
9. In what ways are the popular arts escapist?
10. What are the social functions of popular arts?
11. Explain some of the important ways in which popular art and art differ.
12. Why, after all of his negative comments about the popular arts, do you think Kaplan still feels that they "might anticipate tomorrow's" art? Why is he still "willing to prophesy that even television has art in its future"?

Additional Questions for Composition, Research, and Further Discussion

1. Television comedy in the 1940's and 1950's was often compared with vaudeville. How accurate is this comparison? What are the significant differences between television and vaudeville? Do the differences or the similarities seem to you more significant in the long run?
2. What does an examination of the history of western films show about the ways in which popular heroes have changed in the last forty years?
3. How sick are the "sick comedians"? What is the basis of their humor? Why have they attained such wide popularity?
4. What was the "Golden Age of Television Drama (1950-1960)"? How did it arise, what conditions allowed it to flourish, and why did it disappear?
5. What is the image of the American family currently seen on domestic comedies? How realistic, healthy, and artistically successful does this image seem?
6. Compare any play and the movie version of the play to determine the kinds of changes. Explain the reasons for the changes, both practical and artistic, and evaluate the artistic results.
7. In "Pornography Is Not Enough" (p. 164) Eric Larrabee says that perverted expressions of sex are more pornographic than normal expressions. Yet there have been a number of widely acclaimed playwrights—Jean Genét, for example—who use perversion in their plays. Can you explain what perversion symbolizes

for some of the controversial playwrights? Does it actually function as Larrabee claims it does? Why is perversion such a frequent
symbol in our time?

8. What is pop art? What do serious artists feel they are doing with
   it? How successful are their attempts? Why has pop art become
   so prominently associated recently with dress design?

9. One form of popular art not discussed in this book is religious
   revival music. What are its distinguishing characteristics? To what
   popular values does it appeal? Why?

10. Although country western music is very popular, it has failed to
    gain the respect frequently granted other forms of popular music.
    In what ways is it different from some other forms of popular
    music? Why do serious students of popular arts generally dislike
    this form?

11. Cecil B. DeMille was probably the most successful of all pro-
    ducers of spectaculars. What was his recipe for success? How
    successful was he artistically? Why?

12. Except when it directly adapts Broadway musicals, Hollywood
    has been largely unaffected by the development of musical come-
    dies since *Oklahoma!* Why is this so? What strengths and limita-
    tions do films offer for musical comedy?

13. The cartoons handled by Universal Press Association (U.P.A.)
    have had great influence on modern cartoons, particularly tele-
    vision cartoons. What, exactly, did U.P.A. contribute to the art
    of cartooning? Why were their techniques so quickly adopted by
    television cartoonists? How have their cartoons influenced the
    general kind of humor presented in television cartoons?

14. Home design is a major business in our country, not only for
    builders and designers, but for publishers as well. Examine a
    number of home-design magazines. Try to decide how good,
    artistically, the designs are that are presented, what seem to be
    the limits and guidelines used by publishers in selecting designs,
    and to what tastes these designs actually appeal. Depending upon
    the magazine, how would you classify these designs—as functional
    design, or kitsch, or both?

15. In "The Witness Point" (p. 254) Vernon Young does not discuss
    in detail how film techniques are finally blended together mean-
    ingfully by the editor of a film. What is editing? What does the

film editor contribute to the artistry of a film? How does he decide what to include and what to leave in the cutting room?

16. Television commercials are rarely considered to be artistic. Yet some of them are technical virtuoso pieces. Which ones seem to you to have the highest degree of technical competence? Which have the greatest originality? Which seem to make the greatest use of experimental film techniques?

17. There is very little material in this book on radio. Radio, however, developed its own conventions and expressive possibilities. Try to find the recording of Orson Welles' famous broadcast, "War of the Worlds," October 30, 1938 (Audio Rarities 2355); or read the script of the broadcast (in Hadley Cantril, *The Invasion from Mars: A Study in the Psychology of Panic* [1940]). Analyze the broadcast to discover exactly what conventions of radio Welles used, how he used them, and why the broadcast so successfully (and unintentionally) precipitated a national panic.

18. By comparing the rock 'n' roll of the sixties with the jitterbug of the forties, see what you can discover about what kinds of feelings are expressed in each style of dancing, what attitudes toward dance are inherent in each kind of dancing, and why jitterbug seems inexpressive for the generation of the sixties.

19. Yogi Bear became a popular international hero. What was the secret of his appeal? Why was it Yogi Bear rather than Huckleberry Hound who became the greater popular success? Which seems to you the more perceptive cartoon character?

20. Photographic portraiture is one of the popular arts which has achieved the greatest maturity. Study the work of Yousuf Karsh and try to explain in what sense his portraits are something more than mere photographic records of his subjects. Why is he considered an artist rather than a mere reporter?

21. The documentary film has made more deliberate use of experimental film techniques than other forms of film have. Look at John Grierson's book on the documentary (*Grierson on Documentary*, ed. Forsyth Hardy [1947]), and compare his theory of documentary film with some of the documentaries that have been produced for television—for example, "Air Power," "The Valiant Years," or the documentaries produced by John Secondari for ABC. How well do television documentaries measure up to Grierson's

standards? How do they differ from the usual news special we see?

22. Much has been written in recent years about the image of the United States which we export to foreign countries through our films. Exactly what is that image? How accurate is it? If you were choosing films for export, what would you choose?

23. John Glenn is the greatest popular hero we have had for many years. What aspects of his personality conform naturally to the popular hero of magazine and organization fiction? How was he treated to exploit these aspects? Can you find evidence that some aspects of his personality were deliberately played down to make his image more heroic?

24. Read Betty Friedan's *The Feminine Mystique* (1963). Then compare the image she says most American women have of themselves with the heroines of stories in women's magazines. Does her analysis seem accurate? What do the readers of women's magazines seem to want in their heroines? Do you see any evidence that Miss Friedan's analysis is overstated? Can you find additional explanations for the kind of heroine the American woman idealizes?

25. The *Reader's Digest* seeks to improve the American language by publishing each month a column called "Picturesque Speech and Patter." Analyze the column and decide for yourself what the magazine defines as "picturesque." How good are the figures of speech reprinted there? Justify your decision by comparing these figures of speech with figures you find in modern poetry—in the poetry of E. E. Cummings or Marianne Moore, for example.

26. In "History on the Silver Screen" (p. 225) Gilbert Highet objects to the way history is frequently used in films. Read one of Thomas B. Costain's novels (*The Black Rose* [1945], for example). Then read several well-accepted historical accounts of the same era. Decide how accurately Costain has interpreted history. In what ways has he changed historical truth? Has he done so for popular or artistic purposes?

27. Protest songs, such as those written and sung by Bob Dylan, are a flourishing form of popular music. Analyze a number of these songs. Then decide to what degree and how well they embody contemporary problems. To what extent are they com-

mercializations of serious protests? How can you distinguish between authentic protests and commercial capitalization?

28. The conversation show has long been a sustaining feature of the NBC television network. The *Today* show (1952) generally attempts to use conversation as a means of informing, while the *Johnny Carson Show* (1955) generally tries to use conversation as an art for entertainment. Which of these shows seems to you more successful? Why?

29. Franz Kafka's short story "In the Penal Colony" (1948) is frequently anthologized in collections of science fiction. Kafka is considered a major artist; Ray Bradbury, whose stories generally appear in the same collections, is generally considered to be a popular science-fiction writer. By comparing Kafka and Bradbury, see if you can understand why critics generally make an artistic distinction between them.

30. Science fiction seems to have its greatest popular audience in the film. Why do you believe this is so? How successful are science-fiction films? What are their weaknesses? To whom do these films appeal? Why do they appeal?

31. The Italian film maker Federico Fellini has been involved in at least two American censorship battles—once in 1952 when *The Miracle* (1950), which he wrote, was threatened with censorship, and more recently, when several states censored *La Dolce Vita* (1960), which he wrote and directed. In spite of the public controversy his films have aroused, most critics consider him to be a major artist. What is so controversial about his films? Why does much of the public seem to misunderstand his work? Why do most critics believe him to be a serious artist? Finally, can Fellini expect to avoid controversy so long as he uses the film as his medium of expression?

32. One of the most interesting side effects of mass production has been the growth of the packaging industry, the industry that designs and manufactures packages—such as boxes, bottles, and cans—for consumer goods. What qualities of mass production have given rise to the particular form of popular design in this industry? What constitutes good packaging design? Are the qualities of functionalism and marketability always compatible with each other? In the field of packaging, which quality seems

to be more highly valued? Does John Kouwenhoven's article on vernacular forms ("Stone, Steel, and Jazz," p. 21) give you any help in understanding how to judge the products of the packaging industry?

33. Television is frequently charged with allowing excessive violence in the shows that children see. To what extent does this charge seem justified to you? What criteria can you use to determine whether violence is excessive? Consider both children's shows and adult shows. (Don't forget that many adult shows come early enough in the evening, especially in the Mountain and Pacific time zones, so that children can easily see them.)

34. The *Reader's Digest* frequently publishes condensed versions of novels. From a detailed comparison of three novels and their condensations, try to determine how the staff of *Reader's Digest* goes about condensing novels. What do they omit? How does their condensation change the meaning of the original work? Is there anything wrong with condensing novels?

35. Why are the Beatles so popular? What do they express for teenagers? Why are they objects of admiration?

36. Are the television rating systems, such as the Nielsen rating, good or bad? Do they actually measure preference, or do they merely reinforce the status quo?

37. The curvaceous Hollywood star has been accused of creating major psychological problems for the American housewife. Examine this charge carefully to discover the kinds of problems the star creates, how much the star herself contributes to these problems, and how much is the fault of the film script itself. Some of the biographical material on Marilyn Monroe may be helpful in pursuing this study (see, for instance, Edwin P. Hoyt, *Marilyn* [1965]).

38. In the introduction to *An Approach to Literature* (1964), Cleanth Brooks, John Purser, and Robert Penn Warren analyze sob-sister writing to show the ways in which it attempts to fulfill our desire for literature. Read that introduction, and then analyze a number of stories in pulp and slick magazines to show the degree to which such writers use sob-sister tactics as substitutes for genuine emotion.

A Selected Bibliography

GENERAL

Allen, Frederick Lewis. *The Big Change: America Transforms Itself 1900-1950*. New York, 1952.

Barzun, Jacques. *The House of Intellect*. New York, 1959.

Blum, Eleanor. *Reference Books in the Mass Media*. Urbana, Illinois, 1963.

Boroff, David, ed. *The State of the Nation*. Englewood Cliffs, 1965.

Carpenter, Edmund, and Marshall McLuhan, ed. *Explorations in Communication*. Boston, 1960.

Deer, Irving, and Harriet A. Deer, ed. *The Languages of the Mass Media*. Boston, 1965.

DeMott, Benjamin. *Hells and Benefits*. New York, 1962.

———. *You Don't Say: Studies of Modern American Inhibitions*. New York, 1966.

Denney, Reuel. *The Astonished Muse*. Chicago, 1957.

Ellis, Albert. *The American Sexual Tragedy*. New York, 1954.

Galbraith, John Kenneth. *The Affluent Society*. Boston, 1958.

Hall, Stuart, and Paddy Whannel. *Popular Arts*. New York, 1965.

Hoggart, Richard. *The Uses of Literacy: Changing Patterns in English Mass Culture*. Boston, 1961.

Kronenberger, Louis. *Company Manners*. Indianapolis, 1954.

Larrabee, Eric. *The Self-Conscious Society*. New York, 1962.

———, and Rolf Meyerson. *Mass Leisure*. Glencoe, Illinois, 1958.

Macdonald, Dwight. *Against the American Grain*. New York, 1965.

McLuhan, Marshall. *Understanding Media*. New York, 1964.

351

O'Hara, Robert C. *Media for the Millions.* New York, 1964.

Phillips, Gifford. *The Arts in a Democratic Society.* Santa Barbara, 1966.

Riesman, David, with Nathan Glazer and Reuel Denney. *The Lonely Crowd.* New York, 1950.

Rosenberg, Bernard, and David Manning White, ed. *Mass Culture: The Popular Arts in America.* Glencoe, Illinois, 1960.

Seldes, Gilbert. *The Great Audience.* New York, 1951.

———. *The Public Arts.* New York, 1956.

Steinberg, Charles S., ed. *Mass Media and Communication.* New York, 1966.

The Times Literary Supplement. The American Imagination. London, 1960.

Thompson, Denys, ed. *Discrimination and Popular Culture.* Baltimore, 1965.

Ulanov, Barry. *The Two Worlds of American Art: The Private and the Popular.* New York, 1965.

Warshow, Robert. *The Immediate Experience.* Garden City, 1962.

Whyte, William H. Jr. *The Organization Man.* New York, 1956.

Williams, Raymond. *Culture and Society.* Garden City, 1960.

LITERATURE

Bainbridge, John. *Little Wonder and How It Grew.* New York, 1946.

Barrett, William. "American Fiction and American Values," *Partisan Review,* XVIII (November, 1951), 681-690.

Bazelon, David. "Dashiell Hammett's 'Private Eye,'" *Commentary,* VII (May, 1949), 467-472.

Bradbury, Ray. "Day After Tomorrow: Why Science Fiction?" *The Nation,* CLXXVI (May 2, 1953), 364-367.

DeVoto, Bernard. "Western Fiction," *Harper's,* CCIX (December, 1954), 10-14.

Hart, James D. *The Popular Book: A History of America's Literary Taste.* Berkeley, 1961.

Harvey, John. "The Content Characteristics of Best-Selling Novels," *Public Opinion Quarterly,* XVII (1953), 91-114.

Haycraft, Howard, ed. *The Art of the Mystery Story.* New York, 1956.

Leavis, Q. D. *Fiction and the Reading Public.* London, 1965.

Noel, Mary. *Villains Galore: The Heyday of the Popular Story Weekly.* New York, 1954.

Parkes, Henry Bamford. *The American Experience.* New York, 1959.

Podhoretz, Norman. *Doings and Undoings.* New York, 1964.

Wilson, Edmund. "Why Do People Read Detective Stories?" *Classics and Commercials: A Literary Chronicle of the Forties.* New York, 1950. Pp. 231-237.

MOVIES AND PHOTOGRAPHY

Agee, James. *Agee on Film.* New York, 1958.

Arnheim, Rudolf. *Film as Art.* Berkeley, 1957.

Barry, Iris. *Film Notes, Bulletin of the Museum of Modern Art,* XVI (Nos. 2-3). New York, 1949.

Eisenstein, Sergei. *Film Form,* trans. Jay Leyda. New York, 1949.

————. *Film Sense,* trans. Jay Leyda. New York, 1947.

Fenin, George N., and William K. Everson. *The Western: From Silents to Cinerama.* New York, 1962.

Hall, Stuart, et al., ed. *Film Teaching.* London, 1964.

Hardy, Forsyth, ed. *Grierson on Documentary.* New York, 1947.

Inglis, Ruth. *Freedom of the Movies.* Chicago, 1947.

Jacobs, Lewis. *The Rise of the American Film.* New York, 1939.

Kael, Pauline. *I Lost It at the Movies.* Boston, 1965.

Kauffmann, Stanley. *A World on Film.* New York, 1966.

Knight, Arthur. *The Liveliest Art.* New York, 1957.

Kracauer, Siegfried. *From Caligari to Hitler: A Psychological History of the German Film.* Princeton, 1947.

————. *Theory of Film.* New York, 1965.

Lawson, John Howard. "Theory and Technique of Screenwriting," *Theory and Technique of Playwriting and Screenwriting.* New York, 1936. Pp. 305-439.

Lindgren, Ernest. *The Art of the Film.* London, 1950.

MacCann, Richard Dyer, ed. *Film and Society.* New York, 1964.

Manvell, Roger. *Film.* Harmondsworth, Middlesex, 1944.

————. *The Film and the Public.* London, 1955.

Moholy, Lucia. *A Hundred Years of Photography.* Harmondsworth, Middlesex, 1939.

Pudovkin, V. I. *Film Technique and Film Acting.* New York, 1949.
Reisz, Karel. *The Technique of Film Editing.* New York, 1953.
Ross, Lillian. *Picture, A Story About Hollywood.* New York, 1952.
Rotha, Paul, and Richard Griffith. *The Film Till Now.* New York, 1949.
Spottiswoode, Raymond. *A Grammar of the Film.* Berkeley, 1950.
————. *Film and Its Techniques.* Berkeley, 1953.
Tyler, Parker. *Classics of the Foreign Film.* New York, 1962.

MUSIC

Barzun, Jacques. "Kind Word for Pop, Bop and Folk," *The Reporter,* XIV (May 17, 1956), 36-39.
————. *Music in American Life.* Bloomington, 1962.
Hoffman, David G. "Jazz: The Survival of a Folk Art," *Perspectives: U.S.A.,* XV (Spring, 1956), 29-42.
Lomax, Alan. *The Folk Songs of North America.* New York, 1960.
Spaeth, Sigmund. *A History of Popular Music in America.* New York, 1948.
Swados, Harvey. "Popular Music and the New Man of Skill," *Dissent,* I (Summer, 1954), 269-273.
Ulanov, Barry. *A History of Jazz in America.* New York, 1952.

RADIO AND TELEVISION

Cantril, Hadley. *The Invasion from Mars.* Princeton, 1940.
Graham, Saxon. "Cultural Compatibility in the Adoption of Television," *Social Forces,* XXXIII (December, 1954), 166-170.
O'Brien, Mae. *Children's Reactions to Radio Adaptations of Juvenile Books.* New York, 1950.
Postman, Neil. *Television and the Teaching of English.* New York, 1961.
Siepmann, Charles A. *Radio, Television, and Society.* New York, 1950.
Smythe, Dallas W. "The Content and Effects of Broadcasting," *Mass Media and Education,* ed. N. Henry. Chicago, 1954. Pp. 192-213.
Steinbeck, John. "How to Tell Good Guys from Bad Guys," *The Reporter,* XII (March 10, 1955), 42-44.
Sterner, Alice P. *Radio, Motion Picture and Reading Interests: A Study of High School Pupils.* New York, 1947.

Toffler, Al. "Crime in Your Parlor: TV Programs Under Fire," *The Nation*, CLXXXI (October 15, 1955), 323-324.

Warner, W. Lloyd, and William E. Henry. "The Radio Day-Time Serial: A Symbolic Analysis," *Genetic Psychology Monographs*, XXXVII (February, 1948), 7-13, 55-64.

Weaver, L. S. Jr., R. E. Kintner, and J. L. Van Volkenburg. "Outlook for Serious Music on Television and Radio," *Musical America*, LXXVI (February 15, 1956), 25-27.

Wharton, Don. "Let's Get Rid of Tele-Violence," *Parents' Magazine*, XXXI (April, 1956), 54-56.

Wylie, Evan M. "Violence on TV—Entertainment or Menace?" *Cosmopolitan*, CXXXIV (February, 1953), 34-39.

Wylie, Max. *Clear Channels: Television and the American People*. New York, 1954.

THE COMICS

Bakwin, Ruth M. "The Comics," *Journal of Pediatrics*, XLII (May, 1953), 633-635.

Feiffer, Jules, comp. *The Great Comic Book Heroes*. New York, 1965.

Gruenberg, Sidonie M. "The Comics as a Social Force," *Journal of Educational Sociology*, XVIII (December, 1944), 204-213.

Kolaja, J. "American Magazine Cartoons and Social Control," *Journalism Quarterly*, XXX (Winter, 1953), 71-74.

Muhlen, Norbert. "Comic Books and Other Horrors," *Commentary*, VII (January-March, 1949), 80-87, 194, 294.

Politzer, Heinz. "From Little Nemo to L'il Abner," trans. R. Manheim, *Commentary*, VIII (October, 1949), 346-354.

Schwartz, Delmore. "Masterpieces as Cartoons," *Partisan Review*, XIX (July-August, 1952), 461-471.

Thrasher, Frederick M. "The Comics and Delinquency: Cause or Scapegoat," *Journal of Educational Sociology*, XXIII (December, 1949), 195-205.

Warshow, Robert. "Woofed with Dreams" (review of *Krazy Kat* by George Herriman), *Partisan Review*, XIII (November-December, 1946), 587-590.

Waugh, Coulton. *The Comics*. New York, 1947.

Wertham, Frederic. *Seduction of the Innocent*. New York, 1954.

MISCELLANEOUS

Birch, Lionel. *The Advertising We Deserve?* London, 1962.

Goodman, Walter. *The Clowns of Commerce.* New York, 1957.

Mayer, Martin. *Madison Avenue, U.S.A.,* New York, 1958.

Packard, Vance. *The Hidden Persuaders.* New York, 1957.

Wright, Frank Lloyd. *The Natural House.* New York, 1954.

Meehan, T. "Not Good Taste, Not Bad Taste, It's Camp," *New York Times Magazine* (March 21, 1965), pp. 30-31, 113-115.

Sontag, Susan. "Notes on Camp," *Partisan Review,* XXXI (Fall, 1964), 515-530.

Dreyfuss, Henry. *Designing for People.* New York, 1955.

Kouwenhoven, John A. *Made in America.* New York, 1948.

Nelson, George. *Problems of Design.* New York, 1957.

Pevsner, Nikolaus. *Pioneers of Modern Design.* Harmondsworth, Middlesex, 1960.

Lichtenstein, Roy F. "What Is Pop Art?" (interview, edited by G. R. Swenson), *Art News,* LXII (November, 1963), 24-25.

Loran, E. "Pop Artists or Copy Cats?" *Art News,* LXII (September, 1963), 48-49.

Levi, T. "Biennale: How Evil Is Pop Art?" *New Republic,* CLI (September 19, 1964), 32-34.

Saarinen, Aline B. "Explosion of Pop Art: Exhibition at the Guggenheim Museum," *Vogue,* CXLI (April 15, 1963), 86-87, 134, 136, 142.

McLean, Albert F. Jr. *American Vaudeville as Ritual.* Lexington, Kentucky, 1965.